Praise for
Overland Before the Hippie Trail

Can you imagine travelling for two years without a credit card, cell phone or internet connection? Travelling over 40,000 miles, across Europe and Asia, without an itinerary, a guidebook or a plan? Patricia Sullivan and her husband did this while carrying all they own in a duffel bag, an attaché case and a small suitcase. At the end of two years, she still had a smile for everyone she met, a fascination with how other people lived and her marriage was stronger than ever.

Sullivan has something to tell us about the 1960s, about the nature of travel, about the peoples of the world, about what it means to be American and, ultimately, what it means to be human.

Sharif Gemie, Author of The Hippie Trail: A History

Patricia Sullivan recounts in touching detail an epic round-the-world trip with her new husband Mick through Western Europe and across the Asian continent. In an era predating the "hippie trail" of the late 1960s, their spontaneous, unplanned journey—via boat, train, van, and sundry other means of transportation—immerses the reader in a world that in many cases no longer exists due to the ravages of war and the resulting destruction of cultural monuments and ways of life.

Donna M. Brinton, author/consultant

Patricia Sullivan writes about a world that is still unbelievably huge in its differences of geography and tradition. At the very beginning of our ultra-modern era the continuing seeds of awful political schism are there. And yet, the sensitive humility with which she describes her experience helps us to see that we can all connect through our deeply common humanity.

Adrian Holliday, author of Intercultural Communication & Ideology and Contesting Grand Narratives of The Intercultural

In her memoir *Overland Before the Hippie Trail,* Patricia Sullivan gives us an endearing, fascinating account of traveling the world on the cheap in the 1960s. She and her husband, newlyweds in their twenties, set out from San Francisco with little more than a plan to visit Europe, buy a van, and maybe pick up some teaching work along the way. They end up instead on a two-year journey that takes them from Europe to the Middle East to Asia as early pioneers on the Hippie Trail, stopping here and there in places that today seem at once impossibly remote but also hauntingly familiar. A charming and intimate story of a bygone era of travel.

George Bishop, Jr., author of *The Night of the Comet*

Overland Before the Hippie Trail

OVERLAND
Before the
Hippie Trail

Kathmandu and Beyond with a Van a Man and No Plan

Patricia Noble Sullivan

Noble Press
Berkeley, CA 94705
www.patriciansullivan.com

Ordering Information
Quantity sales: Special discounts are available on quantity purchases by corporations, associations, and others. For details, please use the website address above.

Book design by Six Penny Graphics
Maps by John Byrne Barry
All photographs © Patricia Sullivan

Printed in the United States of America

Library of Congress Control Number: 2022905422

Publisher's Cataloging-in-Publication Data
provided by Five Rainbows Cataloging Services
Names: Sullivan, Patricia Noble, 1942- author.
Title: Overland before the hippie trail : Kathmandu and beyond with a van a man and no plan / Patricia Noble Sullivan.
Description: Berkeley, CA : Patricia Noble Sullivan, 2022.
Identifiers: LCCN 2022905422 (print) | ISBN 979-8-9857519-0-1 (paperback) | ISBN 979-8-9857519-2-5 (ebook)
Subjects: LCSH: Hippies--Biography. | Counterculture. | Europe--Description and travel. | Asia--Description and travel. | Nineteen sixties. | Autobiography. | BISAC: BIOGRAPHY & AUTOBIOGRAPHY / Women. | TRAVEL / Special Interest / Adventure. | TRAVEL / Europe / General. | TRAVEL / Asia / General.
Classification: LCC DS10 .S85 2022 (print) | LCC DS10 (ebook) | DDC 915.044/2--dc23.

ISBN 979-8-9857519-0-1 (paperback)

First Edition

For my grandchildren,
Lucas, Jacob, Eliana, Joshua, Noah

Human Family
by Maya Angelou

I note the obvious differences
in the human family.
Some of us are serious,
some thrive on comedy.

Some declare their lives are lived
as true profundity,
and others claim they really live
the real reality.

The variety of our skin tones
can confuse, bemuse, delight,
brown and pink and beige and purple,
tan and blue and white.

I've sailed upon the seven seas
and stopped in every land,
I've seen the wonders of the world
not yet one common man.

I know ten thousand women
called Jane and Mary Jane,
but I've not seen any two
who really were the same.

Mirror twins are different
although their features jibe,
and lovers think quite different thoughts
while lying side by side.

We love and lose in China,
we weep on England's moors,
and laugh and moan in Guinea,
and thrive on Spanish shores.

We seek success in Finland,
are born and die in Maine.
In minor ways we differ,
in major we're the same.

I note the obvious differences
between each sort and type,
but we are more alike, my friends,
than we are unalike.

We are more alike, my friends,
than we are unalike.

We are more alike, my friends,
than we are unalike.

Contents

Travel 1965–1967

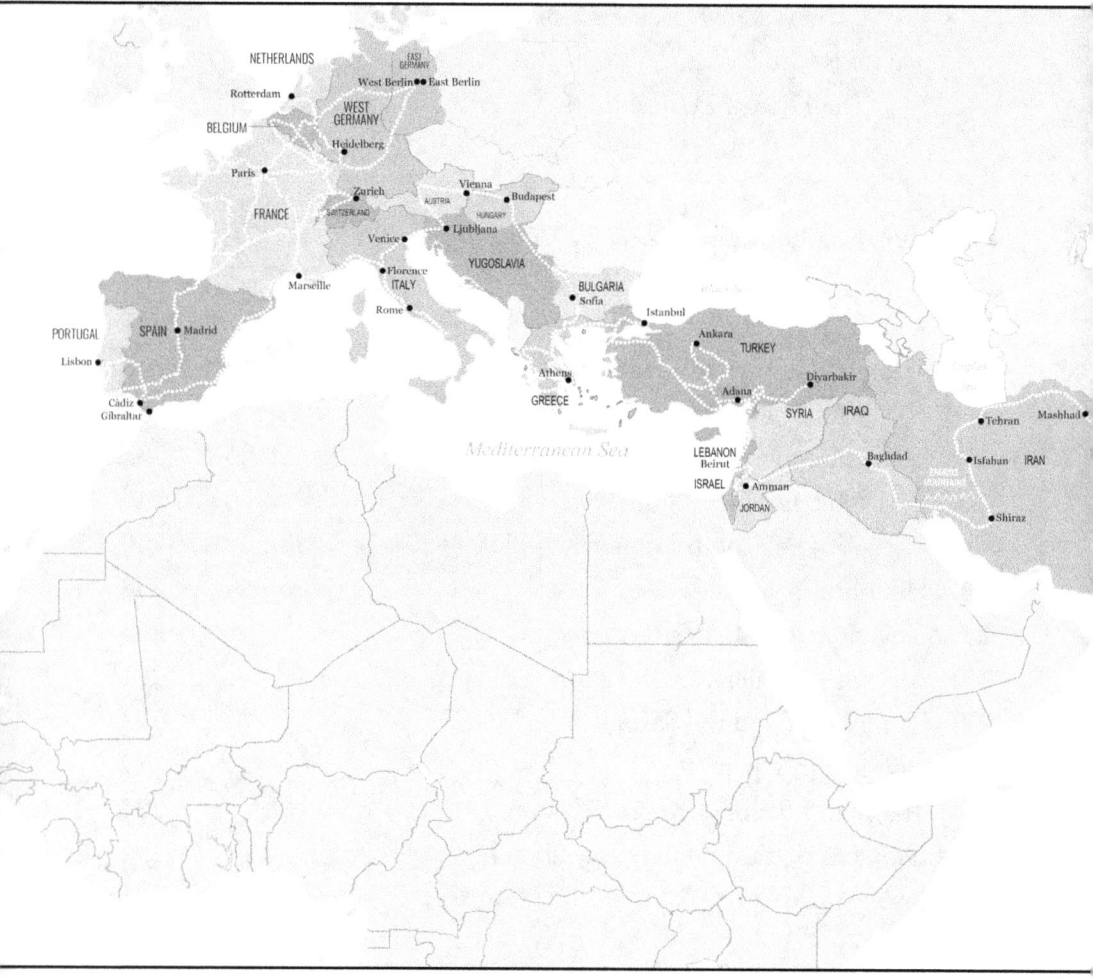

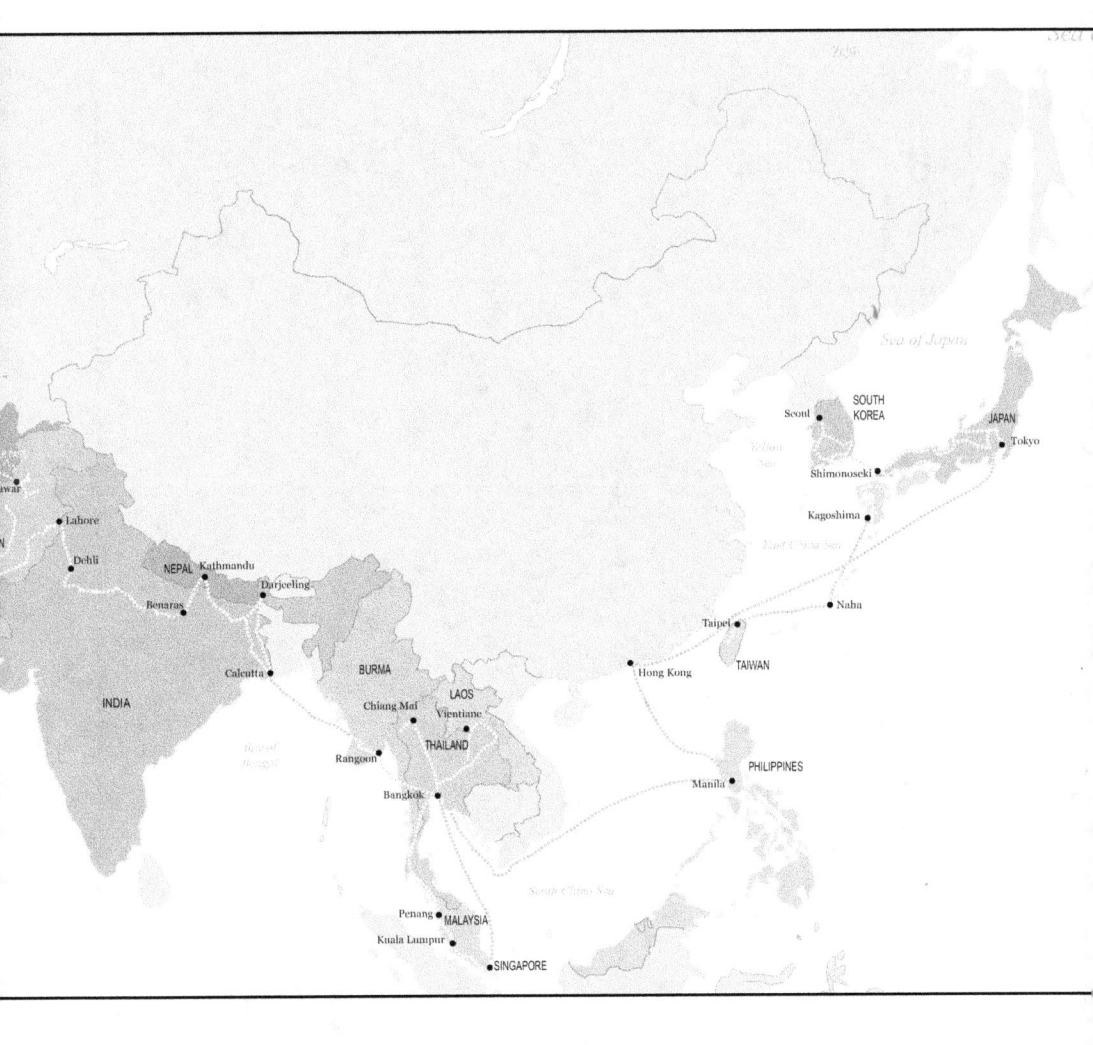

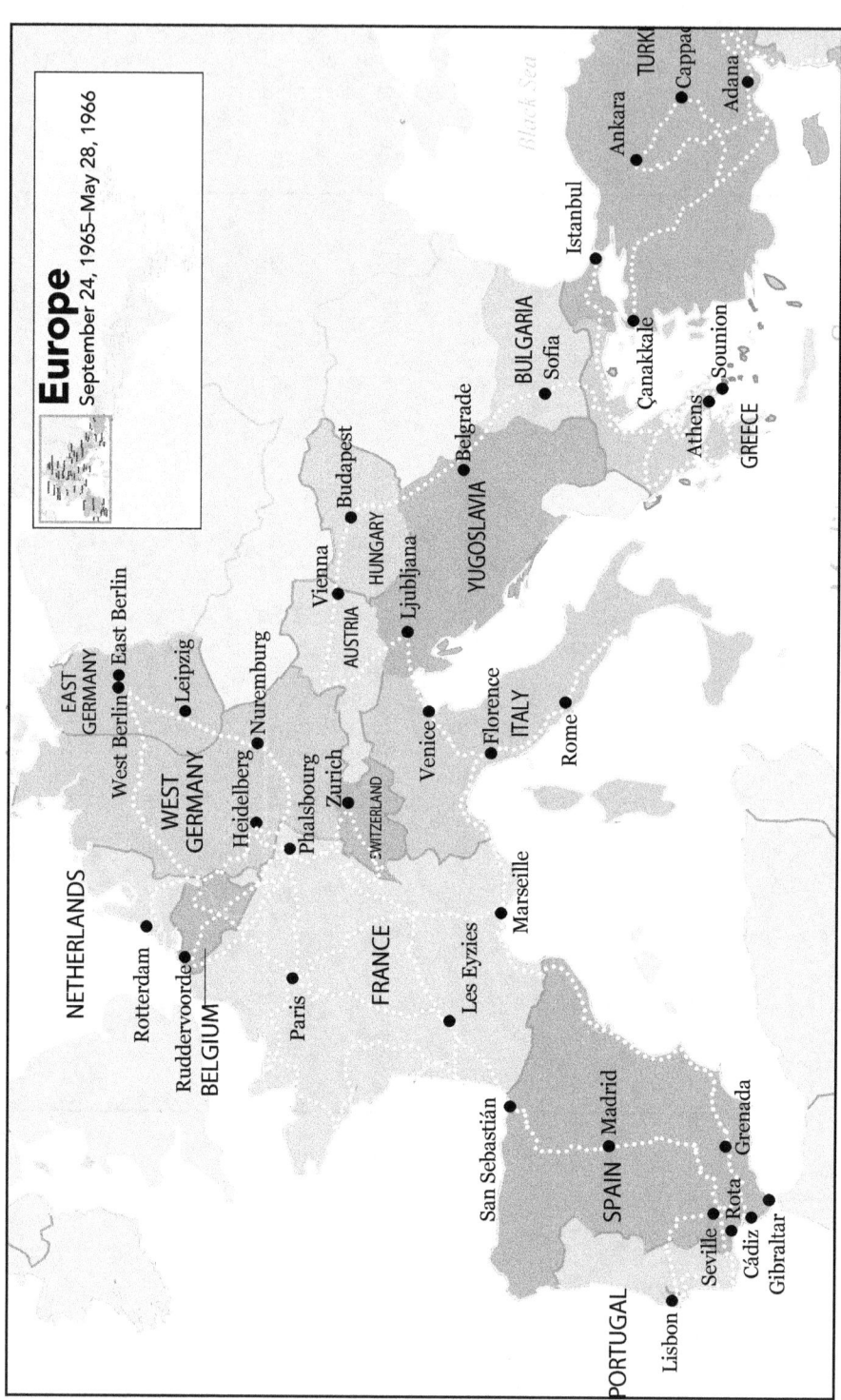

Europe
September 24, 1965–May 28, 1966

Black Sea

TURKEY
Cappadocia
Adana
Ankara
Istanbul

BULGARIA
Sofia
Çanakkale
Sounion
Athens
GREECE

Belgrade
Budapest
Vienna
HUNGARY
Ljubljana
YUGOSLAVIA
AUSTRIA

East Berlin
EAST GERMANY
West Berlin
Leipzig
Nuremburg
Heidelberg
Zurich
SWITZERLAND
Phalsbourg
Venice
Florence
ITALY
Rome

NETHERLANDS
Rotterdam
Ruddervoorde
BELGIUM
WEST GERMANY
FRANCE
Paris
Les Eyzies
Marseille

San Sebastián
Madrid
Grenada
SPAIN
Seville
Rota
Cádiz
Gibraltar
PORTUGAL
Lisbon

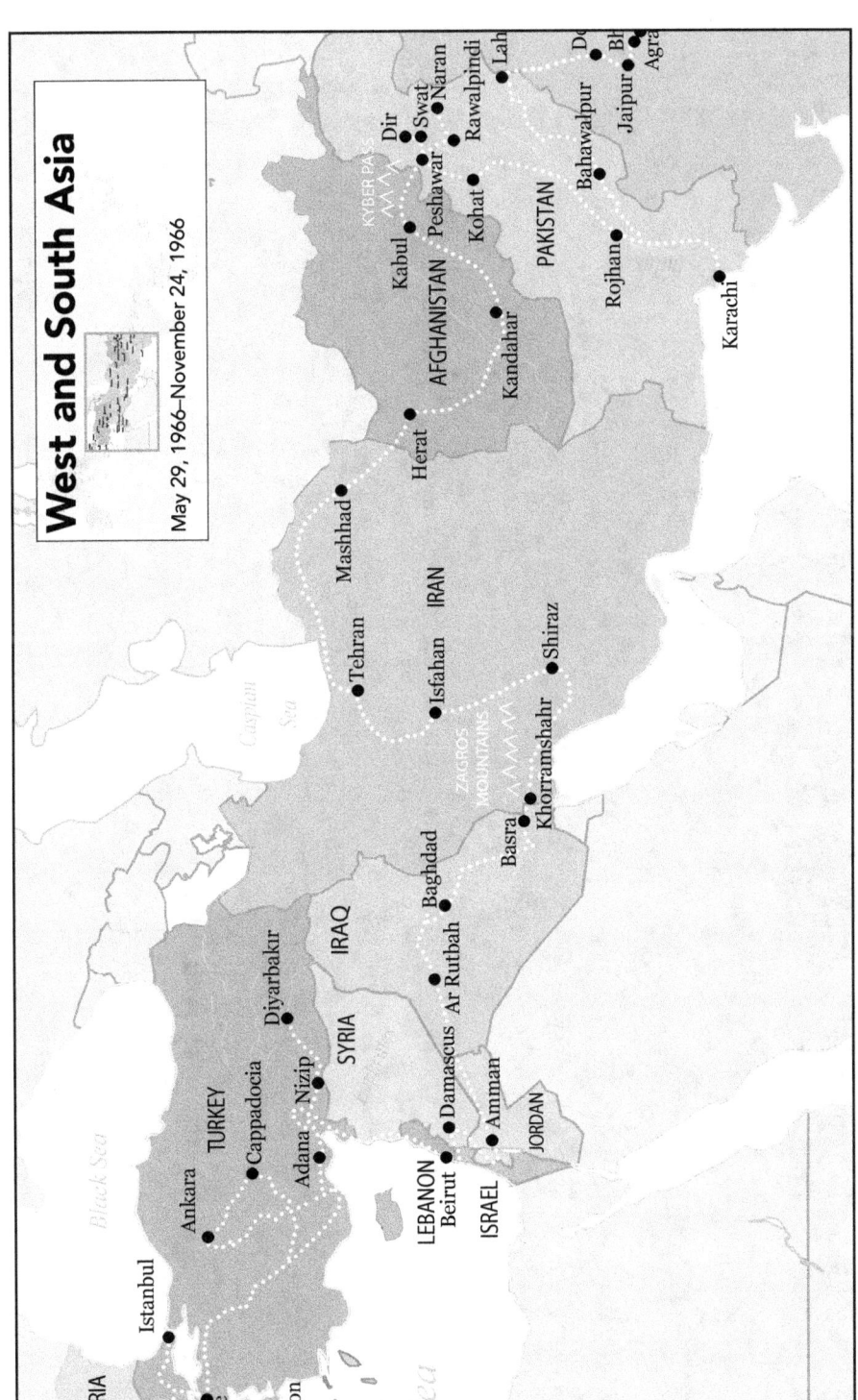

West and South Asia

May 29, 1966–November 24, 1966

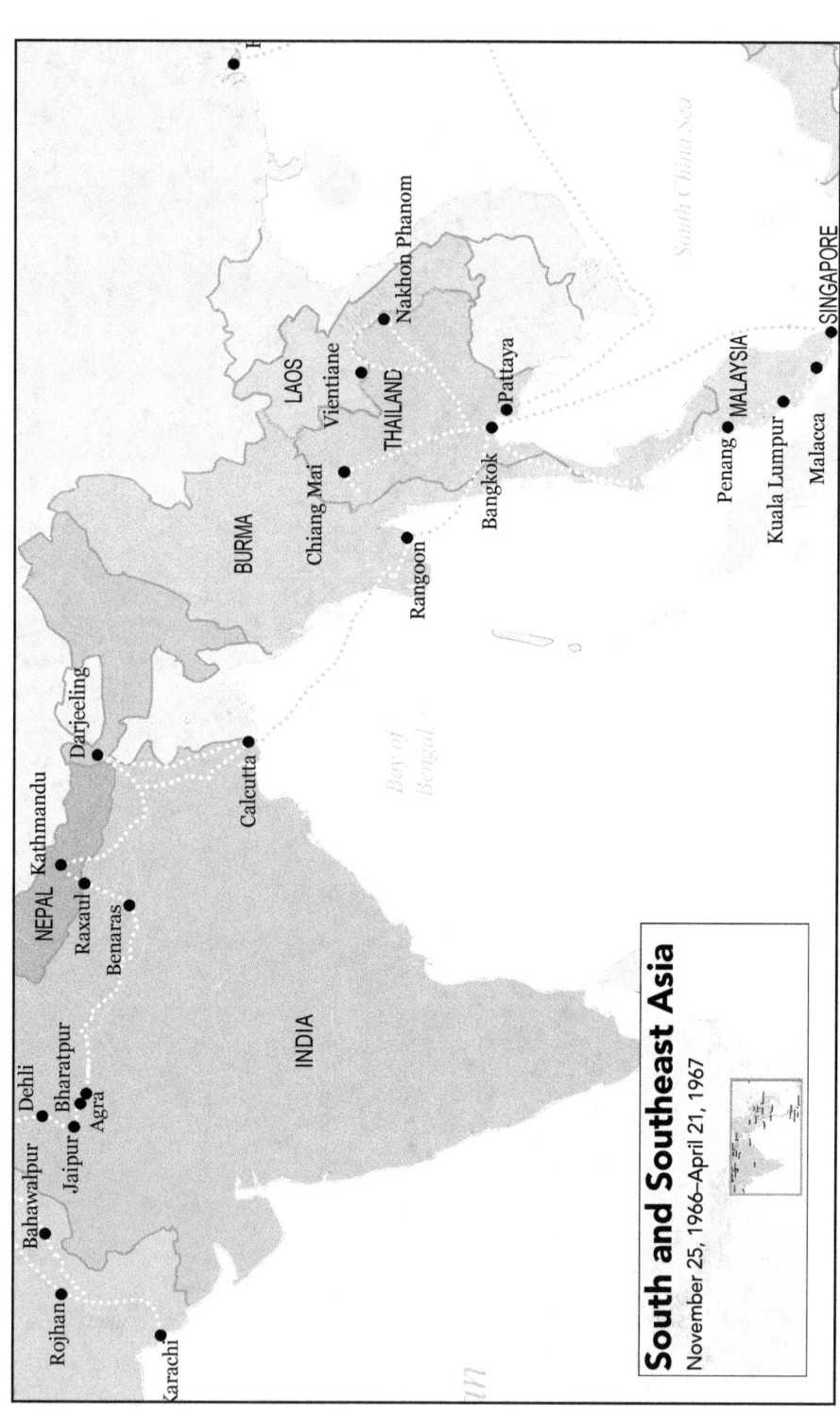

South and Southeast Asia
November 25, 1966–April 21, 1967

Karachi
Rojhan
Bahawalpur
Dehli
Jaipur
Bharatpur
Agra
Benaras
NEPAL
Kathmandu
Raxaul
Darjeeling
Calcutta
INDIA
Rangoon
BURMA
Chiang Mai
LAOS
Vientiane
THAILAND
Bangkok
Pattaya
Nakhon Phanom
Penang
MALAYSIA
Kuala Lumpur
Malacca
SINGAPORE
Bay of Bengal
South China Sea

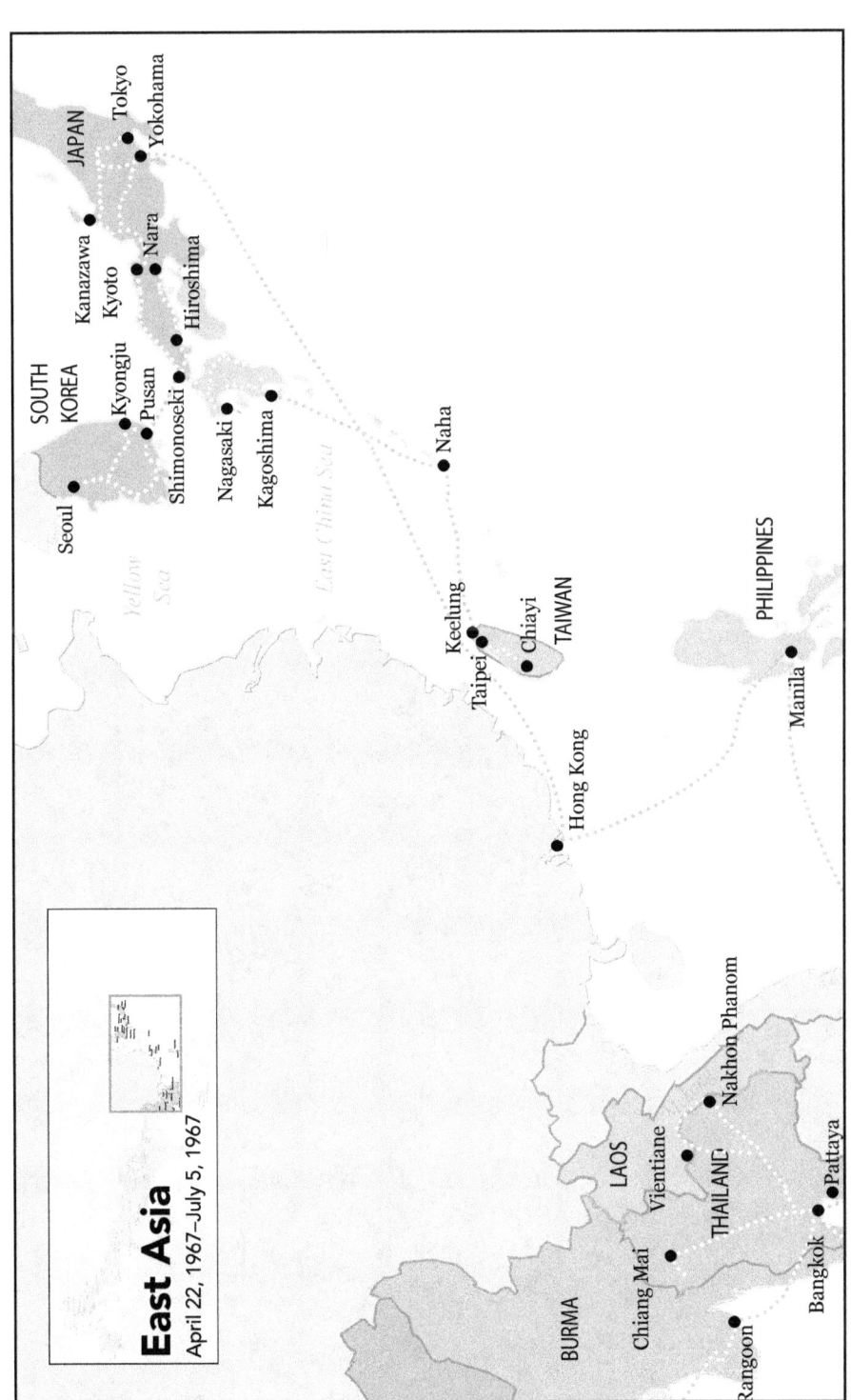

East Asia
April 22, 1967–July 5, 1967

JAPAN
Tokyo
Yokohama
Kanazawa
Nara
Kyoto
Hiroshima
SOUTH KOREA
Kyongju
Pusan
Shimonoseki
Nagasaki
Kagoshima
Seoul
Naha
Yellow Sea
East China Sea
Keelung
Chiayi
TAIWAN
Taipei
Hong Kong
PHILIPPINES
Manila
Nakhon Phanom
LAOS
Vientiane
THAILAND
Chiang Mai
Pattaya
Bangkok
BURMA
Rangoon

Author's Note

In 2009, I pulled from my closet a box containing 118 letters, four journals, one daily trip log, maps, and hundreds of photographs, all from my husband's and my world travels between 1965 and 1967. This was the first time I had read these letters and journals in 40 years. My goal was not to publish a book but to combine these documents into one coherent written account. Four years later I was happy with the result, pleased that I now had a complete record of this important period of my life. I made a few copies to give to my family, while realizing that it was too detailed for a broader audience.

Jump to 2020, the first year of the COVID-19 pandemic, when we were suddenly isolated and sheltering in place. It was then that I decided to revise my earlier manuscript. As I reread my old journals and letters, I was able to become that young woman again, and I could see her grow and change. I could relive some of her adventures as a world traveler in the mid-1960s; I could feel her joys, her frustrations, her excitement.

The world seemed bigger then. It took longer to get from one point to another. Differences between cultures were more pronounced, and of course the amount of information people now have at their fingertips was not available then. We not only had no computers, Internet, or cell phones; we had no backpacker guidebooks with their detailed maps and explanations of out-of-the-way places. On the road, telephones were hard to find, expensive, and difficult to use for international calls. To receive mail, we

had to plan weeks or months ahead, usually by notifying our families of the address of either Thomas Cook & Son or an American Express office, two businesses that would hold mail for travelers.

And yet, maybe because of the isolation from our families and the slowness of communication, we continually sought out other world travelers in campgrounds and cafés. In these places we were able to share information and get new ideas about where to go and what to see. Rather than read about a site and make plans to visit it, we would often stumble upon a temple or a palace or a parade with no forewarning and no expectation of its grandeur. Of course, this was not unique to the times; many travelers find the most exciting moments to be the serendipitous ones.

Rereading my journals reminds me of how much the world has changed since the 1960s, not only in communication but in health care, living conditions, transportation. Regions that seemed peaceful then may now be in conflict. Places that were at war may now be thriving with industry or tourism. Hotels and rest houses that were old or run-down may have been replaced with modern structures. Some changes seem to be for the better, others not. This account gives a snapshot of lives—ours and others'—in this changing world.

Note: I use the geographical term "West Asia" instead of its Eurocentric designation "Near East" or "Middle East." For names of cities and countries that have changed, I use the term in effect at the time I was there—for example, Burma instead of Myanmar, Calcutta instead of Kolkata.

Introduction

Suitcases are open on the floor, the bed is strewn with clothes, wedding presents are scattered around. Frustrated and tired, I stand in my old bedroom in California. "Mom," I call out, "I don't know what to pack. I can't fit everything in." She walks into the bedroom with an understanding smile and says, "Why don't you take one of our old steamer trunks?" Her calm response reassures me. *Perfect*, I think, as my anxiety begins to melt away. That afternoon I carefully pack a trunk and a few suitcases with winter clothes, towels, books, toiletries, and even a few wedding presents.

I was 23 that summer of 1965. Mick and I had been married for six weeks. We both had college degrees, teaching credentials, and a year of teaching experience. And we were planning a trip to Europe. We quit our jobs, sold everything we had, and pooled our money. Our immediate plan was simple: we would go to Europe, buy a camper van, travel around, and hope to find teaching jobs. We had no idea exactly where we'd go or how long we'd be gone, but I wasn't troubled by that. If we couldn't find jobs or if the trip didn't work out for some reason, we could come back home. We might even be back for Christmas.

At least that was what I thought. Mick, though, as I was beginning to realize, had a different view. He was a person who liked to plan way ahead, and his immediate focus was on how to keep us safe and make enough money to keep us traveling, maybe for a year. I hadn't thought much about safety, but Mick not only had purchased worldwide health coverage for us but also had become certified through the Overseas Division of the University of Maryland to teach college-level classes in anthropology and sociology at U.S. military bases in Europe and Asia. He knew that these jobs weren't certain, but he felt that something would turn up.

As I packed my suitcases and trunk that afternoon, I didn't think it was strange that my mother had suggested that I take a steamer trunk rather than encourage me to pack less. In looking back, I think both she and I were imagining this upcoming trip less in the sense of "going out to explore the world" and more like "going to get a job in Europe." Besides, it felt normal to me to travel overseas with a steamer trunk. Though these trunks were now filled with Christmas wrapping paper, winter clothes, and memorabilia, they had been used for years by my parents and grandparents for crossing the Pacific Ocean. I was born into a family of travelers and educators. Both sets of my grandparents had lived and worked in Asia, and I had lived in the Philippines with my family for a year in 1953. More recently, in 1961, I had lived in Taiwan, where my father was teaching. I had delightful memories of living and traveling abroad, but that travel was always with my parents and sisters. This was different. Now I would be with my new husband.

And who was this guy I had married? We had very different upbringings. Mick was the first person in his family to go to college and then to graduate school. When I met him, he had not traveled outside California, but he always knew he would. He remembers opening an issue of *Life* magazine when he was 12 years old and coming across a full-page photograph of the Potala Palace in Lhasa, Tibet. The light from the intense blue sky was streaming down over the mountain. It was dramatic, unreal to him, and it triggered his imagination. Where was this mysterious palace? Were there other places like this in the world? He knew he would find out someday.

Though I had lived abroad and Mick had not, in this we were similar: we both harbored a desire to travel and explore new places. I did not question whether he and I would get along. I didn't wonder whether we would have similar ideas about how to spend our days or whether we would get tired of living so close together in a camper van. I was just thinking of the fun we would have.

How was I to know how much I would learn from people we would meet? I never thought we would be asked about the war in Vietnam multiple times, even in a small Kurdish village in Turkey. I never imagined that we would be invited to meet a maharaja in his palace in India, nor could I have anticipated that we would float on a barge down the Mekong River in Laos. Certainly, I did not know that we would often be completely isolated from contact with our families, sometimes for months at a time, or that along the way we would little by little jettison our belongings, even the trunk.

This trip, which started out on a lark, stretched out for two years and took us around the world: it became a way of life.

Part One

Leaving the USA

September 1965

I had butterflies in my stomach as we waved goodbye to our parents in California. It was early September, and we were off! For the next two weeks, we rumbled along in Mick's truck on a road trip to New York. I had rarely been in a pickup truck and had never slept in one, but I loved rolling out our blankets and sleeping cozily in the open-air bed of the truck. We had already sent our luggage ahead to New York City by Greyhound bus, so we were traveling light. I felt adventurous and free.

We traveled leisurely, with no specific itinerary, visiting friends along the way. One thing I really wanted to do was go to Carlsbad Caverns in New Mexico. Mick seemed happy driving to the Caverns, but he didn't want to go in. Why? I wondered. It seemed so exciting to me. I wanted us to do it together. He told me to go on alone, and I did, reluctantly. I can still remember my exhilaration in seeing the vastness of the rooms and feeling the welcoming coolness as I walked deeper into the cave. But I missed being able to share the experience of seeing the huge stalactites and stalagmites with Mick. I didn't fully understand his feelings until many years later when he told me that he was claustrophobic. Then it made sense.

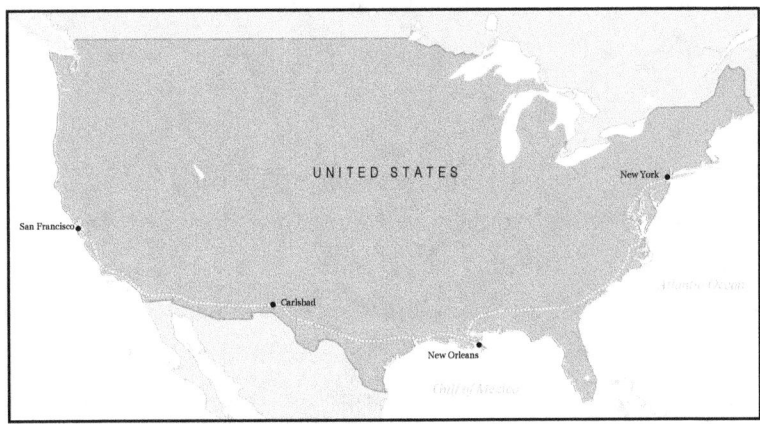

Our southern route from San Francisco to New York

Though we differed in our desire to explore caves, we were both shocked as we drove right through a hurricane that was roaring into New Orleans. Winds howled around us at 80 miles an hour as we dashed into a boarded-up hotel. Later the winds reached 150 miles an hour, and I read that Hurricane Betsy caused more damage in that area than any hurricane had since 1929. That night I stayed awake, peering through the window, aghast at watching metal signs being torn from buildings and sent tumbling down the street, rooftops being hurled to the ground, glass breaking everywhere. I had never seen such a thing. In my journal I wrote, "I was scared to death. Mick managed to sleep a good part of that night—I don't know how!" I knew that he was as frightened as I was, but I was beginning to realize that although we might share similar feelings, we didn't always respond in the same way.

As I look back on this hurricane experience, what astonishes me is how relatively little information was available about weather forecasts. The first U.S. weather satellite was launched in 1960, but it was many years before people could regularly receive national and international forecasts from newspapers or TV. When I was growing up in San Luis Obispo, California, in the 1940s and '50s, I thought of "weather" as something that was only happening over the skies of my own town. I had no images in my mind of the ubiquitous swirls of gathering storms over the Earth that we now see in the media.

WHEN WE ARRIVED in New York City, on September 16, 1965, I donned my new red-and-white-checked wash-and-wear dress, low black pumps, and nylons. Mick put on his jacket and tie. He carried my small green suitcase as we walked up the gangplank of the SS *Rotterdam*, bound for Europe. It took eight days to cross the Atlantic. Eight days! We did not think of this as a cruise; it was just a common way to travel to Europe. At the time, it didn't occur to me to fly.

Our days on shipboard passed slowly and comfortably: we ate, we slept, we talked to fellow travelers, we played shuffleboard, we ate again, we slept again. It was hard to tell the difference between night and day, especially since our tiny room had no porthole. Life was easy; all our needs were taken care of, and I loved it. I didn't think much about what would be coming up; I didn't worry about our next steps.

My mood changed immediately when we disembarked in Rotterdam, the Netherlands. Suddenly no one was taking care of us anymore. We entered the vast arrival room of Central Station. People were hurrying here and there. I was overwhelmed. Mick said

Boarding the SS *Rotterdam*, September 16, 1965

he would get the train tickets to Heidelberg, Germany, while I stayed with our luggage. Luckily, we didn't have much with us since we had sent most of our bags to a storage facility in France. I waited, perched uncomfortably on the edge of our largest suitcase. And I waited more. Finally, Mick came back, empty-handed. "Can't figure it out," he reported, clearly frustrated. I was tired and crabby as I thought to myself, *You can't even find a ticket counter?* In my mind's eye I was a child, sitting with my mother and sisters as my father went to buy tickets. But my father always came back with the job done.

So here we were in this new country, new language, unable to figure out the system, both of us exasperated, and no train tickets. *Maybe I should do it,* I thought. After all, I had studied French and had also traveled a bit by myself in Hong Kong a few years before. So why had I assumed that this was the man's job? Finally, together, we did get our tickets. I didn't tell Mick how irked I felt, and he was probably so upset that he didn't notice. We never did discuss these feelings, but while walking to the train depot, I said to myself, *Let it go. I didn't marry my father.*

Part Two:

Europe

September 1965–June 1966

1.

Setting Up—
Germany and France

"We're looking for a camper van," I said to Bodo, the English-speaking agent at the Volkswagen dealership in Heidelberg. "Maybe a used VW?" We were in luck. An American Army major was selling a VW camper that he had brought to Germany from the United States. He had outfitted it so that his family could travel around Europe, but now that the major was being sent to Vietnam, the family had to leave Germany. At the time, I didn't think about the significance of this man suddenly being sent to Vietnam. I knew that President Johnson had begun sending ground troops into Vietnam and that large numbers of U.S. military advisers were already there. But the war seemed far away to me. I was just feeling excited to be in this city, country, and continent, and relieved that we had already found a camper.

By Monday, we were the owners of a 1963 VW Kombi Camper, which we immediately dubbed "House." At $1,900, the price was more than we had planned to spend, but we didn't hesitate. In fact, we were thrilled. In my journal I mention only briefly that we had bought a camper van, but Mick's letter to his folks was filled with details, some of which I didn't even understand.

15

Excerpt from Mick's letter—September 1965:

> *It has 20,000 miles on it, but at 12,000 miles, the mechanic reversed the*
> *push rods, so 200 miles later it needed a complete overhaul. As a result,*
> *our engine has 8,000 miles SMOH, and it runs perfectly. It has the large*
> *engine—the 1500cc with 50 h.p.... The previous owner also gave us*
> *two <u>new</u> snow tires and a chemical fire extinguisher.... The interior is*
> *all custom with a walk-through to the house section, AM-FM radio, a*
> *kitchen with a 15 gal. water pumper (and a two-burner stove that we*
> *purchased), a good bed, complete lighting system (12 volt), and even*
> *a chemical "potty." It's really a cutie, completely insulated, and all the*
> *back windows, of which there are 7, are curtained.*

The details in Mick's letter to his parents are indicative of his seriousness
and his sense of responsibility. As I was to learn in upcoming months, he
was the one who kept the engine in the best condition; he was the one who
made sure the gas tank was always more than half full; he was the one who
checked the engine fluids and the tires to make sure the van was ready for
long-distance travel. Without realizing it at the time, I had begun to count
on him to ensure that both of us were as safe as possible.

WHILE WAITING FOR THE CAR PAPERWORK to be completed, Mick went to
the University of Maryland European Headquarters in Heidelberg to talk
to Jim, the director of education. Jim hadn't known exactly when Mick
was arriving, but he welcomed Mick warmly and seemed hopeful that he
could set Mick up with teaching jobs. It would take a while to contact the
U.S. bases in Europe to see which ones could advertise a class, but the first
prospect was in Seville, Spain, beginning on November 15. With this news,
I was now thinking seriously of staying in Europe beyond Christmas. If
Mick could get a class during the fall, and maybe another after that, and if
I could teach somewhere too, we'd be set. And now, with our new camper
and about six weeks before the start of a class, I was ready to play.

AS WE HEADED for the South of France, I looked forward to our first night sleeping in our new camper, all snuggled up in the down-filled sleeping bags we had just bought. We stopped in Basel, Switzerland, to get gas and change our deutsche marks into francs. A few hours later, now armed with francs, I went into a store to buy sausage, bread, and wine, but the saleswoman wouldn't take my money. I thought I had misunderstood the price and pulled out another franc, but she kept saying "*Non*" and repeating something I couldn't understand. I was befuddled. Why couldn't I pay? Finally, I realized that it was because we had crossed the border into France. I was trying to pay with Swiss francs instead of French francs. *How embarrassing*, I thought, *I should have known that.*

For the next three weeks we spent a relaxed though busy time, mostly in Paris and Marseille with my sister, who was attending college in France. She was great fun to be with, as well as an extremely knowledgeable guide. What became frustrating, though, was that Mick did not get any confirmation about teaching. My optimistic, even cavalier, attitude about getting a job with the University of Maryland was dissipating.

Journal excerpt. Paris, France. October 19, 1965:

> *All week Mick has been trying to find out about where, and if, he will be teaching. There is only one man who knows, and this man has been very inaccessible. Mick has called Heidelberg (collect of course) at least four times expecting to find out for sure each time. Now tomorrow we're again hoping for sure to reach him. Then we can plan a bit.*

The next day, as I had hoped, Mick did reach Heidelberg, and the answer was yes. The class would be in Spain. I was relieved; Mick was more skeptical than I.

Excerpt from Mick's letter to his parents. About October 20, 1965:

> *Hi,*
>
> *I have discovered that I am set up for a class in Saragosa, Spain, which lasts from 15 Nov to 21 January with two weeks at Christmas. However, because it is a small base there may not be enough men enrolling and the class will be canceled. So we may be in France instead—which is all right with me.*
>
> *M*

With the prospect of teaching in Spain, and now not needing to keep in touch with Heidelberg, I was itching to begin living in House full time. Besides our sleeping bags we now had a Jet Gaz two-burner camping stove, a Jet Gaz heater, a frying pan, a saucepan, two plastic dishes, a Styrofoam icebox, plates, cups, eating utensils, and a washbasin.

Journal excerpt. Uzerche, France. October 21, 1965:

> *This is our first night really camping. We left [Paris] at 8 a.m. this morning and have driven 314 miles. We stopped for lunch at a secluded spot off the road, and then for dinner and the night at this little deserted campground. We had our first dinner in the camper using all our equipment. . . . We're really pleased the way things are set up for living. . . . Oh boy.*

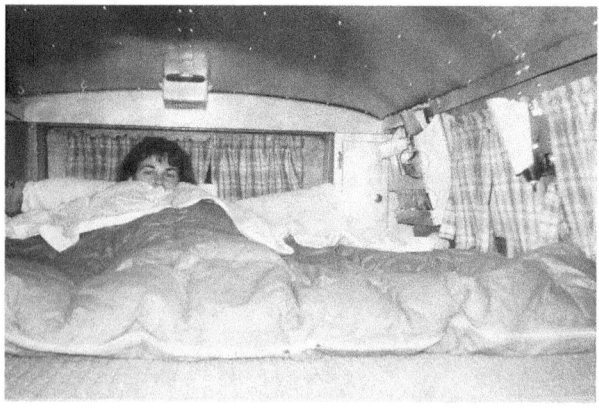

Cozy new bed

One of the ways that Mick and I differed in our approach to traveling in Europe was that I was contented to make day-by-day decisions about where to go, whereas Mick was more focused on long-term planning. He especially wanted to visit prehistoric sites where he could get firsthand experience to make his anthropology classes livelier and more personal. Mick had already written to Dr. Hallam Movius, an American archaeologist working on a site in France, and Dr. Movius had invited us to come to Abri Pataud, a Paleolithic site in the town of Les Eyzies in southwestern France. This is the area of Cro-Magnon remains and the location of the Lascaux cave paintings. It was perfect for us, and, like Mick, I was glad to have a specific aim for our travel in France.

Breakfast in Vézère Valley, France

River bathing

The lush green woodsy area of the Vézère Valley near the excavations was so delightful that we stayed there for eight days. Each morning in this idyllic spot we were greeted by the quiet rustling of leaves and the cooing of little birds. We even had a river to provide us with water for cooking and bathing. Dr. Movius wasn't around, but two of his assistants welcomed us. We ended up eating meals with them and exploring caves, castles, cliffs, and tunnels. Even with his claustrophobia, Mick was able to go in most of the caves, as he was so focused on getting an insider's view of archaeological research.

Journal excerpt. Les Eyzies, France. October 26, 1965:

> *Today we went to the Grotte de Rouffignac—cave of 100 mammoths.*
> *We were the only ones there, so it was a bit spooky. . . . We got into a lit-*
> *tle open-train and went down into the depths of the cave. Our woman*
> *guide knew a bit of English, so we got along with that and my sparse*
> *French. The cave is about 10 kilometers in all—huge! On the ceilings*
> *are many many drawings made by upper-Paleolithic man. There were*
> *beautiful pictures of bison, mammoths, mountain goats, and horses.*
> *Their faces were so sweet and kind looking. I was really impressed. The*
> *animals were very shaggy—hair hanging down from their stomachs.*
> *Also along the walls were bear scratches and on the floors were hol-*
> *lowed-out places where bears slept. The cave was made during the 4th*
> *glaciation period. We could see evidence of different levels of water.*
> *Also on the ceiling were large rounded areas formed by whirlpools.*

As we got ready to leave this delightful region of France, I wrote about the way we got access to the caves.

Journal excerpt. Ruffec, France. October 31, 1965:

> *The caves were usually on a farmer's property, and though the state*
> *owned them, they were run by the farmers who owned the land. To*
> *visit a cave we would go up to some rickety little house, knock on the*
> *door, and a little old lady would peek out and ask us what we wanted.*
> *I really felt as though I was intruding into their home. She would soon*
> *understand that we wanted to see the cave, so she would begin her*
> *little spiel about the cave. Then we'd have our private tour with a little*
> *speech. I couldn't understand all of it, but we would get the gist. The*
> *whole process was quite something.*

As we continued traveling around France, we settled easily into the routine of living together in one small space, adapting to each other's needs. I was relieved to find that we had the same comfort level in terms of keeping the camper clean. Every morning we would sweep out House and fold up the bed to turn it into a table and seats. We'd open both side doors so that we could stand outside, set up the stove on the door shelves, heat up water for coffee, and bring out the bread and jam. We had similar ideas about when to go to bed and when to get up in the morning. We agreed on how to use our time when sightseeing, whether we were learning about Impressionist paintings at the Jeu de Paume museum in Paris or visiting the World War II beach landings on the Normandy coast.

Although the easy life of going where we wanted whenever we wanted was exhilarating, the lack of information about teaching continued to be nerve-racking. We both had a gnawing feeling that the class might not work out. Even though Jim had said that there would be a class in Spain, he had not contacted Mick with any more details. Classes were supposed to begin on November 15, and in Mick's November 8 letter to his parents, he added, "*I won't know until tomorrow where I'm assigned, and even then, they may not know.*"

Without knowing whether Mick would be teaching or not, we couldn't make plans, but even more important, we didn't know how to allocate our money. Being parsimonious was easy for me, though. I liked keeping a daily account of our expenditures, a detailed task I had begun the day we arrived in Europe. My travel log indicates that during the week of October 22–28, our average daily expenditure for the two of us was $5.84. For the week of October 29–November 11, it was $7.83. I was most pleased to realize that we were spending less per person than Arthur Frommer touted in his popular 1957 book *Europe on 5 Dollars a Day*. Frommer's five dollars was based on the cost of a hotel and meals for one person, while our average daily expenses included every bit of money we spent, not only for the major items of gas and food but also for such necessities as camera film, museum entrance fees, souvenirs, and stamps. It tickled me that we were spending so little money. (Admittedly, for daily averages I didn't count the $1,900 we had spent for the camper van.)

Five days before we thought we'd be going to Spain, we heard from Heidelberg that the class was not to be. Mick wrote to his parents, "*We are scheduled to teach in Phalsbourg, France, beginning November 15. The base in Saragosa, Spain, closed down and we were switched. However, we have put in for Sevilla, Spain, for the semester following and there is a good chance we may get it."* He gave the military APO address to his parents, but added, *"The class could fall through if minimum enrollment is not met, and as such I wouldn't want mail sent yet."* He concluded his letter with a list of things to send us assuming we would have an APO address. Among the list were my Kodak Instamatic camera, our transistor radio that was broken (*"If you have time and the spirit moves you, perhaps you could have it fixed?"*), and a list of 29 books for teaching.

2.

A Job and a Dorm—France

Though in some ways I looked forward to staying in one place as we arrived at the United States Air Force base in Phalsbourg on November 11, I knew I would miss being on the road. But since Mick's classes were only on Monday and Wednesday evenings, I assured myself that we would still have plenty of time between classes to explore the region. Belgium, West Germany, East Germany, and Switzerland were all within easy reach.

We had been married for almost four months and had been camping in House most of that time, but now that we had picked up our trunk from storage in Marseille, I wanted to unpack it. I wanted to use the place mats and matching napkins and other niceties that were still put away. I wanted to live in a real house, but we couldn't find anything available in the town of Phalsbourg to rent for only two months. When the people at the base offered us two rooms with a bath in the Bachelor Officer Quarters (BOQ) for only $10 per person a month, I reluctantly agreed, at least for the first month. We unloaded our trunk and suitcases and moved in, and after that I never did look for other housing. It seemed too difficult as well as unnecessary for only another short month.

The BOQ was not where I had imagined living. It was devoid of life. The building opened into a long hallway with apartments on both sides, like a boring dormitory. We had one room with a double bed and dresser, and another with a small couch, a desk, and a kitchenette along

23

one wall. It was roomy enough, though bare. At least the building was quiet; it seemed that no one else was living there. I tried to make this barren room look more like a home by putting a few things on the walls, but it didn't help. Maybe the weather added to the bleakness of the room; it was cold, and the sky was always overcast. On the positive side, our rent included all electricity and heat, maid service, and clean sheets and towels once a week. Another advantage was that the price of food on the base was amazingly low. On November 12, the day after we arrived, I wrote in my journal, "We went into the commissary today and were so excited that we bought T-bone steaks for dinner (.73 a pound). We also had ice cream with chocolate sauce."

Journal excerpt. Phalsbourg, France. November 14, 1965:

> *I meant to write yesterday because we woke up to the most exciting thing. Mick looked out the window and gasped. The ground was white and snow was falling. It was beautiful. It snowed continuously all day long, and we were both so excited we could hardly stand it. This morning it was snowing when we woke up but it soon stopped. Now, however, it has started again—2 PM. I love to watch the flakes falling or rather floating gently to the ground. I hope it keeps it up all winter. Mick is studying and preparing for his class now. It starts tomorrow. I have been sick with flu or diarrhea or intestinal something for the last two days. Today's better, though. We're still in this horrible BOQ housing.*

For me as a Californian, that first snowfall was exciting, but my thrill of seeing it was short-lived.

Journal excerpt. Phalsbourg, France. November 18, 1965:

> *We are still in the BOQ. Things are sort of at a standstill now because of the weather yesterday. Sleet and ice. Terrible. Everything was covered with ice. Roads were so slick that one could barely walk, much less drive. So the base was closed [that day] and Mick's class was canceled.*

Though I had given up my plan of finding housing in town, I continued to dislike living on the military base. I missed the good times we'd had in Paris, in Marseille, and while we were camping. To compensate, I made a point of going to the small outdoor market in town, using my beginning-level French to buy chickens and vegetables for light cooking. While in town, at least I could pretend that I wasn't living on a military base. But when I found that the base offered a French class two evenings a week on the same days that Mick was teaching, I signed up. It helped minimally. I studied for my French class and tried out new language skills at the market, but I still felt removed from learning about France and French life.

Time on the base continued to drag. When we had been traveling, we shared our daily routines. Together we decided where to go, what to eat, and what to spend money on. But now Mick was under a different pressure than I was. He had his job, his students, and classes to prepare for. He was meeting new people. He was busy. I knew no one, and I didn't feel like trying to make friends.

Things looked up for me when I heard that the elementary school on the base needed a substitute teacher, but my hopes were soon dashed. The principal couldn't accept my California credential because I didn't have civil service certification. I continued busying myself with reading, writing, and studying French, but at the same time, I withdrew more and more into myself. A mixture of thoughts swirled around my head. Who was I and what was my role now? I was newly married with a new last name that didn't quite feel like me. I was living in a temporary place where we had a tiny cooking space but none of the new kitchen items and other wedding gifts that were packed away in my parents' basement. What was a "wife" anyway? And what did wives do on this base? Cooking? Cleaning? Sewing? My mother had not only done all that—she also was the major organizer for clubs and community activities in addition to teaching school for many years. But I wasn't her, and I didn't want to get involved in any groups on the military base.

I did not feel that Mick should be spending more time with me; on the contrary, I felt that what he was doing was exactly right. Making money to keep us traveling was crucial; it was his job. But what was my job? I grew up in an era when it was assumed that the wife's responsibility was to support her husband and keep the relationship healthy. If there were marital issues, she should be the one to smooth things over, not to complain. I did not think my role was to keep Mick happy, but I didn't know how to fit into this life. I felt stuck and lonely. I didn't talk to Mick about these feelings; I was embarrassed to admit them. Besides, they didn't seem important enough to warrant a discussion.

A BOOST TO MY MORALE came unexpectedly. Two weeks after we arrived in Phalsbourg, our van needed a new battery and some other repairs, and the best place to get it done was at the VW shop across the border in Germany. Mick was busy with classes, so I decided that I could take the van into the shop. In fact, I looked forward to the adventure. As I drove off alone toward Germany, I felt free and loose, ready to tackle anything. I was confident in my use of French as well as in my ability to manage the border crossing and the repair shop negotiations in Germany. When I found out that the shop needed to keep the van for a few days, I spent the afternoon exploring the town and had no problem finding the bus station for my return trip to Phalsbourg. Three days later, I returned to Germany to pick up the van, this time going by train, again by myself. The job of handling these tasks gave me new confidence and a revived outlook on life. And it was fun.

OUR CASH WAS RUNNING LOW. The van repairs—new battery, new generator and voltage regulator, plus my train and bus fare—came close to $100. Before I left for Germany, Mick had written to his mom, who had agreed to be our banker, and asked her to send us money from our bank in California. Until it came, we didn't have enough money to drive anywhere. It was a few weeks before we finally received Mick's mom's letter with a personal check from our bank. We thought it would be easy to cash the check, but no—it was complicated and time-consuming. The only place we could cash it was at the military base. And they would only give us American money. We took some of the U.S. dollars to a French bank in town to exchange them for francs but kept a goodly supply in U.S. dollars. This routine, of getting spending money in the correct currency, continued to be a problem, always a headache. During those months in France, we alternately needed French francs, Swiss francs, deutsche marks, and Belgian francs. It would be many years before credit cards, ATMs, and the euro eased the lives of travelers.

Friends in Switzerland

FINALLY, ON DECEMBER 9, now with money in our pockets, we left for Switzerland for four days. How I had missed the excitement of exploring new places!

The cold, blustery wind in Zurich seeped down the neck of my jacket, but I was enveloped in warmth as soon as we stepped into the restaurant. Warmth came not only from the crackling fire in a corner of the dining room but also from people chattering away as they shared pots of fondue. We had not yet tried this dish, a specialty of the restaurant, and so were pleased to be seated at a table with three other people. To our surprise, they all spoke English, and they immediately demonstrated the art of stabbing pieces of bread in the bubbling pot. We talked all through the meal, comparing governments, social issues, and politics. I learned a lot about Switzerland and was surprised when one of the diners said that Switzerland was the world's oldest democracy. I didn't refute it, but I wondered if it was older than the U.S. At the time, I didn't even consider bringing up ancient Greek democracy or the political systems of other ancient nations. But I was stunned to hear our dinner companions say that women did not have the right to vote in Switzerland. Not only that, but one woman did not think it mattered. She explained, "Well, if my husband and I agree, then it's redundant. And if we don't agree, we cancel each other out." I was so surprised that I didn't even think of asking something such as, "What if a woman is not married? Shouldn't she be able to vote?"

I was also surprised that our new restaurant friends were so aware of and so interested in American political events. Two years previous, in 1963, Martin Luther King Jr. had given his "I Have a Dream" speech during the March on Washington. President Johnson had recently signed the Civil Rights Act of 1964 as well as the Voting Rights Act of 1965. The Johnson administration had begun bombing Vietnam; the war was heating up. At that time, there were not many antiwar rallies in the U.S., but there were sit-ins and teach-ins on college campuses. I knew that changes were being made in my country, but I didn't realize that people in other countries, like these in Zurich, were also affected by what was happening in the U.S.

When the cheese started to get brown at the bottom of the pot, one couple invited us to their home for wine and Romansh cake. We stayed up late into the night, continuing our stimulating conversation. The topic of Vietnam kept coming up. I agreed with our hosts' opposition to the war, but I was conflicted. I felt like I should support my country, but I could neither explain nor justify President Johnson's actions. The best I could do was say that I too did not think the U.S. should be involved in this war.

That night, after an engaging evening, we climbed into House for a comfortable sleep parked in their driveway. Over the next few days, we continued to strike up conversations with people in Lausanne, Interlaken, and Basel, and I realized how much I enjoyed this type of interaction. I liked visiting historical sites, but it was meeting people, hearing their stories and perspectives, that fascinated me. By listening to others, I understood more about myself, was able to broaden my perspectives, and could see my own country in a new light. I was also feeling less shy about adding my own thoughts to a conversation.

After these stimulating few days in Switzerland, in which both Mick and I had engaged in open discussions that included expressing our antiwar feelings, we were driving back to Phalsbourg when we turned the radio dial, looking for a station in English. Up came the Armed Forces Radio.

A: *What's communism like?*

B: *Oh, you know.*

A: *No, what's it like, anyway?*

B: *Well, it's sort of like bad breath or body odor. Once you have it, even your best friend turns against you.*

A: *Oh. How many people are there in Russia?*

B: *About 250 million.*

A: *Imagine 250 million people with BO.*

B: *Yeah, what a place! Aren't you glad we have a democracy? Don't you wish everybody did?*

I couldn't believe what I was hearing. Was this supposed to be a joke? It wasn't funny at all. I did realize that it was a takeoff on a popular ad for Dial soap ("Aren't you glad you use Dial? Don't you wish everyone did?"), but what poor taste. I was taken aback as I realized that the U.S. military was sending this propaganda out on radio waves to anyone who could understand English. It was even more upsetting since we had just had such stimulating conversations in Switzerland. And here we were, living on an American military base. Mick was able to focus on the positive aspects: the relief of having a source of income and the joys of being a teacher. But for me, coming from an antiwar perspective, the only way I could justify living on the base was to remind myself that it was the University of Maryland that was paying Mick, not the military, and that classes offered by Maryland were helping military men explore new ideas while working toward a degree.

Checkpoints in East Germany

SINCE MICK HAD a few weeks off for Christmas vacation, we decided to drive to Paris to visit my sister, but first we headed in the opposite direction, toward East Germany. Our route took us through the ancient city of Nuremberg, a place I associated with the Nuremberg Trials that had occurred 20 years earlier. Nuremberg, where several Nazi leaders had been tried and executed; Nuremberg, one of the cities that had been bombed during World War II: it was not what I expected.

Journal excerpt. Nuremberg, West Germany. December 17, 1965:

> *What a beautiful city! The old town wall, moat, and towers still remain.*
> *There are something like seventy towers left around the city. We went*
> *into the gorgeous old church in the center with its intricate fountain*
> *nearby. It's sure nice that at least a few of the items of beauty are left*
> *since the bombings of the war.*

Having heard fearful tales of the communists, the Iron Curtain, and
the Soviet Bloc as we were growing up during the Cold War, we both felt
some trepidation as we drove north from Nuremberg (West Germany) across
the border toward Leipzig (East Germany). Germany had been divided for
20 years, and American tourists *could* enter East Germany, but few did.
It seemed to be an off-limits area. We were especially looking forward to
visiting Berlin, which was a divided city situated completely within the
borders of East Germany. The Berlin Wall had been erected four years
earlier, in 1961, and we had heard tales of East Germans being shot as they
tried to flee to West Berlin. But our sense of adventure took over. We knew
that we were leaving "the West" and the diplomatic protection of the U.S.
government when we went behind the Iron Curtain. But mostly we were
more concerned with whether we could get visas at the border.

Journal excerpt. Leipzig, East Germany. December 19, 1965:

> *We got to the border at about 11:30 today and got through the many*
> *gates without much trouble. It took us about 1½ hours to get a visa*
> *and all. We certainly didn't expect to spend as much money as we had*
> *to. The visa cost $5.00 and we had to buy insurance for the car, which*
> *was $3.75. Evidently the German Democratic Republic doesn't honor*
> *the green international insurance card. Also we bought gas coupons*
> *(30 liters for $3.20). The main thing that came upon us unexpectedly*
> *was that we were told that we could not camp, and that we would*
> *have to pay for our bed and breakfast there. So the lady took $7.20*
> *from us and gave us directions to reach our destination in Leipzig. Of*
> *course they pick out our hotel. So here I am writing in our hotel room*

near the Hauptbahnhof. When we signed in, the man at the desk asked us for our 19 marks. We told him that we had paid already and showed him our paper. He was quite astounded at that and didn't know what to do—but anyway we refused to pay. We barely have enough money to get to Paris as it is.

Mick's journal excerpt. December 20, 1965:

While in Leipzig where we had to sleep, I lay awake concerned over "House." At approximately 5 a.m. while reading "Studs" [Lonigan] the door was quietly unlocked and opened. Who me, scared? Hell yes I was! I started to get up (probably to run) but whoever it was immediately left. Have no idea what was up. We left at 6 a.m., or should I say "blew the place." We had been given 6 marks to buy breakfast (part of the deal), and we took off with the marks and bought on our own. Hot dark bread and wurst with a meat spread—yummy.

After Leipzig, it was an easy drive to East Berlin, though the roads were often either cobblestone, badly pitted, or dirt. We did not see many cars and no Volkswagens. Once in the city, the only way to drive from the Soviet sector (East Berlin) into West Berlin was through Checkpoint Charlie, the only crossing point at the Wall. We were, in a sense, going backward, since we were entering West Berlin from the east rather than the usual way for Americans, which was to visit East Berlin from the west.

Excerpt from Mick's journal entry. December 20, 1965:

The borders controlled by E. German military and police are rather ominous. The entrance to W. Berlin was as formidable a barrier as I have seen. Having passed one point, we drove to the car inspection area where House was gone through again. She passed her check ... we then drove to another checkpoint, showed all our papers and were passed through. Another point was then crossed, and finally the last station. The last, making a total of five not including the W. German inspection, was interesting. Two concrete barriers on runners were set in position to completely block the road . . . there were long rows of barbed wire enclosures patrolled by armed men day and night. . . . All had machine guns.

After the rigor of getting through Checkpoint Charlie, we found a place to park House in West Berlin and then walked back into East Berlin for the day.

Looking into East Berlin from the American sector in West Berlin

Journal excerpt. December 22, 1965:

We spent about 45 minutes for customs at the wall . . . then we just walked around E. Berlin for most of the day. We walked to Brandenburg Gate to see it from that side. We ate lunch at the Mitropa at the Bahnhof. Then we went to the Pergamon Museum for several hours. It's an excellent museum of Middle Eastern artifacts from Bronze Age times. East Berlin seems much less lively than W. Berlin. There are fewer cars, fewer people on the street, fewer gay store windows, fewer lights. We had this feeling all over East Germany. On our way back . . . we went into the Russian War Memorial—a large cold room with only one rock "altar" (maybe 5 to 6 feet high) in the center. Also a few flags. We went back to Checkpoint Charlie, crossed and left Berlin.... We drove all the way to the border last night [144 miles] and slept on the West side. We had to go through more car searching, etc., at the [German] border. We were scared that we would have to open our Christmas presents, but they, like all the other guards, just frowned, looked dubious, and then let us go. Good thing!

Family in Belgium

BACK IN PHALSBOURG, I could hardly wait until our next short trip, and it didn't take long. We took a four-day trip to Ruddervoorde, Belgium, to meet and learn about relatives Mick had never met. His grandfather Camille had left Belgium around 1900 when he was about 17 years old. He went back to Belgium in 1908, got married, and immediately returned to the U.S. through Ellis Island. Though Camille visited Belgium a few more times in his life, his wife, Julia, never did. At that point, neither had any of his children or grandchildren. But since Mick was interested in learning more about his own heritage, he wrote an introductory letter to his father's cousin, Maria. She immediately wrote back saying that she would truly enjoy our visit.

We had planned to sleep in House that weekend, but Maria welcomed us with a big smile and open arms, insisting that we stay with them. When she led us up narrow stairs to a chilly bedroom, I saw the most inviting bed I had ever seen. It was piled high with a down comforter over a feather mattress. As Maria left us to freshen up, we lay down gently on this bed to try it out. I sank into the covers and breathed deeply, wondering how I had ever existed before. This was nothing like the bed I had slept in as a child, where I was weighted down with three heavy woolen army blankets.

On the first day, we visited Camille's younger brother August, who was 74, and his wife, Margarita, in their tiny farmhouse. It was chilly inside August's house, but steam from the soup pot on top of the wood-burning stove helped warm the dark room. When Maria explained who we were, August and Margarita both grinned from ear to ear as they squeezed our hands. August couldn't believe that he was actually meeting his brother's American grandson.

Tante Emma's *spellewerk* and bobbin

Over the next four days, we were taken from house to house, meeting cousins and second cousins, aunts and uncles, in both Ruddervoorde and Courtrai. Camille's younger brother Gustave was 73 years old; his only living sister was Emma, 80 years old. Tante Emma was still making lace doilies (*spellewerk*), as she had been doing since she was about 10 years old. We watched her weaving very fine lace, using about 20 or 30 four-inch bobbins made of bone for each doily. She sat with a leather pad on her lap, moving the bobbins so fast that her fingers were blurred. She said that it took her about 100 hours to weave a 15-inch lace doily. None of the younger relatives were making doilies, and she said that the bobbins weren't being sold anymore. In fact, her bobbins were 70 years old. This seemed to be an art that was quickly dying, so I was exceptionally thrilled when she gave us one of her doilies and a bobbin.

Every day we ate, talked, and even danced around the house in Zorba the Greek style. We were amazed at the amount of information the family had about the California relatives and chagrined at how little the Californians knew about the Belgians. At one event, the Belgian relatives brought out a family tree that was almost up to date and asked us for the latest information about the California side of the family. Communicating was difficult, but we got along with a mixture of French, English, German, and Flemish until 22-year-old Fernand arrived with his girlfriend. With his excellent English, we didn't struggle anymore to communicate.

As we left Belgium on Sunday, many of the old people had tears in their eyes, as did I. One lasting effect of this visit was that several of Mick's California relatives, having heard our stories, later visited Belgium, thereby strengthening the relationship.

Mick holding new *klompen* (wooden shoes)
at the family gathering in Belgium

In 2011, many years after this trip to Belgium, we had the fortunate opportunity to meet Fernand again when he and his wife, Gerda (who had been his girlfriend in 1965), were visiting Los Angeles. We had a delightful time recalling memories from 46 years earlier. The most surprising to me was hearing Gerda's recollection. She remembered that I was wearing Levi jeans, of which she was envious because she could not buy them in Belgium. I didn't remember that I had worn Levi's then, and I did not know that Levi's were unavailable in Belgium. I do remember hearing, though, that it was good to carry a few pairs because they could be sold for extra cash.

A WEEK AFTER WE returned to Phalsbourg from Belgium, Mick's class was over and we were headed to Spain, since Mick was told that Naval Station Rota, near Cádiz, would be offering a class. As I began to pack, I was surprised at how much we were carrying. Though we had sent back several of our books, as well as some souvenirs and other items through the APO service at the base, we still had a lot. We didn't lack for containers, though;

we still had our two suitcases, Mick's canvas duffel bag, a briefcase, and of course my steamer trunk. Cumbersome as the trunk was, it was handy, and we could hoist it up to the roof rack of our camper. I knew we were carrying a lot, but I wasn't ready to get rid of more since I wasn't sure what lay ahead for us. Even so, I was also beginning to realize that, looking back over the past four months, what was important in our travels was not what we were carrying, nor even the places we visited. What was memorable were the people we had met: the couple in Switzerland, the extended family members in Belgium, the archaeologists in France.

Excerpt from Mick's letter to his parents. January 1966:

> *Hi,*
>
> *We'll write as soon as something is definite in Rota [Spain]. Don't know a thing yet. Anyone who must depend on a job certainly shouldn't work for this system. And yet, it is the uncertainty that makes it so exciting to me. I love this vagabond life and have no desire to settle anywhere.*
>
> *M*

Journal excerpt. Ussel, France. January 23, 1966:

> *Yesterday morning we left Phalsbourg for good. We're terribly anxious to move on, to meet new people, [learn about] new customs, etc. Mick's new class (if it materializes) starts a week from tomorrow.*

3.

Waiting and Wondering—Spain

Spain! Blue skies, green rolling hills, gorgeous mountains, sandy beaches, whitewashed houses with red tile roofs: it was all so welcome. This was the first time we had seen donkeys and mule-drawn carts on the road, often laden so high with grain that we could hardly see what was pulling the cart.

Journal excerpt. San Sebastián, Spain. January 25, 1966:

> For the first time in at least two months we are able to cook outside. Now it is 9 P.M. and still we have the doors open. What a great feeling after living in ice, snow, wind, and cold for two months. (The temperature got down to 0 F a few times in Phalsbourg.) . . . As soon as we crossed the Spanish border we saw the sun peeking out. . . . We drove on to San Sebastián . . . and have a gorgeous camping spot high on a hill. We took a little hike before dinner—what a view! On one side of the hill was the ocean; on the other were San Sebastián, the mountains, and a few scattered villages; the sun was just setting; the lights one-by-one sparkled on. We're terribly excited about the prospects of living here for two months. Today was a good beginning.

Seville was teeming with people in the late afternoon. I wanted to walk around and soak up the energy, but first we needed food for dinner. In France we could easily find a *charcuterie* for meat, but here we drove and drove around town and didn't see a store that looked right. We finally parked the car and walked, but still couldn't find anything. I had no idea where to go. Maybe, I thought, food was only sold in the morning at open markets. We'd have to wait until tomorrow to look again. But we were so hungry we continued walking until we finally saw a small store that had a few bins of fruits and vegetables and some canned goods on the shelves. None of it looked very good, but we bought a half-kilo of peas for eight cents. Then down the street we found a *panaderia* with freshly baked rolls. This would be a good enough dinner, but as we were walking back to the car, we caught an aroma of something delicious. A vendor was selling piping hot fried shrimp and fish. I had no idea how to ask for a few pieces of fish, and since I'd been doing the marketing in French for the past four months, it was hard to bring up the words in Spanish. I finally blurted out the same words I had used for the peas, "*Un medio kilo, por favor,*" and pointed to both the shrimp and the fish. It seemed to work. The woman smiled as she handed me a package that looked way too big, and I promised myself that I would immediately begin studying Spanish again. My high school Spanish had receded to some dark place in my head.

Living on the Beach

"BAD NEWS," THE DIRECTOR of the Education Department said. "We advertised the class, but only six people signed up. The minimum is 12, so we can't offer you a class." What a shock. We had arrived at Naval Station Rota with high hopes of Mick getting a job. Even though we knew that the class offer depended on enrollment, we had assumed that we would be living in Spain for the next few months. Mick had even asked for his check from Phalsbourg to be mailed to Rota, and we had already written to our parents with our new address in Spain. So now, since we didn't have enough money to go anywhere, our only choice was to stick around and wait for the check to arrive. The department director said it would be fine for us to pick up mail there; it should come soon.

We thought about telephoning our parents about not having a job in Spain but then decided against it. Making an international phone call not only was expensive—it was also a hassle. First, we would have to find a post office where we could order the call. Then we would have to wait in a little booth until the operator put the call through. If we finally did get through, we had to shout to be heard over the static. It wasn't worth it.

After about an hour of moping about, the idea of staying in Spain without Mick teaching a class began to sound just fine. Maybe we'd stay through the winter. Maybe I could get some money teaching English. I could put an ad in the *Diario de Cádiz* or go around to schools to see if I could set up English tutoring classes. That night we camped on the beach near an abandoned World War II bunker. We went running on the sand. I felt free and excited; I wanted to jump in the ocean, but it was still a bit cold for swimming.

The next day, though we knew the check would come soon, Mick was worried about not having money in hand. He wrote to his parents, explaining the situation.

Excerpt from Mick's letter to his parents. January 29, 1966:

Hi,

The check from Maryland has not arrived yet and may be held up because of class cancellation. To ensure that we don't starve, could you send $20.00 and as soon as Maryland comes through I'll send it back. We eat on $1.00 for both, but gas is .70 a gallon. All our money goes into the car—it is everything to us—home, car, etc. If it goes, we go. Remind Mamie [Grandma] I have a birthday soon. I hate to be a moneyman, but we will need two heavy-duty tires and I'll just apply her present to the cost. We still have our PX cards, so I can buy them here for a cheaper price. We hope to send you a few of our acquired and read books, as they add weight and take up space in "House." As

you can see, things are up in the air around here, but then this trip
wouldn't be as exciting as it is if it weren't for a little confusion.

M

On our second day in Rota, we looked for a new place near the beach to camp, one that was more secluded since we had been on the road for almost a week and wanted to shower outside. It didn't take us long to find the perfect spot surrounded by trees just behind a newly built apartment building. Only a few people had moved in, so it was quiet. The next day we planned to hang out: to cook, wash clothes, and clean out House. We thought no one was around the new building, but around midday someone walked over.

Excerpt from letter to my parents. Rota, Spain. January 30, 1966:

Dear Daddy and Mom,

At around noon we saw a man approaching. We were sitting in the sunshine as I cut Mick's hair. We thought the man would tell us to leave but instead he just talked a bit. He was fascinated by our car. He kept walking over and staring inside, telling us how "bonito" it was. [But] the best thing was that he took us inside one of the "motel" units, pointed out the bathtub and shower and turned on the hot water for us. He also said we could fill up our water supply. Boy, oh boy! Nothing could sound better for people who have no shower than to have someone tell us we can use their shower. We jumped at the chance!

Love,

Patti

For the next few days, we stayed at this beach, enjoying the solitude and the proximity of hot water. We rearranged the cupboards and closets in our camper van, sorting out a pile of books and clothes to get rid of. Though we had already sent several boxes home from Phalsbourg, we realized that we still had too much. Luckily, the education director had said we'd be able to use APO services while waiting for the check.

The more time we spent camping on the beach, the more life slowed down. I still had not put an ad in the paper for English tutoring. I began to think that it might be better to try to set up an English class for Spanish employees at the Naval Station. A couple of days after that, we decided we wouldn't look for jobs after all, but just travel around Spain after the check arrived. Maybe we'd stay in Spain for a month or so, and then make our way to Greece and Turkey. Or we might go to Morocco. Maybe Tangiers.

Our daily routine was slow and satisfying. We would check the mail everyday (not finding any) and then go to the market. Since we had no refrigeration, we'd often cook a midday meal while the food was fresh. We had two burners attached to our Jet Gaz tank, so we could boil, fry, or heat food in two pans at the same time. Often, though, we used only one burner since the second one didn't have much of a flame. Still, we cooked simple, tasty meals, especially when the weather was warm, it was not too windy, and there was water nearby for heating or boiling.

In the afternoons we'd read, relax, wash, and clean up. Though our money was slowly dwindling, we weren't too worried. We lived on about 50 pesetas a day (the rate was 60 pesetas to one dollar). Seamlessly, we fell into roles that would continue throughout our travels. Mick tended to the van; I kept records of our expenses and other daily information. We continued to share cooking, shopping, and cleaning, though mostly we each washed our own clothes.

ON FEBRUARY 2, WE saw a sign for horse riding stables at the Naval Station, so we went in to check them out. Though we didn't ride any horses, we did have a good talk with Jim and Gail, the Americans in charge. They invited us to their house for dinner that night. I was looking forward to this, not only for dinner and the chance to talk more, but to see the inside of a Spanish house. From the street, all I had seen were chipped, dirty-looking whitewashed walls, but every now and then I had an enticing glimpse through an open door of a tiled courtyard.

That evening, as we walked through the narrow hallway into the court-yard leading to Jim and Gail's house, I was enamored of the delicate tile work and the garden with bushes and flowers. The quietness contrasted with the hustle and bustle of the street outside. From their small and cozy living room they took us up a narrow flight of stairs to the roof, where we could look down into the courtyards of several houses. Women were cooking at outdoor kitchens and washing clothes at a community well; children were running around. What a difference from the secluded places we camped in. The glimpse of these families casually intermingling made me a bit homesick, but not enough to give up my camping life.

The most intriguing part of the evening was learning about the Guardia Civil. We had seen these guards, always walking in pairs, ever since coming to Spain. They seemed to be everywhere: in towns, by the highway, along the beach. We had heard that they were a force to be feared, especially during this time when General Franco ruled the land, but we didn't know much about them. That night I wrote about what Jim and Gail said.

Journal excerpt. Rota, Spain. February 2, 1966:

[The Guardia Civil] is [General] Franco's more-or-less "personal" army. . . . They are the "highest law of the land." They supersede any and all of the other policemen in Spain. They carry out Franco's orders and are personally responsible to him; no one else is above them. We heard of a case where a Guardia Civil ran over a gypsy boy on a bicycle. The boy was killed, so the [guard] stopped to talk to the gypsies there. When he stopped, one of the men came toward him with a knife. The [guard] shouted to stop, but the man kept coming. So the [guard] shot him with his rifle. The rest of the gypsies came toward him with knives so he shot them all. After that incident 12 men lay dead in the road. The Guardia Civil had no trial or any reprimand. All he had to do was pay for the ground they were buried in.

I didn't believe all the stories about the Guardia Civil, but I decided that it wasn't something to test. Whether true or not, they were frightening to hear. The stories didn't deter us from camping, though, since we felt that they didn't apply to us. We were not Romani or Spanish, but foreign travelers. However, we decided we would pay due respect if we encountered armed men! That feeling was soon to be tested.

THOUGH THE CAMPING PLACE near the newly built apartment building was excellent for a few days, more people began moving in, and we couldn't continue to use the water of the kind man we had met earlier. We didn't want to go to a campground because they were all too expensive (45 pesetas/night), about the same price as getting a hotel room, so our daily routine now included driving around looking for a place to camp. We became quite selective in our search: the best spots were near the beach (because we liked the view), secluded (so we could wash and dress outside), and quiet (so we

could relax). In addition, it had to be a new place since we didn't want to attract attention by parking in the same place on consecutive nights. Sometimes it took an hour or more to find a place that wasn't

guarded and wasn't on a private road. A few times we were chased away from a spot. There was one beach where we felt comfortable staying more than one night. It was off the main road and not in anyone's way. The only action we saw were men with their packs of burros who came by in the early morning to load up with sand.

One afternoon we saw one of the burro men again. He eagerly approached us, even letting me ride on his burro. Mick had quite a conversation with him. I don't know how much education the man had, but with his minimal English and Mick's minimal Spanish they covered a lot of ground. The most surprising was that the burro man asked about "the Negro problem" in the U.S. "Wow," Mick said later. "I didn't know this was a worldwide topic!" This was the second time we had been asked about civil rights actions in the U.S. The first time, in Zurich, wasn't as surprising since it had been a part of a long evening discussion at the Swiss restaurant. But now, hearing this man on the beach in Spain, I was becoming more aware of how broadly the actions of the United States were felt by people outside the U.S. I would have liked to know where the burro man got his news and how he compared the issues in the U.S. with those in Spain, but we didn't have the language ability to delve into such issues. It was clear, though, that he not only was interested in what was happening in the U.S.; he had definite opinions about Americans at the nearby Navy base. He didn't like all the new bars in town, and he was angry that several Spaniards riding bikes had recently been killed or injured near the base.

LATE ONE NIGHT, AFTER our first few nights at this beach, we heard a banging on the side of the car. Mick sleepily stuck his head out the window. Two rough-looking men with bandoliers across their chests stood outside. We had seen the Guardia Civil from a distance but had never interacted with them. "No camping on the beach," one of the men said to Mick in Spanish. "You have to leave." "OK, I understand. Can we leave in the morning? We have no place to go right now," Mick responded in his basic Spanish. After a bit of cajoling, they seemed appeased and left. We stayed awake for a while that night wondering what we would do the next day, hoping that they wouldn't come back, and afraid that they would. I thought about the Guardia Civil stories we had heard. But the next day, we still couldn't find a good place to camp, so we went back to the same beach. We parked in another part of the beach, hoping they wouldn't see us. But it happened again: that night, two men banged on our door. I didn't know if they were the same men or not, but they didn't tell us we had to leave. They just shined their flashlights into the car, looked us over, and said a few things that we didn't understand. With that we felt relieved enough to return the next night. But so did the Guardia Civil. The visits continued, always in the middle of the night.

After a few days we got used to being woken up and checked out. I wondered what they thought about us. Were we just two people breaking the law, or were we two young foreigners who didn't know any better? Did they wonder if we were German (because of our German license plate) or American (because of the USA sign on the back of House), or would that even matter to them? Maybe they shined their flashlights into the camper because they wanted to see what it looked like inside. Whatever they thought, they didn't seem to want to shoot us. We decided to view them as our protectors. Sometimes they would let us stay; other times they said we'd have to leave because we were blocking the men and their donkeys, even though we were careful to park out of their path. It got to be a routine for both the Guardia Civil and us. We smiled at them and began to recognize those on the regular beat. For the most part, they let us stay.

AS OUR TIME CAMPING on the beach stretched out, the issue of money became more critical. We couldn't imagine why Mick hadn't received the check from Heidelberg, since we had been told that it would come right away. At that time, of course, there were no ATMs for instant access, nor did we have any local bank where money could be deposited or taken out. One morning Mick was so frustrated that he drove out to the base and asked if he could contact the education office in Heidelberg. I had decided to stay in town and wander about, but when he picked me up, he told me how complicated it was to make a call. A technician set up the call on a one-way radio transceiver. "Heidelberg, Heidelberg. This is Rota. Over." "Hello, Rota. This is Heidelberg. Go ahead. Over." "I have Mick Sullivan here who wants to talk to you. Over." And the technician handed the transceiver to Mick. "Hello, Jim. I haven't received my check yet for the class in Phalsbourg. Do you know when it was sent? Over." And the conversation continued with Mick holding the radio transceiver and pressing the button alternately for talking and listening. When he told me about the transceiver, I couldn't believe that military personnel still communicated between bases in this way. It was clumsy and outdated. Didn't they have telephones? Whatever the reason, at least Mick got to talk to Jim, who said he would look into the money issue.

For those first 10 days in Rota, we rarely drove anywhere besides the food market. Since we had already spent $30.29 for gas driving from France to Rota, we now doled out pesetas sparingly. We watched every penny, mostly living on bread, oranges, and bananas. Sometimes we could get artichokes, and now and then we bought eggs or a chicken. From January 30 to February 6, we spent $7.53. That was almost all for groceries, but it also included $1.20 for 32 liters of gas and 51 cents for mailing letters. Every day we hoped the money would come from Heidelberg.

Trip log

One Saturday, while waiting for Monday's mail, we spent the day at the house of another American couple, Larry and Betsy, whom we had met a few days earlier. It was nice to meet people our age; we hit it off right away. They were quite interested in our camping experiences, and we were interested in their life in Spain. Betsy had asked me if we'd like to use their washing machine, and I gladly took her up on the offer. I gathered all the clothes we had, washed everything in her machine, and then carried the load up to the roof to dry. Our clothes ended up blowing in the breeze along with the clothes on everyone else's rooftops. It was a perfect sight: the bright sun, the blue ocean, and dancing clotheslines everywhere.

Journal entry. Rota. February 6, 1966:

> *We are still camped at the beach, still receiving nightly checkups with flashlights by the Guardia Civil and still waiting for the check from Heidelberg. Tomorrow is the day we expect (and hope for) it to come. We think we can last until Tuesday, though. We have 57 pesetas left (60 pesetas = one dollar). Tomorrow is Mick's birthday, and I feel horrible because I can't buy him anything—not even a cake! Maybe our money will come.*

The next day, Monday afternoon, we did get some money in the mail, though it was not the check from Heidelberg. Mick's mom had sent us a money order for $100. We still had to wait for the check from Heidelberg, but at least now we were able to drive the car and even buy a few extras.

Excerpt from Mick's letter to his parents. February 7, 1966:

> *Howdy,*
>
> *Well, today we received your letter and money and were darned glad to have it. I'll start by saying that of course we can't accept it as a straight gift and that as soon as the money comes from Maryland I'll return yours. We still have some money in the bank, and the truck [sale] will also bring us some.... Our tentative plans ... are as follows: leave here end of February, drive to Rome, up to Salzburg, perhaps Prague, down to Vienna, across Bulgaria, and into Yugoslavia. Then into Greece, where I hope to teach. On to Turkey and then down the Tigris and up the Euphrates rivers, through the Near East and to Aqaba in Jordan. There we hope to hitch a ride on a freighter to wherever he's going.*
>
> *M*

Mick's journal entry. Rota. February 7, 1966:

> *My birthday and one I won't forget ... with [the] $100 [we] filled our tank with gas—$1.16—and our bellies with ice cream and candy. Mailed our packages and ate dinner on the beach. Went to a show and returned to our house with the Guardia Civil and the Shore*

Patrol to provide guard over us. Tomorrow we drive to Cádiz for Jet Gaz, other essentials, and then back to the base for a supply of packaged protein, which will last us in times of stress. So we are now affluent.... Trish made my birthday a happy one with two presents: a box of chocolate-covered raisins and Hershey bars.

We needed to refill our Jet Gaz tank with cooking gas, a task that we thought would be quick and easy. It wasn't. We couldn't find the place. We had an address in our Jet Gaz booklet, but no one could give us directions to get there. By midday, after driving all over, we still had not found the shop, and everything was closing for the afternoon. We knew they wouldn't open until about 4:30, and we were tired, angry, and frustrated. We really needed that cooking gas! But we decided to give up looking and instead go shopping and sightseeing. I bought Mick a leather tie and a bota bag for his birthday, and a leather belt for myself. We took a tour of the Moorish cathedral; we hired a horse and buggy to take us to the archaeological museum. The streets were lively and teeming with people, since a fiesta was coming on Sunday. The spirit was infectious, and I finally felt relaxed. That evening we even found the Jet Gaz shop and got our tank refilled.

While we were now carefully doling out our dwindling pesetas, the stress of waiting for money was exasperating. Neither of us had ever been in a situation like that. Even though we knew we had money in our California bank, and we knew we would eventually get the check from Heidelberg, it didn't relieve our anxiety. We could forget it for a while as we walked around town or went to a museum, but the underlying anxiety permeated our daily lives. The surprising thing, though, in retrospect, was that we didn't take out our frustration on each other. Maybe it was because we only had each other to rely on. Or maybe it was because we both knew that we always had support from our parents. Whatever the reason, in my letter to my parents, I didn't even mention my anxiety over money.

Excerpt from letter to my parents. Gibraltar. February 10, 1966:

Dear Daddy and Mom,

This will be the longest time that we have lived only in our car. We're doing quite well, I think. I should think that it would be quite hard to live in such close quarters with anyone else. After all, we are very rarely outside of arm's distance from each other, and if we are, it is usually for less than an hour. This is really living together. We are both very happy with everything, though—no problem. Yesterday morning [in Rota] we didn't see each other for about 45 minutes. I got gas and went shopping and Mick got the mail. When we met again, we had so much to tell each other that we were just bubbling and jumping to get it all out!

Love,

Patti

Monkeys and Baths in Gibraltar

THOUGH WE STILL HADN'T gotten the check from Heidelberg, I was itching to get away, so we figured that we could use the money left from Mick's mom's $100 for a short trip. Since the van needed a checkup, we decided on our first destination: the Rock of Gibraltar, where there was also a VW garage. The drive to Gibraltar was a quick three hours. As we rounded a hill, there was the gorgeous sight of the Rock and the Strait. I was amazed by how large it looked. The customs process for leaving Spain was quite tough, though it didn't compare to East German customs. Our car was searched thoroughly; one man continued to mutter "*Muy bonito*" as he looked at all the items stored away in our cupboards and closets. We heard that it would be much more difficult to leave Gibraltar than to enter, and we soon discovered why. The city turned out to be a shopper's paradise. There were Swiss watches and clocks, German Hummel figurines, Chinese ivory knickknacks, Spanish Toledo jewelry, Moroccan tapestries. It seemed like we could find anything from anywhere, and the prices were low! That first day we just walked around to get our bearings and make a plan for the next few days. We looked all over for a camping spot but couldn't find one, so we decided to park behind the VW garage for the night. It wasn't very pretty, but at least we'd be there when they opened in the morning.

That next morning, we were first in line to get the work done on House, soon finding out that it needed new shocks, clutch bearings, and an exhaust manifold. While the work was being done, I decided to stay in House to read and write, since it was raining a bit and there was no comfortable waiting room in the garage. Mick wanted to walk around and watch the men work. As I was settling in to write, I suddenly felt a strange sensation of movement. The van was shaking a little back and forth. I looked out the window, and sure enough, I was slowly being hoisted up above the heads of the mechanics. I don't think they knew I was inside. At first, I felt a bit panicked, but then I realized that the van wasn't going to fall off the hoist and I was perfectly safe as long as I didn't open the door to get out. And why would I? I had everything around me that I needed. While I was writing a letter, Mick called up to me, "Hey, it's teatime. Let's have some coffee." Sure enough, all the workers had gone to get their tea, so I set up our stove to boil the water, then leaned down and handed the coffee to Mick. I drank mine while comfortably hoisted above everyone's head.

WE ENDED UP STAYING in Gibraltar for three nights. We couldn't find any good place to camp, so we parked in a road pullout area for the second two nights, where we got a kick out of the friendly macaques that climbed on us and on our camper.

On one of the days as we were driving around the Rock, we saw a sign advertising a public bath. Since it was chilly and our camping spot obviously had no amenities, a bath sounded idyllic. We each paid the equivalent of 21 cents and ventured in, Mick on one side of the building, me on the other. The bathwater was wonderfully hot and deep. I wanted to soak with the water right up to my neck, but the tub was so long that my feet couldn't reach the front end when my back was at the other end. I kept trying to relax and get comfortable, but I couldn't stop from slipping down. I stayed as long as I could stand it, then dried off and walked out to meet Mick. I told him about my struggle with the long tub, and he said he had had the same problem. We both laughed at the thought of each of us trying to soak while fighting to stay above the water.

Macaques abound

What's a WT?

IT WAS IN GIBRALTAR that we began to sense a new image of ourselves as travelers. We met a couple from Rhodesia (now Zimbabwe) who were on the road with their 12-year-old daughter. They had been living in their VW camper for two years and were in the process of returning to Africa. I was amazed. Two years? Traveling with a child? Returning to Africa? We had been living in Europe for four months, but that seemed like nothing compared with this family. Up to this point, I had thought of myself as a young person traveling in Europe, living out of our VW camper van, getting some jobs, and having fun. My not-very-thought-out plan had been that we would continue traveling for a few more months. Maybe until summer. But two years? That seemed like forever. We were not like this family from Rhodesia; we were just two people having fun. But were we in the same category? My view of our vagabond life was beginning to change.

After leaving Gibraltar, we went back to Rota to check the mail. There was no paycheck yet, but it didn't dampen our spirits this time since we weren't ready to leave Spain. That night, while at a campground in Cádiz, we were again inspired, this time by a couple from New Zealand who were older than us, both retired. We spent a good part of the evening in their van, looking at maps and talking about places to go, things to see. They had been camping all the way from India. Mick, who had been fascinated with maps all his life and whose high school friends had not shared his longing for travel, was now thrilled to meet people who shared his interests. In his journal, he wrote that it was so exciting to meet "moving, adventuresome people with international ideas."

Mick's journal entry. Cádiz. February 13, 1966:

> *[We met] a retired engineer and his wife [who] began their journey in Bombay and are now in Cádiz. We learned much from them. He said, "It's too bad you've started so early in life on your travels; you'll never get over it now!" He is right. This is my life from now on out! I'm now meeting the people who share my view on life. I'll see the world before I'm through.*

For the next 10 days, we stayed on the road: watching a bullfight in Cádiz, tasting Tío Pepe in a Jerez bodega, enjoying Seville again. But we continued to rehash stories of people we had met in campgrounds; their lifestyle choices and places they had traveled excited us. I wanted to meet more people like this, and in a campground in Portugal—which enticed us with its hot showers—I wasn't disappointed. We walked around the campground, looking at various people's setups and passing on information about where to go, where to camp, what to see, and what to look out for. The people we were most drawn to, a couple from Seattle, had a camper like ours. We had dinner with them and talked until about 11 p.m. It was hard to sleep that night, as we were so energized by a feeling of kinship with these travelers.

Something else struck us at this campground: people were referring to themselves as "WTs": world travelers. WTs were people living out of camper vans or car-camping with tents. They were meeting in campgrounds, swapping stories while poring over maps. They were going to Africa and Asia; they were headed toward India and Nepal or Morocco and Egypt. They were coming from Australia, the U.S., Germany, England.

My mind was expanding; I sensed something large. Was there really a new movement, a loose confederation of world travelers? Were we part of it? If so, how could that be, given that we had made our own traveling decisions by ourselves? We hadn't joined a group. But maybe that was what this movement was: a lot of people like us who had left their homes, who were itching to see the world, who were not worried about getting jobs, who were traveling with no timetables, and who were not ready to settle down. Maybe we really were part of a larger event. The concept of WT felt right. There was one thing we knew for sure: we felt most comfortable when we were with other travelers, looking at maps and talking about where to go next.

WHEN WE RETURNED to Rota, we contacted Betsy and Larry again, and invited them over to House for dinner. It was the first time we had entertained dinner guests.

Excerpt from letter to my parents. February 27, 1966:

Dear Daddy and Mom,

We had a couple over for dinner night before last. The dinner was lousy, I thought, but Mick was very appreciative. I'm not used to cooking for four people, and there wasn't enough. We used all the rice we had.... Mick asked Betsy if she'd like sugar in her coffee and she said yes. I knew all the time that we didn't have any!... Also we only have 3½ plates—one melted halfway. We only had two cups, so they drank their coffee out of glasses they had brought. I was out of napkins and forgot to even offer them toilet paper. Mick had to sit on his little suitcase because we only have room for 3 to sit.

Love,

Patti

Though we were enjoying our days, underneath everything was a growing anxiety about money.

Journal excerpt. Saturday, February 26, 1966:

> *We are still waiting for our check from Heidelberg. Mick has called them [again] and they have drafted us a new one. I guess ours got lost in the mail. We're hoping for Monday morning now. It has to be there!*

The check did not arrive that Monday, and now we had become so anxious to leave Rota that we thought we'd go without the check and have it forwarded. I did not want to wait any longer. We were both at the end of our rope, though still we didn't take out our frustration on each other.

On Monday, February 28, I wrote in my journal, "We're still waiting for the check. . . . Tomorrow we'll leave whether it comes or not." The next day was March 1, and the check was *not* in the mail. Despite our decision to leave that day, we didn't. We kept thinking that if we left, we might never see the check, so we stayed a few more days, checking the mail each day. Finally, on March 3, the check was there!! Four hundred and fifty dollars. We could hardly believe that it had come. After waiting more than *five weeks* for a check that we thought would come in a few days, we could finally leave Rota.

That day, after picking up the check, we bought two new tires, a toolbox, and a water jug. That night, Larry and Betsy had us over for dinner. They served us huge porterhouse steaks, fried potatoes, celery and carrots, Brussels sprouts, and ice cream and cookies. It was the most we had eaten at one sitting for months. Larry and Betsy had been especially good friends during the time we were in Rota. They had given us food, done us favors, and just been nice. The next morning, with a new lease on life and money for the gas tank, we left the beach, the market in Cádiz, and our Guardia Civil protectors. And we drove 213 miles to Granada.

On Our Way

THE ALHAMBRA WAS MUCH more impressive than I had imagined. As we were buying our entry tickets, two American students asked us if we were from the Madrid tour. We said no, and they responded that they were supposed to be guides but they couldn't find the group. They were from New York and were spending a year in Granada. They said they would like to take us on the tour, as it would help them prepare for their upcoming test. What luck for us! We spent the whole day with them, marveling at the delicate architecture, the exquisite gardens, the arches and pillars, the fountains and pools. It was hard to leave. In Granada I bought a copy of *Tales of the Alhambra*, and I couldn't put it down.

This was the second time that I purposely began reading a book that focused on a place where we were staying. The first was *The Hunchback of Notre Dame*, which I began reading in Paris. In fact, the excitement of reading *Tales of the Alhambra* ushered in the beginning of a new practice: whenever possible, I would read a novel or historical piece or whatever I could find that was situated in the location we happened to be in. Of course, we always bought maps and sightseeing information when available, but picking up a historical novel or a history book added another dimension and led to a broader understanding of the place where we were staying.

OUR LAST DAY in Spain was March 7. We had heard from Heidelberg that there would be no class in Greece or Turkey, but there was a chance of teaching in Verona, Italy. We were sorry that we had to leave Spain without going to Morocco, but it seemed more important to be ready for a possible teaching job, should one come through. We had already told our folks to write us in care of American Express in Vienna but that they might also reach us as we passed through Marseille or Rome. We were looking forward to a new phase of camping life.

4.

A Community of Travelers—Italy

After 10 relaxing days, mostly in Nice and Marseille, Mick got sick. His temperature was so high that both of us felt like our bed was on fire. The next morning, he stayed in bed, mostly asleep, and I decided that I might as well drive to Rome as we had planned. We were 320 miles away, but one of the nice things about living in a camper is that one person can stay "home" (in bed) while the other continues the journey. And you both get there. We had been sharing the driving for the past few months, but this was the first time I was the only driver for the whole day. I didn't mind the driving; it was easy and relaxing. Mostly I worried about Mick, but I thought he would get better with some rest. A few days later Mick's fever disappeared; he just felt exhausted.

In Rome we got mail, including a letter from the office of the University of Maryland in Heidelberg. Mick opened it immediately, hoping to read about arrangements for teaching in Verona, but the news was not good. Jim had not been able to arrange a teaching job in Italy. Even worse, he said there would be no job in Greece or Turkey for the term. It looked like our plan to travel and teach was falling apart. Spain had not worked out, and now Italy and Greece were not working out either.

We stayed in Rome and Florence for several days, seeing the sights, reading guidebooks and history books. I began *The Agony and the Ecstasy*, which drove me to examine more of Michelangelo's work. We decided that even if Mick didn't get any more teaching positions, we would keep on traveling at least until summer. I came to this decision in part because of the intoxicating atmosphere in campgrounds. Spring had arrived and the weather was warm. Not only were the trees and flowers beginning to bloom, but the tents were popping up in green, blue, and yellow hues. Languages also blossomed: we were hearing Italian, French, German, and English. What a change from camping in the U.S., where there seemed to be one color for tents—drab khaki—and one language spoken: English.

Florence campground with trunk on top of House

In the campground in Florence, people would put up their tents or open their camper doors, maybe set out little tables and chairs, and then wander from campsite to campsite, finding out where people were from and what languages they spoke. We had become used to the routine in Spain and were looking forward to it. As before, people shared stories about where they had been and where they were going. It was exciting not only to compare people's experiences but also to think of the whole world as a place to explore. The whole world! We came away inspired with the thought of going east and made immediate plans to drive north to Austria, then through Yugoslavia, and then into Greece. After that, we'd drive on to Turkey. We were open as to what would happen after that. We'd have to watch our money, but we could do it. We loved the feeling that we were part of a multinational community of travelers in Europe.

Though we enjoyed meeting people in campgrounds when we were in Italy, as we continued driving through Eastern Europe, we rarely stayed in them. They seemed too expensive and not necessary. Instead, we would look for secluded side roads or fields. The lengthening afternoon shadows would be the sign that we needed to look for a pull-off spot to prepare our dinner, clean up the dishes, and turn the table into a bed before dark. Even now, 50 years later, when afternoon shadows begin to lengthen, I feel the tug of "time to pull over and find a safe place to sleep."

5.

International Flavor and Tasty Mushrooms— Yugoslavia

Ljubljana was the capital of the Socialist Republic of Slovenia, one of the six republics that formed Yugoslavia. During the Cold War, Yugoslavia had not been one of the countries "behind the Iron Curtain," nor was it a part of the Eastern Bloc; rather, it was a member of the Non-Aligned Movement. But as we had been brought up during the Cold War, our thoughts were colored by stories of Marshal Tito and the communists. We wondered how we would be viewed. Were we the enemy to them? Did the children grow up hearing horrible stories about Americans? Did people have enough to eat? Were they all oppressed? As we drove into Ljubljana, we were pleasantly surprised. We didn't see rich-looking homes, but we didn't see slums either. We saw a variety of newspapers for sale: *Pravda*, the *New York Times*, and *Le Monde*, to name a few. We saw flags of the United States, Russia, Germany, Italy, and other countries. I hadn't expected such an international flavor.

Later that afternoon, we learned much more about Yugoslavia. The previous summer, one of Mick's friends had said, "If you're ever in Yugoslavia, look up my friend Denis in Ljubljana. He'd love to meet you." It was with some hesitation (Who is this guy? Would he really want to talk to us?

Will he still be at the same address?) that we entered a large office building and met Denis, the former editor of the widely circulated newspaper *Delo*. Denis had excellent English, and he seemed as eager to talk to us as we were to him. He quickly put us at ease as he spoke about his country, its independence, its open borders, its policy of free trade and freedom of the press, and its form of representative government. He compared the American newspapers he had seen in the States to the local papers, commenting that Yugoslavian newspapers contained many more critiques. An hour sped by as we talked nonstop. All the while I was realizing how narrow my impressions of Yugoslavia had been. The next day, we stopped in a supermarket where shelves were filled with foods from a variety of countries, further eroding my preconceived notions. The prices were lower than those we had been paying in Italy, so we stocked up on canned goods, starches, fruits, and vegetables.

WHEN WE BOUGHT OUR camper van, we were pleased that it had a chemical toilet that hid under a cushion on the seat just behind the driver. With the cushion in place, the seat was part of the dining room table arrangement, and that's usually how we left it. In fact, we never did set it up as a chemical toilet, since that would have meant keeping chemicals sloshing around in water in the bucket. In addition, I didn't know exactly what kind of chemicals we were supposed to use or where we would buy them. But we also had special plastic bags that came with the camper that would attach to the toilet seat.

Though we rarely used the toilet, I did find it especially convenient one day. We were in a large city, parked downtown on a busy street, and I really needed to use the toilet. There were no public facilities around, so I went inside our camper, closed the curtains, and attached a plastic bag to the toilet seat. Even though no one could see inside House, I felt embarrassed sitting there since I could hear people talking as they walked by. The problem came later. What to do with the plastic bag? I got out, feeling conspicuous as I carried my bag, walking up and down the street looking for a garbage can. There was no waste receptacle in sight. I didn't want to leave the bag in the gutter, as I thought a dog might open it, and I didn't want to keep carrying it around in the camper, so I kept walking. After a long, unsuccessful search, I reluctantly placed the tied-up bag in a remote part of an alley near some other garbage and walked off. I didn't look back.

ONE LATE AFTERNOON near Belgrade, Yugoslavia, as the daylight began to wane, we drove up a little cobbled road and pulled off in what seemed to be a secluded spot. As we got out to open the side doors, we noticed four or five little faces peering at us from the bushes near the road. The children kept getting braver and coming closer, and soon we were laughing and doing our best to communicate in sign language. It wasn't long before a man that we assumed was their father approached the car, and when he saw the "USA" sign on the rear bumper, he smiled and invited Mick to come with him into their house.

I was only a little worried about seeing Mick go off with the man; mostly I wondered why I hadn't been invited. I did want to see where they were going, but I stayed near the car with the shy but curious children. Before I was truly worried, I saw Mick returning with a small group of men and woman and a few older children. Mick was holding up a bag of fresh mushrooms and lettuce as he introduced me to the father, the mother, the grandpa, the grandma, and the next-door neighbor. The father's English was good enough for us to understand that his brother lived in Chicago, where he was doing research on mushrooms. We were surprised to learn about this connection between communist Yugoslavia and the United States; at home we hadn't heard anything about such research opportunities or such information sharing between our two countries.

That evening I cooked up a delicious mushroom dinner, with a gaggle of giggling kids accompanying the sizzling of our mushrooms. As the food cooked, we let the children examine our cooking setup and peek inside our camper. After dinner, the parents came out again and invited us back to their house for coffee and sweets. Then they took us on a short walk to a place where they had dug out a large section of the mountain to store their mushrooms. I absorbed the pleasant, musty, yet fresh aroma in the sweet darkness in the cave. The father explained that they were using new growing techniques provided by his brother in the U.S. We had an animated conversation with our hosts that evening; they joked about their government, laughing as they referred to themselves as "good capitalists." Before we left for the night, the father said that we should move the car to the front of their house, that it would be safer there. I preferred the more secluded spot we had chosen, but we did as he said. On the next morning, they invited us in again for coffee. While there, Grandpa asked Mick if he could exchange a dollar bill. Mick gave him the dollar, and he gave Mick 1,300 dinars. It was much more than we would have gotten at the bank. Apparently, the black market was quite lively.

Belgrade family who invited us in and gave us mushrooms

6.

May Day—Bulgaria

Three days later we were in Sofia, Bulgaria, an Eastern Bloc country, satellite state of the Soviet Union, and member of the Warsaw Pact. Despite this, maybe because of our experience in Yugoslavia, we didn't worry. In fact, it seemed adventuresome and somewhat daring to be traveling behind the Iron Curtain in "enemy" country, according to our Cold War perspective. It was May 1, which, to my mind, meant dancing around a maypole and leaving flowers on the front doors of neighbors' homes. I had no idea that May 1 was anything bigger than that. I was in for a surprise.

Excerpt from letter to my parents. May 6, 1966:

Dear Daddy and Mom,

The whole city was decked out for the holiday, with red banners, flags, and huge pictures of Marx and Lenin and other men. Practically every house and building was decorated. There were also huge posters showing "the workers" (men and women in overalls). All morning long there was a parade, but it was the most unique parade I've ever seen. It was a real "workers" parade. The people marched. There were very very few spectators; in fact, you weren't allowed to get onto a sidewalk for seeing the parade unless you had a pass. We don't know how one gets a pass; all we know is that we weren't allowed in. However, there were throngs of people milling around who, we soon found out, were *in the parade. When the parade started, we found ourselves in the middle of it! In fact, the only way to get anywhere was to march with the parade. Someone gave me some red paper flowers, which everyone had, and away we marched. The streets were filled with mobs of people, but there were only a few people watching. Soon we came to the grandstand. On the top row stood about ten big party officials, and as we passed the stand, everyone in the parade chanted and raised their flowers. Then the officials waved with arms outstretched. I also raised my arm and shook my red flowers, but I was a bit more timid than the men around me. I felt strange saluting, but I felt worse <u>not</u> saluting when all other arms were up. So after we had marched past the grandstand, we ducked out onto the roped-off sidewalk. We stood there right across from the grandstand to watch the rest of the parade. It was all the same—crowds of people marching by and chanting or shouting as they passed the party officials. There were also huge pictures of Marx and Lenin that were carried, raised above the crowd. The whole thing was fascinating.*

Love,

Patti

Patti (lower right corner, facing camera) in the
parade. Sofia, Bulgaria, May 1, 1966

I felt not only out of place in the parade but also uncomfortable being hemmed in by so many people. I was glad that we didn't seem to be identified as Americans, since many of the posters were denouncing the United States for being in Vietnam. But I also felt thrilled that I could blend in or at least not be singled out.

After the parade, we wandered around a bit, stopping in two different cafés. In each one, people came up somewhat hesitantly, clearly recognizing us as outsiders, wanting to talk. Usually they thought Mick was German (because of his beard?) and I was French (my hair/my clothes?), until we spoke English and said we were Americans. I was surprised when we were told that everyone was required to march in the parade. If they didn't, they might lose their jobs. No wonder we had seen such huge crowds! One of the men who talked to us said he was not a communist, so he had no way to get a better job. He was not happy with the government, and he wanted to find out if other parts of the world were any better. Another man said they were not free to talk and that if anyone came up to us after we left the café, we should say that we were talking about all the wonderful tourist sites in Bulgaria. It was hard to know what to think about these conversations. Certainly, it would be disenchanted people who might seek us out. We had no idea as to how many people would agree with the ones who quietly, and somewhat nervously, spoke to us.

7.

Dancing and Partying—Greece

After few hundred miles on the road, and a welcome break for a picnic and wash-up, we entered Greece. It had been two weeks since our last pickup of mail in Vienna, so we were thrilled to be handed a small stack of letters at the American Express office in Thessaloníki. Though we spent several happy hours reading news from home, there was nothing from the University of Maryland about future classes for Mick. Another blow. Even so, we weren't ready to stop traveling; the more we talked to other travelers, the more we wanted to keep going, maybe all the way to Asia.

Excerpt from letter to my parents. May 6, 1966:

Dear Daddy and Mom,

You mentioned going to India and the Orient. Well! This is our big dream, but whether or not we can fulfill it now is another matter. There are several things yet to be decided. The biggest is money, of course. . . .
We have to come home somehow, and we would rather go to S.F. by way of the Pacific. We have heard of people getting rides on freighters in exchange for work. Sounds a bit unrealistic, but one never knows. We have begun inquiring about freighters to see where they go, where they stop, etc. Everything is certainly up in the air now, and we aren't too anxious to break up our leisurely life by returning to the U.S. rat

race. Neither of us feels like stepping into a time-consuming teaching job. But money does run out. We are living on $200 a month—gas, food, everything. Our limit is supposed to be $50 a week, but last week we spent only $30. Pretty good, huh? We eat well, too. . . . Back to getting home—we could also drive to India (we know many people that have driven that route), where we could possibly sell our beloved House for ship tickets. Evidently cars can be sold in India for a very high price, but I wonder how many Indians would want a "House." So, as yet we don't know anything. I don't think we could afford to drive to India unless we have another job before then, but the U. of Maryland seems "out" as far as jobs go. Too bad.

Love,

Patti

Hair washing in the stream

My last comment in the letter to my parents was premature, since in Athens Mick finally got good news: he was scheduled to teach an anthropology class in Adana, Turkey, beginning on June 6. Great news! With this deadline, we could be more relaxed about staying in Greece for a month. The not-so-great part was that Mick wouldn't know whether enough students signed up for the class until June 1. At that point, he could pick up a letter in Istanbul that would give the final word. Though we knew we couldn't count on this class yet, it was still encouraging to think that teaching with the University of Maryland might still work out. But even if it didn't, we would keep on traveling.

THE CAMPGROUND OUTSIDE ATHENS was very well situated, mainly because the bus regularly came right by the camp. As with our Florence campground, we could easily visit tourist sites all day, leaving House safely in the campground. We wouldn't have to negotiate city traffic or park House on city streets. Though we didn't think the camper would get broken into, it seemed prudent to leave it parked at the campground.

ONE EVENING WE WERE enticed by the aroma of chickens roasting outside a little café near our campground. We decided to buy one to take it back for dinner, but instead we ended up going inside to eat. What an evening it turned out to be! First a man came over to our table to talk with us, and then the group at his table invited us to come sit with them. We joined them, and as the evening progressed, the café livened up. Greek music was blaring from the jukebox and people started dancing. One of the men began playing the spoons, something new to me. Spoons, as a musical instrument? I marveled at his ability to get so much rhythm and tone just out of spoons clacking together. Then Western music began playing, and the people at the table pushed Mick and me out onto the dance floor. No one else was dancing, and I turned red as a beet when I felt that everyone in the restaurant had their eyes glued on us. We did our best at a combination of jitterbug and slow dancing, and when we finished, a Greek man asked me to dance. Here I was again, embarrassed at being the center of attention. The man was an excellent dancer, leading me smoothly and firmly, but for the first part of the dance I kept stumbling as we whirled around in what he later told me was a German waltz. After that, everyone began dancing, so I felt less onstage and more comfortable. We ended up having a delightful time until late in the evening.

Just before we left to walk back to our campsite, the people at our table said they wanted to have a party for us next Saturday. A party? For us? I was astonished, and I wondered if they really meant it. After all, we had only just met a few hours before. Yes, we had been friendly and had had a great time, but I doubted whether these people at the restaurant—nice as they seemed—were serious. We told them we couldn't come, as the next day we would be driving down the peninsula to Sounion. I thought this explanation would be the end of it, but they responded by saying that that was no problem, it was only Monday, and we could be back by Saturday. Then they gave us a sheet of paper with directions for a taxi driver. We couldn't read the Greek, but we said we would try to see them next weekend. Though I thought it was presumptuous for these people to tell us when we had to be back in Athens, it was certainly gracious. I also wondered if the party would really happen. If it did, though, it would be fun to meet these local people again.

The next day we drove south to Sounion, to the very tip of land. We found a spectacular camping place high on a rocky ledge near the sea, not far from the remains of the temple dedicated to Poseidon. It was so delightfully beautiful and relaxing that we stayed four days. On the first day we scrambled down the cliff to a little secluded beach. I was soaking up the warm sun, feeling the soft sand under me, enjoying the quietude, when a group of five middle-aged women and one man set down their towels and bags near us. That didn't bother me, but I was surprised when the women immediately stripped to their bras, underpants, and slips, and went swimming and wading. When they got out of the water, I was again surprised that they so unabashedly walked around in their underwear. It was quite funny, I thought, and certainly odd. Maybe Europe was socially ahead of California.

The big news in Sounion was that there would be a solar eclipse the next morning. We got up early to gather with a small group of campers. There were six of us: one man that we had met earlier in the campground outside Athens and two young women with an older man, all from somewhere in Scandinavia. Someone had rigged up a hole in a can and another person had a smoked glass. I wasn't sure what to expect as we all waited quietly.

It was eerie. The temperature slowly got colder, and the light receded. The animals stopped making noises and everything was still. So quiet. I felt as though my eyes were deceiving me, as the darkness then came quickly, but with a deep blue cloudless sky above. We waited breathlessly, taking turns looking through the hole in the can. Then the moon passed, and the light began returning. We were all astonished at the effect the eclipse had on us. We were subdued; no one wanted to break the silence. No other humans were around. I felt like we were alone on the planet as we stood on those desolate cliffs overlooking the sea.

Later that day, as Mick was walking down on the beach, he saw the Scandinavian women and the man with whom we had watched the eclipse. As they walked out of the water, he immediately noticed that the women had been swimming topless. Brazenly, he walked over to greet them, and when they invited him to their camp to look at maps, he didn't hesitate to follow. ("What?" he told me later. "Of course I would follow topless women.") Surprisingly enough, as soon as they got to their camp, all three of them took all their clothes off. At the time, I was still up at our campsite, but when Mick didn't come back, I decided to walk down to the beach too. And there was Mick—fully dressed—surrounded by two naked women who looked to be about 18 to 25 years old. Then I looked at the man—who seemed to be about 50—and saw that he was also completely naked. He and Mick were poring over maps, talking about possible travel routes to the east. All this activity seemed perfectly natural and normal, but naked?

ON SATURDAY, AS PLANNED, we returned to the Athens campground. We wondered whether we should try to get to the party that we had been invited to a week earlier. Maybe they wouldn't remember that they had asked us to come. Furthermore, could we even find that house? With some hesitation and a bit of trepidation, we decided to go. After all, it would be another adventure.

We left by bus, following the directions that we could barely understand. The first bus got us partly there, but when we changed buses, we realized that we were going back the same way we came. Obviously, we had gone too far, and it took us at least an hour to backtrack and find the house. As we walked up to the door, we could tell that it really was a party. The people inside, some of whom we recognized, greeted us with hugs. We listened to rock-and-roll records, watched our hosts cook, and danced a variety of Greek dances (following along as best we could). The Greeks we had met seemed so open, so musical, and so welcoming. I loved every minute. Since we didn't speak more than about five words in Greek, and few people spoke any English, there were some bumpy times, but the laughter got us easily through the evening. When the food was put on the table, people all started feeding one another. I was taken aback when someone picked up a fork, stabbed some food, and stuck it in my mouth. We ended up getting fed more than the others, and we both ate way too much.

After dinner, everyone divided more or less into two groups: the older people in the kitchen talking and the younger ones in the living room dancing. The surprise to me was that I ended up being pulled into the kitchen with the older group. At 24 years old, I felt like I should be dancing with the teenagers; they seemed to be having more fun. But the older group was where our hosts thought we belonged, so we obliged.

Though it was getting late, the party didn't seem to be winding down at all, but we were concerned about getting downtown in time to get the regional bus back to our campground. As far as we knew, the last one left downtown Athens for our campground at 12:30 a.m., so we told our hosts we should leave the party by 11:30 on the neighborhood bus. They were convinced that there was no need to leave that soon, that we could stay at least until midnight with no problem. We didn't, though. Our hosts walked us to the neighborhood bus, told the driver where to let us off downtown, and said goodbye. By the time we had changed buses and arrived downtown, it was 12:15 a.m., but the bus that went by our campground didn't come. Maybe it had left early, or maybe we had the time wrong. We didn't know if another one would be coming, so we waited. And waited. Several came by, but none with the right number. There were no taxis, so we had no other way to get back to the campground in the middle of the night.

We waited some more. Finally, after 45 long minutes, a bus stopped that was going our way. With relief, we got safely back to our camp and into bed by 2 a.m.

WHILE IN ATHENS, WE cleaned out more of the books, papers, and clothes that we didn't need anymore. Again, as in Spain, the education office at the U.S. Army base let Mick use APO for mailing boxes. It felt good to have more space in the camper. In fact, the more we traveled, the less we found that we needed. This practice of traveling light was one I would judiciously follow the rest of my life. Even then, I realized that what was important about traveling was not what I had packed, but the people we were meeting along the way.

It was at this time, somewhere in Greece, that we decided to get rid of my grandparents' steamer trunk. I had carefully packed it with clothes, books, kitchen items, towels, toiletries, and other items that now seemed excessive. The trunk had been traveling with us for eight months, usually strapped on top of the camper. We didn't need it anymore, but we had no one to give it to and nowhere to leave it. We debated quite a bit about what to do with it, finally agreeing that it would be OK to leave it near the road. I was reluctant, since this seemed like littering, but I convinced myself that someone who could make good use of it would find it. When we came to a deserted spot, we lifted the trunk down from the roof of our camper, placing it somewhat off the road but near enough to be seen. As we drove away, I looked back at the trunk, thinking of how I had packed it so carefully the previous summer and how much I now realized that I didn't need to carry those things. I was also thinking of all the world journeys that the trunk had made, mostly on ships crossing the Pacific Ocean. I hoped that my grandmother would feel that it was a good thing that we were leaving it in that spot, that we weren't abandoning it but, on the other hand, were allowing some lucky person to find a treasure.

8.

Leaving Europe—
European Turkey

On May 28, we said goodbye to Greece and crossed the border into the European part of Turkey. As we drove on toward Istanbul, we saw women and girls wearing ankle-length black cloaks and scarves or hoods. Camels and water buffaloes were near the road. Most surprising, though, was our first Turkish campground, Mocamp, located behind a BP gas station several kilometers west of Istanbul. It had a swimming pool, free showers with hot water, hot water in every sink, free gas for cooking, and a large room with tables, chairs, pots and pans, and about six gas burners. Most of all, it was exceptionally clean, and the toilets even had toilet paper. We settled in immediately and, as usual, began talking to other campers. Two of the groups were going to Pakistan. The more we talked to them, the more we knew that was what we would do. We would not return to the U.S. yet, even if the class in Turkey fell through. To cement this decision, we bought a new map. It covered the territory from Turkey to India.

Of the travelers we met at the Istanbul campground, we had the most fun with Dave, Kathy, and their three-year-old daughter, Lizzie. Dave and Kathy were about our age, also from California. I was amazed that they could travel with a small child. For Lizzie this was a regular life; she seemed perfectly happy as she ran around giggling with people in the campground. Everyone played with her, and she seemed perfectly content to be the center

73

of attention. When Dave and Kathy were busy cooking dinner or wash-ing clothes, they would put a child's harness on Lizzie and tie her to their camper so she couldn't wander off. I had never seen such a harness, and it seemed a bit like putting a leash on a dog, but it certainly did bring peace of mind to Dave and Kathy. They, like the two of us, were headed east. We weren't sure where or when we might meet again, but just in case our paths crossed, we wrote down the addresses of various post offices between Turkey and West Pakistan (in 1971, West Pakistan became Pakistan) where we might pick up mail.

DURING OUR PREVIOUS EIGHT months of travel, we had often encountered situations that were new to us, but as we continued traveling, we were confronted with events that we couldn't explain. One afternoon in Istanbul, as I was walking down the street, an older woman wearing a veil and long coat suddenly grabbed my purse, pulling at it as she shouted at me. I held on tight, but it didn't seem like the woman wanted to rob me. Maybe she was upset by what I was wearing. Or maybe by my uncovered head. Several other people stopped and stared at us but gave no indication that anything was wrong. The woman finally let go and walked away, still shouting. I was taken aback, more surprised than scared, but I decided to view it as a onetime incident rather than a reflection of society.

ON JUNE 3 WE heard from the University of Maryland about Mick's class: it was a go. Relieved, we left Istanbul immediately for Incirlik Air Base near Adana, Turkey. The class was to begin on June 6, and we were more than 400 miles away. Despite being in a hurry, we decided to cross into Asia by way of the Dardanelles, a strait that separates Europe and Asia, rather than the Bosporus in Istanbul. This route was a little longer, but it would allow us to visit the archaeological site that was generally considered to be ancient Troy. We knew that there was a ferry across the narrowest part of the Dardanelles to the town of Çanakkale on the Asian side. It all sounded fine to us, but when we got to the port, the ferry had already left. The next scheduled one wouldn't come back for an hour. Normally an hour's wait wouldn't have fazed us, but since we were in a hurry, we arranged to have House ferried across the strait on a small boat that looked more like a raft. I didn't think the van would fit, since another car was already there. But with the help of a few men guiding us, we inched our way on. The boat was so small that our bumper, tied to the edge, hung over the water. As we set out across the strait, the waves increased, splashing all of us. We docked safely, a bit wet and ready to cross Anatolia. To the west, our last views of Europe faded into the distance.

Crossing the Dardanelles

Getting off the raft on the Asian side

Part Three:

West Asia

June–September 1966

9.

A Job, a House, and
a Landlady—Turkey

It was a short drive from the port of Çanakkale in western Turkey to the site of Troy. I wandered through the ruins of this legendary city but was disappointed that there wasn't much to see other than a few low excavated walls and rocks scattered around. There was no indication that this might have been ancient Troy. For me, it was more exciting to see camels along the road as we drove through Anatolia. We had arrived in a new part of the world. Women and men wearing *shalwar kameez* (baggy pants and a loose shirt) walked along the highways. Many of the women had their faces or heads covered, and most turned their backs as we drove past, whether from the dust or because they didn't want to be seen. People often flagged us down for rides, but we didn't stop. Driving by them seemed impolite and selfish, since we had room in our van, but we justified this because we didn't know the customs and didn't speak Turkish. Even so, I felt uncomfortable and unfriendly passing them by.

We drove steadily through Anatolia for almost a thousand miles, and after two nights, on June 5, we arrived at Incirlik Air Base, outside the town of Adana on the southern coast of Turkey. Mick started his anthropology class two days later. He wasn't wild about going back to teaching again, especially since we had both become used to the rhythm of continual travel.

On the other hand, we were very glad that he had this job. Without it, how could we keep on traveling?

Along the highway

Turkish village

Excerpt from Mick's letter to his parents. Adana, Turkey. June 22, 1966:

Hello All,

Traveling certainly broadens our perspective of the United States and the world as a whole. I hadn't realized how "boxed in" we actually are in the U.S. in regards to our understanding of other cultures. I could travel like this for the next five years at least and never tire of it. . . . As long as the jobs keep coming in, and I hope they will, we'll keep right on going.

Mick

When we arrived at Incirlik, we were again confronted with the issue of housing. I wanted to find a place in town, but the military was offering us a room in the Bachelor Officer Quarters (BOQ) for about a dollar a night. How could we pass it up? Not only was it cheap and immediately available, but also the base offered a swimming pool, a movie theater, miniature golf, and a bowling alley. Since we had been on the road for the previous five months, the "comforts" seemed amazing, even if we never wanted to bowl or play miniature golf. As we moved our things in, I vowed to look for another place in town.

Incirlik Air Base is only about five miles from Adana, so it was easy to get to town. I took the local bus so I wouldn't have to worry about parking or driving in town. During the first week that Mick was teaching,

I ventured into town twice to get a sense of where we were. Most women wore Western-type clothes, though a fair number wore *shalwar* and a few covered their faces. I was conscious of my dress and always wore blouses that covered my shoulders and arms, and skirts or pants that were not too tight. On these first downtown walking trips, however, I learned—the hard way—not to walk too close to men. It seemed like every man that walked toward me would end up rubbing shoulders with me as we passed. One man shocked me by grabbing my bottom as he walked by. After that, I skirted all passing males, even walking out into the street to avoid them.

Patti in an *araba*

The more I wandered around Adana, the more I wanted to live in town, despite obnoxious men. I liked the feel of this quiet town, and I liked using *arabas* (horse-drawn carriages) to get around. Being on the base was too confining for me. It separated me from the Turkish people, and I kept thinking about how isolated I had felt when we lived on the base in France. However, the base did offer me a chance to learn Turkish, so I signed up for a language class and began studying Turkish daily. I also kept my eyes and ears open for a place to rent in town.

During our second week at Incirlik, we heard about a house that was available. A Peace Corps volunteer (PCV) who was living there would be gone for the summer, but he wanted to keep the house for when he returned. We went to look at it and immediately liked it. We paid the landlady the whole amount of rent—$32—for the next six weeks and moved in. The place was perfect for us; we had our own space in a Turkish house. Our landlady spoke no English, which made for an ideal situation in terms of my learning Turkish. I described the house in a letter to my parents.

Excerpt from letter to my parents. Adana. June 26, 1966:

> *Dear Daddy and Mom,*
> *We have quite a large yard inside a high brick wall. The trees inside are so thick that when I look out of our upstairs window, all I can see are treetops—I can't see the walk or the wall. We have two rooms upstairs—a bedroom and an "everything" room. Downstairs is an open courtyard, a kitchen, "bathroom" (hole in ground), and shower room. We do almost everything, except sleep, in the open courtyard.*
>
>

Love,

Patti
>

There was no way to lock the house, but that didn't seem important to us. We didn't expect anyone to walk through the garden to the backyard. We were surprised, therefore, on our first night to be awakened by the sound of people walking into the house. It turned out they were friends of the Peace Corps volunteer and were as surprised to see us as we were to see them. In fact, we ended up sharing the house several times with other PCVs that summer. People just seemed to wander in from time to time. It made the summer more interesting.

I liked being close to neighborhood life. I didn't mind the hot days and nights, or even the mosquitoes and flies that dominated the house. By living in a neighborhood in town and by meeting PCVs, we ended up learning more about life in Turkey than we would have if we had stayed on the base. More important for me, living among Turks that summer brought to the fore cultural biases and practices that I hadn't realized I had. Some of the situations I encountered were exacerbated by a lack of language, as with the episode with my purse in Istanbul. In that case, had I been able to understand what the woman was saying, I might have understood what was happening. But other times my lack of understanding had little to do with language. Rather, it was that others did not share my expectations. For instance, when we rented the house, I thought of the rental as a business agreement. I didn't expect our landlady to concern herself with our personal well-being. But when we returned from a short trip on our first weekend, we were met by a distraught landlady. She said she was worried to death, thinking that we might have had some sort of accident. As for me, I was surprised that she even knew we were gone or that she cared. Realizing this, I began to act more like a guest, or like family. After this first weekend, we always kept our landlady informed of our whereabouts.

Our Adana house behind a corner bread store

Another situation at our landlady's house occurred one day when I clearly stepped outside the bounds of appropriateness. We had a piece of flatbread that was a few days old and quite hard. I tossed it in the garbage can. It wasn't long before our landlady was at our door, the offending bread in her hand. Her message was clear, even with my meager command of Turkish: "How could you throw away good bread?" she admonished. Even if it was hard, it could be used in various ways. I felt humbled and embarrassed. Of course, she was right; I did not realize how thoughtless I had been. From then on, I was careful not to throw away any food that could still be eaten or used in cooking.

It was not only relations with our landlady that made me realize my cultural biases. I often watched children playing and neighbors ambling on the street outside our house. One of the neighborhood men had no legs, but he was able to scoot around on a low makeshift wooden platform with rollers. He would push himself along the street with his hands. One day some young boys began teasing the man by grabbing the rope attached to his scooter and spinning him around until he fell off. The man could do nothing to stop the boys as they laughed at him and ran away. No one stopped the boys, even though several adults watched, some of them also laughing. I was aghast that these boys were allowed to harass this man with no interference from the adults nearby. Then I realized that my shock arose from my own culture and experience in a way that—I assume—was not shared by those around me. Of course, I had no idea how those adults felt. I just know that no one seemed bothered, and no one stopped the boys or helped the man up. Obviously, I couldn't tell exactly how the man was feeling, but the look on his face seemed abject and resigned. I also realized that part of my shock was seeing the primitive cart the man was using. My feelings were mixed. I was glad that he was able to get around outside, that he was not kept cooped up in his house, but I also felt that he should be respected and not be teased or played with like a toy. I wondered what the neighbors felt. There was so much that I didn't understand about life in this neighborhood.

Historic Sites and a Hamam

MICK'S CLASSES WERE ONLY two days each week, so, as in France, we used these four-day weekends for traveling outside the city. Our first trip outside Adana was to the capital, Ankara. What a city! And how different from Adana! Ataturk wanted this city to be a symbol of modern Turkey, and it certainly was. We were impressed with the tall white buildings, tree-lined boulevards, wide streets, and neat houses. What also surprised me, though, were the many American military personnel walking around. Ankara seemed almost like an occupied city.

Our trip to Ankara was not only for pleasure. Though we had just arrived in Turkey, we needed to prepare for travel after Mick's class, and Ankara was the only place to get visas. It was an easy process; in fact, we got three in one day. The Syrian visa cost $1.52, the Lebanese visa was $2, and the Iraqi one was only 22 cents. At all embassies the staff were friendly. Those at the Iraqi Embassy were the most gracious; they served us coffee and gave us numerous maps and pamphlets. Before giving the visas, however, all three embassies made certain that we had not been to Israel—or "so-called Israel," as one staff person said—and that we were not planning to go. They made it very clear that if we went into Israel, our visas would not allow us into their countries. We had heard from other travelers, though, that if we wanted to enter Israel, the border guards would give us a visa on a separate piece of paper rather than stamping our passport.

It seems unbelievable to me now, in the 21st century, that Mick and I shared one passport. After we got married the previous July, we applied for the passport with our two photos on one page. It was not only allowed but expected, and I never thought to question the policy. Never did it occur to me that one of us might need to be—or even want to be—separated from the other. Even more surprisingly, I did not notice that our single passport listed only Mick's full name, birthday, height, birthplace, hair and eye color. I, on the other hand, was described simply as "wife Patricia." Not even a last name!

The brochures that the embassies gave us in Ankara focused mostly on history or government; they were informative but too general for our needs. For people who were traveling like us during the 1960s, there were no appropriate guidebooks for this part of the world. Even if we were given advice from residents in the area, it was not very helpful, since most people who hadn't traveled like us couldn't anticipate our needs. The most useful information came from other travelers. When we met them along the route—at campgrounds, restaurants, coffee shops, or bus stations—the questions were always the same: Where are you headed? Where have you just come from? Where's a good place to camp? What are the roads like? What's exciting to see? World travelers had the intimate details that we needed, especially those who had just come from the direction we were headed. And everyone wanted to pass on "the latest find," whether it was a temple, a restaurant, or a friendly shopkeeper. It wasn't until 1973 that the first edition of *Lonely Planet* was published; it was written by a couple who had traveled much like us, from London to Australia "on the cheap." It was even later than that when books such as *Rough Guide* and *Let's Go* were available.

Camping in southern Turkey

ON THE WAY BACK to Adana we made a quick stop in Cappadocia. I had not heard about this fascinating region. I was amazed at the rock churches in Göreme and the structures that looked like mushrooms or fairy castles. Some of the caves date back to the fourth century; many of the Christian frescoes are from the 11th century. We didn't have enough time to linger there; I hoped to go back there again when we had more time. In fact, we did not get back to Cappadocia that summer, but years later I did make numerous delightful trips to Cappadocia.

THE RICHNESS OF TURKEY'S ancient history was one of the exciting things about exploring the country. Since Mick was teaching anthropology, it was especially important for him to get personal insights that he could add to his class lectures. We did manage to visit several sites, but not all of them turned out as we had hoped. On June 23 we drove north to visit the large Neolithic site of Çatalhöyük, 261 miles away. The first 24 hours of the trip turned out to be disastrous. Though we had been told that the archaeological site was open and that Mick as an anthropology teacher could visit, when we got there the people who controlled the dig had not arrived, so we could not go in. We had to be satisfied with peering over a fence, where we saw an excavated mound that revealed a few low walls. This didn't help Mick much for his lectures, but at least he had seen the site and its surroundings with his own eyes. As for me, I was feeling sick with some sort of intestinal problem, so I was not enjoying much of anything.

That night, we camped in a field that looked perfect: it was flat, there was a small line of trees to provide shelter and privacy, and it was green and beautiful. We fell sound asleep right after dinner. In the morning, I opened the door to step out, and I gasped. There was water almost up to the bottom of the door, about a foot deep. Evidently the field had been irrigated during the night, so as we lay sleeping, the water slowly rose around us. By morning, we were parked in the middle of a lake. We tried to drive forward, but the tires spun uselessly. We were mired in the mud. Mick decided to wade through the watery field to look for help. I sat in the car wondering how long we would be stranded and how long it would take until the water receded enough for our tires to get traction. I didn't think Mick would ever find help, but soon I saw him coming back with a man on a tractor. Mick had wandered around until he found a farmer, somehow had made himself clear about the problem, and had asked if the man could help us. It worked, and we were soon out of the muddy lake. The man reluctantly agreed to take a bit of money for his time and friendly assistance. What a relief and a surprise to meet kind people like this!

The next day, June 24, made up for the Çatalhöyük problems. We drove to the nearby town of Konya, where we bought a small sheepskin rug for ourselves and a goat hair rug for Mick's mom. I loved shopping at open markets with all the people strolling around, noisily bargaining over items. Besides the rugs, we bought two very lightweight carved wooden spoons for only 40 cents each. I didn't know what kind of wood they were made from, but I figured they would last at least a few months. As it turned out, more than 55 years later we are still using these beautiful spoons, almost daily. The wood has become worn on the edges, but amazingly, the paint is still colorful.

The best part of this short trip was our return. We drove along the Mediterranean coast between Silifke and Mersin, an area dotted with ancient castles, both on and off the shore. That night, we found a small campground in Korykos, and the next day we had time for the beach. It was gorgeous. We planned to return as soon as we could.

Patti on the beach; Korykos castle offshore

A few days after we returned from Konya, our landlady asked me if I would like to accompany her to the bathhouse (*hamam*). I was intrigued, especially when I found out that this *hamam* had been built in the 16th century, but I was also apprehensive since I had no idea what to expect. In all my time in Turkey, however, this turned out to be my most unusual experience. My landlady and I walked in together, but as soon as we entered the *hamam*, she disappeared into the next room, leaving me to negotiate this new setting by myself. I wondered why my landlady had left me alone, but then I realized that she probably couldn't imagine how foreign everything seemed to me. I didn't know where to pay, how much to pay, where I should leave my clothes, or even whether I should get completely naked. I stood utterly perplexed next to a row of boxes presumably for storing clothes and valuables, when a group of women began to surround me. It was awkward, frustrating, and embarrassing to have no idea of the procedure, but the women seemed anxious to help me. I wished that my Turkish were better, but at least I could understand some of what they were saying.

Journal excerpt. Adana, Turkey. June 27, 1966:

The bath consisted of two large marble-faced rooms. When we walked in, a large crowd of women gathered around, all explaining to me the prices—everyone trying their Turkish on me—all at the same time. It was supposed to cost 10 lira for a bath and a washer-massage woman. I didn't have that much, so I only paid 7½ lira. I had to undress with about 20 women staring at me, some dressed and some not. Then I walked into the second room, which was very steamy and much hotter. There were naked women all around the room, sitting by little basins, pouring water over themselves and washing. I went into a side room where a big droopy-busted woman took charge of me. First she washed my hair. I had brought my own shampoo, but she just picked up the large bar (sort of like Fels Naptha) and scrubbed my hair and scalp. She washed it as though it hadn't been washed in months. Then she combed through it with a very stiff comb, pulling out gobs of hair. Then she started scraping me down. She went over every inch of my body with a heavy coarse cloth, and as she did so, she rubbed off a layer of brown skin. It rolled off! I really felt dirty. After that she soaped me. For the scraping we had been on the floor, I lying down and she sitting beside me, flopping me over when she finished with one side. For the soaping I stood up and she soaped all over. All through this, she kept throwing pans of hot clean water over me, getting hotter as we continued. After soaping she washed my hair again, this time using

> *my shampoo. I think she started enjoying it because she squeezed half the tube out each time. The suds were rolling down my body. Then we were finished. She came out with me to the outside (cooler) room and helped dress me, comb my hair, etc. Of course again there were over 20 women crowded around us. I think some just came in off the street to see the foreigner! I was a little embarrassed because my underclothes were so much fancier than the others I saw. I'm still wearing my lacy bride-underwear, of course.*

As I walked home after this bath, I felt cleaner than I ever had before. And lighter. Maybe I had lost a lot of skin! Mick said I looked pink all over, and I felt sort of prickly, but I still was ready to do it all again.

Tents and Villagers

THE NEXT WEEKEND, WE drove east to Gaziantep, a distance of 154 miles. As we left Adana, we seemed to be in a different country, at least in terms of the way women dressed. I had become used to seeing women with their heads covered, but now I was surprised at the extensive covering of women along our route. Many were so draped in black that not even their eyes showed. As we approached Gaziantep, we saw low mud homes stacked along a hillside. We felt like explorers as we negotiated the streets and marketplace. One of the market stalls was piled high with copper trays, bowls, and urns. People laughed and gathered around us as we made our way through the market, buying a few items.

Gaziantep market copper stall

Lunch in Gaziantep restaurant

Though people were friendly to us, we were wary about camping alone that night. We liked having privacy but didn't know if it would be safe. After driving around a bit looking for an appropriate site, we finally settled on a gasoline station just outside the center of town. There were lights there as well as a few people, but we saw a spot where we could be somewhat private. We drove in, and I hesitantly asked the station attendant if we could park near his station that night. He seemed delighted. As I struggled to explain myself in Turkish, he brought out two chairs so we could sit outside to enjoy the evening air.

The next morning, we thanked our gas station attendant, said goodbye to all the people who had gathered around us, and drove south toward Carchemish (Kargamış), one of the most important centers of the Hittites in the late Bronze Age. We had heard that the extensive ruins included pottery shards dating back to 3000 BCE. As it is located on the Euphrates River very close to the Syrian border, we didn't know if we needed formal permission papers to enter, but since it was only 60 miles away, we thought it was worth a try. The drive turned out to be fascinating.

Village south of Gaziantep, near Nizip

Before arriving in Carchemish, as we passed a village near the town of Nizip, we heard music and saw people dancing in colorful clothes. It was so different from the dark cloaks we had been seeing that we stopped to see what was happening. I wondered if this was a Kurdish village, or maybe Arab? Or perhaps the people were dressed up for a wedding? We parked the car and walked over.

Journal entry. Nizip, Turkey. July 2, 1966:

> *It seemed to be a festival of some sort. The men brought us chairs, and we gladly sat and watched. At one point, a wagon came and all the dancers rushed over to greet the occupants. I thought it may have been a wedding, but later I decided it may be a circumcision, as one of the ones who brought so much attention was a baby. Someone also brought a fancy cradle into the room where the baby was taken.*

Village women dancing, near Nizip

On the deserted road south of Nizip, we had our first flat tire. Mick put on the spare and said he thought the valve had gone bad and that he should probably get a tube for future road trips. I guess we were lucky that we hadn't had a flat up to this point. I was reminded again how secure I felt knowing that Mick was conscientious about thinking ahead and keeping our van in good order.

AS WE APPROACHED CARCHEMISH, the road came to a stop at the gate of a military camp. The gate was open and there was no sign preventing us from going in, so with some trepidation we drove into the camp. Immediately a man appeared and flagged us down. We told him that we were teachers and we wanted to look at the archaeological site, and with that he said we could enter as long as we took along two of their military guards. Two boys (at least they looked like boys to me) hopped into our van and we took off. I didn't know if they were supposed to protect us or whether they were there so that the Turkish military could watch us. We never did find out. Our conversation was hampered by my lack of Turkish, even though I was using everything I had learned. I understood one of the young men to say that he would be shot if he went over the border into Syria. Or maybe he said that he could be shot if he allowed us to cross the border. Either way, he was serious, and the implications were drastic. These two young men in uniform, however, plus two others who appeared, seemed to enjoy themselves as we all tromped around the site. One of the young men leaned down and picked up a faintly colored potsherd and gave it to me. I thanked him and took it, all the while thinking that this should never be allowed.

Threshing wheat near Urfa

After leaving Carchemish, we headed eastward again, toward the town of Urfa (Şanlıurfa), a few hours away. As we drove, we became more and more comfortable about stopping to talk to people. We would pull over, get out of the car, and walk across fields into villages and camps. One impromptu stop was near a tiny mud village where we saw a family threshing wheat. The farmer seemed proud of his work; he smiled as he posed for a picture. As I was taking this man's picutre, another man walked over to us and invited us to come in for some tea. As usual, we gladly accepted, not knowing what was going to happen but trusting that it would be interesting.

As we approached the village, people surrounded us, first taking us into a spotless white room that was filled with objects that seemed to be laid out for presentation, including beaded and woven hangings and quilts. I first thought this might be for a wedding celebration, but the women pointed to two babies who lay amid the items. Was this maybe for a circumcision? I so wished I could talk to these women who were proudly showing us this room and its contents. Just outside the room, a woman whose chin and arms were covered with tattoos was spinning wool. She gave us a small demonstration, smiling as we took her picture. Several men then indicated that we should follow them, which we did.

Patti and tea in the "men's room"

Journal excerpt. July 2, 1966:

> *Then the men took us up to a main room where they served us tea. It seemed as though every man in the village came. They all greeted us, saying "Hoş geldiniz" ("Welcome"). Though sign language speaking is difficult, they managed to get across one main topic: America-Vietnam (motion of shooting). [All I could say was] "çok fina" (very bad), and they full-heartedly agreed. What can one say? This has been one of our most often asked questions, and it's impossible to talk about it with a language barrier.*

Again I was stunned. Even in this tiny mud village, people brought up the topic of American involvement in Vietnam. Where did they get their information? From newspapers? Listening to the radio? I wasn't even sure if the village had electricity. But in some way people had access to world news, and I was getting a glimpse of the United States through their eyes. It was clear to me that they saw my country as a world power that affected them.

In Urfa we decided to camp in a gas station again since it had worked out well in Gaziantep. We chose a station just on the edge of town where there was little traffic. Again, the people seemed as interested in us as we were in them. And, as in Gaziantep, one of the men brought out chairs for us. We sat in our chairs that warm evening, watching the camel traffic go by, feeling safe sleeping at this station. We told the men that we would be going to Diyarbakır the next day but would like to come back to sleep there the next night. They seemed happy to have us. I wonder if they were surprised that we would go on a 239-mile round-trip drive in one day.

We left our gas station campsite at 6 a.m. the next day, a hot dry morning. The terrain was flat, and there was little traffic other than a few people on donkeys or camels. Since the road was paved, we drove leisurely, especially contented because we knew where we would be sleeping that night. When we didn't know where we would park for the night, we were always somewhat anxious in the afternoon.

When we reached Diyarbakır, it was still morning, but most of the stores were closed for some reason. We walked around the city walls, most of which were intact. The day had become extremely hot, and we were so thirsty that we drank 11 bottles of some kind of carbonated drink. I had no idea what these drinks were made of, or if the bottles were sterilized, but I was so thirsty I didn't care. To cool off a bit, we drove down to the Tigris River, where a man was throwing dynamite into the river to kill the fish. When the fish floated to the top, he grabbed them and barbecued them. He invited us to eat some of the fish, which we did, and it was quite tasty, but the flies were so bad we didn't stay long.

On our drive back from Diyarbakır we were intrigued by a group of dark tents near the road; I assumed the people were nomadic Kurds. We stopped and, in the way that had now begun to be our habit, got out and walked toward them slowly, ready to turn around if people seemed hostile or scared. As we approached one tent, two women warmly—though shyly—beckoned to us. Their tent was sparse; there were no walls or doors, only a screen in back for protection from the elements. A few small flat-woven carpets lay on the dirt with bits of straw strewn around. Water was stored in a bloated goatskin tied outside the tent. There was a hammock for the baby, some piles of blankets, and cooking equipment scattered around. I wondered how long they would stay in one place; it looked like it would be quick and easy to pack up and move.

Tent encampment near Diyarbakır   Patti meeting the women

With my meager Turkish and no ability in Kurdish, it was a rough guess as to what the women were saying, but still we had a conversation animated with laughter and sign language. The younger woman barely spoke, but she giggled all the time. She posed a striking figure, with amber eyes, bare feet, and tattoos on her face. The older woman, with henna-red hair peeking out of her blue scarf, talked as she continued mixing dough in a pan. The younger woman, after showing us how she spun wool, asked if we were married and how long we had been married. When I said, "One year," she responded, "No babies?" She seemed to feel quite sorry for me, as she held out her baby. I cradled him gently, touched that she let me hold him. I wonder if she thought that I couldn't get pregnant, while she had already proven that she could. I suppose she had no idea that birth control pills existed.

Women and baby in the tent

As we drove away from the camp, I realized what an honor it was for us to be invited into these women's tent. This type of impromptu visit would probably not be possible for a man traveling alone. As a young couple, and particularly with me being a woman, we must have been seen as friendly, curious, and harmless, just as they appeared to us.

After another night at the gas station in Urfa, we headed back to Adana on a different route, veering north to the town of Maraş. There was little vehicular traffic, but the drive was not devoid of activities. Men, women, and children ambled by with camels and donkeys. Groups of women were busy washing clothes in streams. Though the chore of washing is never-ending and routine, it is also a time when women catch up on the news, laugh, and talk as they cement relationships.

Near Maraş   Women washing

I was most surprised that day to see bears being led down the road. They looked quite docile, though I didn't want to test that conjecture. We could not communicate with the people, so I had no idea where the bears were coming from, where they were going, or whether they would be trained for entertainment somewhere. I just hoped that this practice was on the wane.

Bears on the road

Maraş was a copper center. The market was arranged so that each section displayed a different product, and we could see the production from beginning to end. For the first time, I watched wool being sheared, then separated, then fluffed up, then "twanged" with a bow and string. In a few minutes it went from looking like a dirty matted clump to being light and fluffy. Later it would be spun and woven.

THE CONTRAST BETWEEN OUR weekend travels and life on the air base was striking. Many of the American military men on the base would ask me how I liked Turkey, and when I replied in the positive, they seemed amazed. One man said, "What do you see here? Nothing to do." I kept hearing how much they hated being there and how they were counting the days to when they could get back to the "Great PX" (the U.S.). I commented on this in a letter to my parents.

Excerpt from letter to my parents. Adana. July 11, 1966:

Dear Daddy and Mom,

Many people mistake us for Peace Corps volunteers. They ask if we are teachers, and since we are, they assume we are PCVs. Most of the PCVs in Turkey are English teachers, so they refer to the PCVs as "teachers." Here in Adana they think we are either PC volunteers or Germans. They know that we are not American military. I suppose it's because we smile and are friendly, try to mix, and buy their food. The American military are specifically told not to mix with the Turks! Even the Turkish people working on the base know we're not military people. Last week we got something to eat at the snack bar, and when the fellow brought us our drinks, he said, "Are you Turkish?" I thought he was kidding because we certainly don't look Turkish! When I said "No," he said, "Are you German?" When I explained that we were just tourists, here for a few weeks, he nodded with an "I knew it" look. That same morning, Mick was asked again if he was German, and so he asked the Turk why he didn't think he was American. The Turkish fellow said, "Because you smile and are happy." When Mick told me that, I felt so ashamed of the Americans living here. It makes me terribly sad. Americans <u>are</u> very friendly and happy, but these [Americans] seem to hold a grudge against all Turks, and they don't show their happy, friendly side. It makes my heart break to see what a picture Turks have of Americans.

My letter ends with:

> I can't believe we've been married almost a year. It's gone by so quickly!
> We haven't even had all those adjustment problems that I heard we
> were supposed to have during the first year of marriage. Maybe it's
> because we have more adjustments to make in our ever-changing
> environment.
>
> Love,
> Patti

Fortunately, we met a few people—through either Mick's class or my own Turkish language class—who were not so negative about life in Turkey. One of them, Dave, was a young and energetic 19-year-old from a military family who looked for opportunities to get off the base. A couple of times we went to the beach with him and a few of his friends. I loved snorkeling for the first time, lazily watching colorful fish in the warm Mediterranean Sea. One day, we heard that there were old jugs and vases lying on the sea bottom near a little island, so we asked a fisherman to row us out there. We dove down and saw what appeared to be Greek or Roman amphorae. We didn't see any whole jugs, just the necks and tops with two handles, all covered with algae or other growth. We didn't know if they were ancient or not, but it was fun to speculate.

THAT SUMMER I WAS 24, and I still felt like a kid just out of college, so I was surprised when some people treated me in a more grown-up way. The first time I had that feeling was back in Greece when we were at a party. Mick and I had been expected to stay in the kitchen with the older people while I felt more like singing and dancing with the teenagers in the living room. Now, in Turkey, I had a similar feeling when we were snorkeling in the Mediterranean with the three American boys ages 15, 18, and 19. I felt somewhat like "the mom," since I was doing the cooking for the group. I wrote home about it.

Excerpt from letter to my parents. July 20, 1966:

I notice the boys treating me in much the same way as I've noticed so many young people treating you, Mom. There is the [talkative] type who is always around asking if he can help. . . . There is the type that stands around watching me and talking, perhaps not feeling quite belonging to the crowd (like the younger brother in this group), and the ones who are having a wonderful time with their own friends and only come around me when the food is served. I think it's interesting because actually I am only a few years older than they, but for the way they treat me I could be 30 years older. In a few more years, or after they are out of college, the difference in our ages would make us "the same age," but now, it is almost as though we're a generation apart.

The letter continues: *We just celebrated our first anniversary— only we didn't get to eat our frozen wedding cake. Will it still be good for our second anniversary? Mick is still upset because he didn't get to eat any at the wedding.*

Love,

Patti

I wanted to learn more about Turkish life and culture but was hampered by my lack of language and the lack of insightful reading material. The books we had about Turkey were informative but too general and superficial for my questions about daily life. And it was hard to find knowledgeable, positive, and informed people who could speak English. The Peace Corps volunteers were excellent at filling that role, but there were not many PCVs around. Then Dave introduced Mick to Hasan, a Turk who worked on the Incirlik Air Base who was friendly and talkative. As soon as he was introduced to Mick, Hasan said that he was free that weekend, and could we all meet him in Mersin for lunch? I was delighted, as I was anxious to meet someone who could give us more answers to the many questions I had about Turkish life. I was in for a surprise.

On Saturday, Mick, Dave, and I drove to the appointed place in the seaside town of Mersin, where we found Hasan with his young son. I was expecting to go to a restaurant, but Hasan said that his brother would have lunch for us. We could drive to his house; it wouldn't take long. Hasan and his son got in our van, and he directed us to the main highway out of town. After several miles on this main highway, Hasan told us to turn right, onto a smaller road. I asked him how far it was, and he said, "Not far, just a ways more." We drove on. Pretty soon he said to turn off this road onto an even smaller dirt road. Again, using the Turkish honorific title *bey*, I asked, "How far, Hasan Bey?" And he said, "It's not too far." We kept going. Soon the small road became a dry rocky gulch in a small ravine. From time to time, we had to get out of the car to move some of the boulders. As the car bounced over the rocks, I said, "Hasan Bey, are we almost there?" I was now getting a little worried, beginning to wonder what in the world we had gotten ourselves into. "We're almost there," Hasan answered. And soon, just as he said, a small house appeared on a hillside, and there was Hasan's brother and family waiting for us. We scrambled out of the car and were guided toward a platform under a large tree. It was an idyllic setting: grapes, olives, bread, yogurt, wine, and some kind of roasted little bird were spread out on a cloth on the platform. The whole scene seemed surreal, probably made more so because of the wild goose chase that I had thought we were on.

On the drive to his brother's house, Hasan talked nonstop about his views on family, marriage, and child-rearing. He first explained that his views were old-fashioned, that only about 30 percent of the population would agree with him. I wanted to hear a Turk's view on local culture, so I kept detailed notes on what he was saying.

Clearing boulders from the road   Lunch picnic with Hasan (left), his
with Hasan, his son, and Dave   son, his brother, Mick, and Dave

Hasan had five sons, but four of them had died. (He didn't mention then that he also had a daughter.) His only living son—the one with us on the drive—was then about seven or eight years old. He said he would like to marry his boy at age 15 to a 14-year-old girl. She would then come to live with his family. This was important, Hasan Bey said, so that the boy would have plenty of time to have sons of his own. Hasan hoped his son would have his own son by the time he was at least 20.

Hasan Bey said that girls of course should never meet their fiancé until their marriage day. He had one daughter, who was 17, and he would be picking a fiancé for her. After he picked out a boy, he would follow the standard practice—that is, "spy" on the boy for a few days to make sure he was "good." The spying often happened in the *hamam*. The boy's mother would give the same kind of once-over on the prospective bride, and when both parents agreed, they would set the wedding date. After the ceremony, the women would wait outside the home until the boy showed the sign that the marriage had been consummated. If there was no physical proof of consummation, the new husband would be allowed to leave right then. As Hasan described this, I was trying to imagine the scene. How long would the women be outside waiting? Would the new husband show off the blood on the sheet? How many new bridegrooms would actually walk away if there was no blood? What would the bride do if that happened?

Hasan Bey continued with his views on people. He said that people could not change much. They died the way they were born, and that was best. He also said that women were not allowed to see a doctor, since doctors were male. There were female midwives for pregnancy, but he said that a woman would rather die than let a doctor see her. If a doctor must be called, he would have to make a diagnosis while only seeing her arms and back. Hasan enlightened us on one more account: women had no brains, he said. They had a lot of hair, but nothing under it.

Throughout this whole outrageous talk, I kept quiet. Partly it was because I was being polite, and partly it was because it was hard to get a word in edgewise. It also seemed pointless to argue with him. I took to heart that he was, as he said, "old-fashioned" and that other Turks would not agree with everything he said. At any rate, his views made the car trip unforgettable.

ON JULY 30 WE took our last weekend trip in Turkey: back again to the village near Nizip. This time we invited Rosalie, a woman I had met in my Turkish class, and her husband, Cliff, to go with us, since they had been fascinated with our stories. Before we left Adana, I asked my Turkish teacher to write a message to give to the villagers, asking for more information about the room with the babies and wall hangings. I wondered who made the items and what were they made for, and if there was a ceremony involved in their presentation.

When we reached the village, people came running out, greeting us as though we were old friends. The villagers took us up to the men's room, where we talked, drank tea, and were entertained by a flute player. I gave the men the message that my Turkish teacher had written, and two people slowly pored over the note all the time we were in the room. As they read it aloud, it sounded to me like a first grader sounding out words. They didn't respond to us at all. Maybe they spoke more Arabic than Kurdish or Turkish. Or maybe they hadn't learned to read very well. Or maybe it was just that they couldn't communicate an answer to us.

When we were having tea, a boy with Down syndrome was brought into the room. He was put in the center of the room, where he danced, sort of sang, and mimicked people, making sounds that seemed unintelligible (at least to me). Everyone laughed and pointed at him. He seemed to be "the entertainment." I was aghast. How could a child be treated that way? But as I thought it over, I wondered if I was being too critical. At least the boy had a place in society. It was better than being shut up in a house. This was another time in which I was confronted with an unexpected situation that made me question my assumptions. Even so, my sense was that this was wrong; I am still haunted by the image of this boy being brought in for our enjoyment.

Our wall hanging held by the woman who made it, and Rosalie (top right)

After we left the tearoom, the men led us again to the same room we had been in before. This time, I had a better look at the intricate wall hangings. Most of them were about five or six feet long and about two feet wide. Some were backed by diagonal squares of woven straw sewn together and covered with small patches of cotton, silk, or felt. Some were edged with tufts of dyed feathers. Many were decorated with bits of plastic, tin lids, shells, paper cutouts, beads, bottle caps, hair. One even had part of a razor sewn in. I suppose that anything the weaver could find lying around might end up in the artistic piece. When our hosts put two colorful hangings into our hands, I felt honored. I tried to give them some money, but they wouldn't take any. They finally agreed to accept a tin of tea, a jar of jam, and a can of crackers.

As our time in Adana was ending, we began to pack for our upcoming travel. We still didn't know if Mick would get a teaching job, but we had already decided on heading east and had gotten our visas for Syria, Lebanon, and Iraq. We'd get the rest later. As we were repacking and stocking up on canned foods, I realized that we had an unused storage spot: the toilet box. We hadn't been using the toilet bucket (which hung from a plastic toilet seat inside the box) on our trips to the Turkish countryside; all we ever used were the plastic bags that went with the toilet. With the realization that we had unused space, the toilet box under the seat cushion became the pantry. We took out the bucket and filled the box with canned meats (stews, chili con carne, etc.) and soups. These canned foods would add to our meals if we couldn't find enough local bread, rice, fruits, or vegetables along the way. It might feel a little weird to lift the toilet seat to pick out dinner, but we'd get used to it.

We hoped to leave right after Mick's class was over, but we had to wait for all our documents to arrive. The main one was the *carnet de passage* from Germany. The *carnet* would allow us to avoid customs and international duties by stating that we wouldn't sell the car. It was crucial at every border, but it wasn't the only document we needed.

Another excerpt from a letter to my parents. July 20, 1966:

> *A week from today is Mick's last class, so our time here is almost up. We don't know exactly how soon we'll be leaving, though. There are many things we've had to do before leaving, and some aren't finished yet. We're still waiting to hear from the German registration office for the renewal of registration, the German touring club for our carnet, the British overseas insurance (which is the only office we could find that would insure cars driving to India), the office in the States for our health insurance renewal, and a few other things. We started all this paperwork when we first got here, but somehow things take a long time. Anyway, everything is on its "last leg," so we should be able to leave by Monday or Tuesday, August 1 or 2.*

On August 1, Mick was relieved to find out that he was on the schedule to teach sociology and anthropology classes at the Air Station in West Pakistan. The classes would begin on September 13, so we would have about five or six weeks to get there if we could leave right away. On August 4, though, I wrote, "*We're waiting for our carnet to come in the mail. We think it's been sent, so we're hoping for it in tomorrow's mail.*" It didn't come that day, however, or the next, or the next. The van was all packed and ready to go, and we couldn't stand waiting around. So, on August 9, when the *carnet* still hadn't come, we drove 40 miles south to Karataş, where we camped on the beach for two nights. Mick had started to feel sick before we left, and his fever spiked while we were at the beach. As had happened before, he sweated profusely during the night. In the morning, our sheets—and both of us—were soaking wet, but he felt better. I did my best to dry out the sheets and sleeping bags, but even with this to deal with, I was happier to be camping on the beach than sitting around at home anxiously waiting for the mail.

WHEN WE GOT BACK to Adana on August 11, our friend the mailman said that the *carnet* had arrived an hour after we had left on the 9th! Relieved, we went back to our house and told the landlady that we had received the paper and were finally leaving. She began to cry; she had thought that when we went to Karataş, we had left Turkey without saying goodbye. I felt so bad! She had been more like a mother than a landlady. As we got into the car for the final time, she kissed me twice and tearfully watched us drive away. I was crying too. We left town immediately, *carnet* in hand.

10.

An Eastern Paris— Syria and Lebanon

Even with all the emotion of leaving, it was exciting to be on the road again, to have all our things organized and tucked away in House. Our two-month stay in Turkey had given us time to learn more about one country, but I was now looking forward to seeing new places. We would have almost a month on the road; we had our map, and the van was ready. We drove south through the Cilician Gates, along the path to Syria taken by the Hittites, the Greeks, Alexander the Great, the Romans, the Mongols, and the Crusaders. That first night, August 11, 1966, we stopped at an excellent free campground at the Syrian-Turkish border, up in the mountains near the border guards, with pine trees, lights, a water pump, and even garbage pails. A most welcome retreat.

OUR ROUTE TOOK US along the coast road straight south through Latakia in Syria, then through Tripoli in Lebanon, and finally into Beirut. I had heard that Beirut was a beautiful modern city, even referred to as "the Paris of the Middle East," but it was even more striking than I had imagined. The city had an international feel, with tall buildings and wide avenues. I felt like we were back in Europe. There were tourists everywhere, so even though we were foreigners, we didn't seem to stand out as we wandered around the city. It felt good not to be stared at. We heard people speaking Arabic, French, and a bit of English. French was the language we heard the most. I was glad I had enough French to communicate our basic needs. We stayed for three days.

One of our tasks in Beirut was to get visas for Jordan. We accomplished this without difficulty. Surprisingly the Jordanian visa cost only eight cents, much less than I had expected. We were watching our money carefully, as we had to get all the way to West Pakistan with what we were carrying. Even buying *Newsweek* for 37 cents was a bit of a stretch but was such an immediate and welcome pleasure that we bought one. The last time we had seen kiosks with news magazines in English was in Greece three months before.

The only untoward thing that happened in Beirut was when we were leaving the building where we had gotten visas. Mick decided to walk down the stairs, but I got in the elevator, not realizing that I was alone with a man who had been unabashedly and annoyingly touchy and flirty with me a few minutes earlier. While we were in the elevator, he tried to kiss me. I pushed him away and he backed off, but I was shaken and angry. When we reached the ground floor, I blurted out to Mick, "That man tried to kiss me." The man was still right there, so Mick went after him. As he wrote in his journal: "I cornered the fellow and was so mad I couldn't act. I simply grabbed one of his hands and hit the other with it (silly thing to do) and told him 'Hands off.'"

After getting the car serviced for the trip to West Pakistan, we drove out to the ancient city of Baalbek (called Heliopolis by the Greeks), about 50 miles east of Beirut. I was astounded by the magnitude of the temple ruins and the marbles. I also realized that in the past year, we had rarely been outside the boundaries of the ancient Roman Empire.

On August 16, we left Lebanon and drove through Syria again, where we stopped for one night in Damascus. We didn't see any campgrounds, so we pulled into a gas station as we had done in Turkey. It was just as delightful. The attendants brought out chairs and cups of tea for us, and we chatted as well as we could with minimal shared languages. The next morning, one of the attendants who spoke a little English took us around the city. We were so pleased that we had discovered this safe way to camp.

Baalbek, Lebanon

Later that day, just before crossing into Jordan, we stopped at a gas station to use up the remainder of our Syrian money by filling up not only our gas tank but also our extra gas can. Mick watched this transaction carefully, since the price was not clearly displayed, and he saw that the service attendant did not give us all the gas that we had paid for. Mick asked the man to give us the rest of the gas. The attendant got quite indignant, insisting that he had given us the right amount. Even though this was happening in Arabic, it was not hard to get the gist of his message. With the man getting more and more angry, and Mick himself trying not to yell, Mick decided just to get away to avoid a worse situation. In his frustration and haste at backing out, he ran into the gas pump, putting a small dent in it. Now the attendant was even madder. He started yelling and pointing to his gas pump. Mick got out of the van to see the damage, and while the attendant was screaming and I was becoming increasingly frightened, a boy stuck his hand into our van and grabbed Mick's watch from the front seat. I was sitting right there and saw him take it. I jumped out to tell Mick, and we both left the screaming gas attendant and ran after the boy. I didn't go far, since I didn't want to leave the van alone, but several other men who were standing around watching the show also started running after the boy. Suddenly a soldier appeared who spoke some English. He cornered the boy and got Mick's watch back, and then the other men began beating the boy. Meanwhile, the gas attendant was still screaming about the dent in the gas pump. The soldier suggested that we give him 50 cents (in Syrian money) to fix the pump. We gladly did that, but the attendant continued yelling and gesturing to the pump. The soldier then said to Mick, "Just get out of here fast." We did.

11.

Saltwater Swim and a Dress—Jordan

After our Syrian gas station encounter, the drive to Jordan was calm. We drove through the area west of the Jordan River, now generally referred to as the West Bank. At that time it was part of Jordan, but a year later, in June 1967, the region was captured by Israel during the Six-Day War. We spent three days in this region, one each in Jerash, Jericho, and Bethlehem. We almost didn't get into Jericho because there was an entrance fee of 250 fils (worth about U.S. $6 in 2020). We stopped at the entrance kiosk debating about whether to spend the money, and when we told the ticket-taker that we weren't going in because we couldn't afford it, he said that not only could we go for free but he would be our guide. This was another of the many unexpected delights of travel. We thoroughly enjoyed the visit, which ended with this young man, who was about our age, taking us to a place where we could swim for free in the Dead Sea. We shared our lunch with him, and I ventured out into the water, where I bobbed up and down like a toy in the salty water. I could even "stand up" straight in the water without touching bottom. After the salty swim, we bathed in a clear freshwater stream just on the edge of the Dead Sea—a perfect way to end the day.

Swimming in the Dead Sea

Mick and our Jordanian guide washing off the Dead Sea salt

That night, as we drove around looking for a place to camp, we saw a shady lime orchard that looked enticing. We pulled over. The owner came out, welcomed us, and said that we could park there for the night. It had looked like a perfect camping spot, but as it turned out we hardly slept. It was extremely hot—probably over 100—with barely a breath of air. After a few hours' struggling to sleep, we pushed open the door at the back of House a little. Then biting gnats began buzzing around us. It was a horrible night. I don't know if the owner realized how poorly we had slept, but in the morning as we were fixing our usual House breakfast (bread, jam, and Nescafé), he invited us to swim in his pool. It couldn't have been more refreshing! The morning was so hot, we didn't even need to dry off. As we left the below-sea-level orchard, slowing making our way up toward Jerusalem, we were both glad to be on our way again.

WHILE DRIVING THROUGH this part of the world, I was hit by a surreal and somewhat magical feeling of *Where am I?* The words "Jerusalem," "Bethlehem," "Mount of Olives," and "Garden of Gethsemane" brought back childhood memories of listening to Bible stories in Sunday school. I associated these place names with events that were far away and long ago, but here we were, surrounded by people living their normal lives.

Bethlehem

Journal excerpt. Bethlehem, Jordan. August 19, 1966:

Bethlehem is only about 10 miles from Jerusalem. You can't go direct because of the Israeli border. We visited the Church of the Nativity. Underneath the main altar is a cave where Jesus was supposed to have been born. It's all very dark and misty. There is a table there where the wise men were supposed to have laid their gifts. I'd really rather picture the birth out under the stars than in this dark and incensed grotto.

Excerpt of letter to my parents. August 24, 1966:

Dear Daddy and Mom,

We really enjoyed Jerusalem and Bethlehem. I was most amazed at Jerusalem. It's still a walled city (the old part) with teeny tiny cobble-stone streets filled with women carrying jars on their heads and men calling out their wares. No cars can fit inside the walls, which makes it nice. The city, though, is very smelly and dirty in places. We walked down the Via Dolorosa and up to Mt. Calvary. Mt. Calvary is hard to imagine though because it's inside a church. You climb up steep steps to get to a little upper floor and that is supposed to be where the crosses were. It doesn't seem like a hill at all. A lot of the Christian places are too touristy, but the city is fascinating. The most beautiful place there is the [shrine] Dome of the Rock. It has a huge gold dome and is built over the spot where Muhammad ascended to heaven. I think it is interesting that both Jesus and Muhammad were supposed to have ascended to heaven only about one mile away from each other. The rock where Muhammad ascended has a large hole through several feet of solid rock where he was supposed to have gone. The rock where Jesus was supposed to have ascended on the Mt. of Olives has only a footprint—which doesn't really look like a footprint.

Love,

Patti

That night, while we were camping in a lonely rocky site in Shepherd's Field a few kilometers from Bethlehem, a man walked toward us with something draped over his arm. As we got out of the car, smiling to greet him, he unfolded the items. They were gorgeous: two women's dresses, clearly worn but still in excellent condition. One was made of heavy black cotton with an intricately embroidered front panel and skirt, gold satin embroidered sleeves, and skirt decoration with silver thread. It was hand-sewn, beautifully done. The man seemed

Buying a Palestinian dress

to indicate that it was a wedding dress, possibly his wife's or daughter's. It was obvious that someone had taken great care to preserve both dresses. The man wanted to sell them to us for $6 each (about $48 in 2020), but I didn't want to buy them because they seemed too personal. *He should keep them*, I thought. We kept saying no, but he continued in such a distraught way that we finally agreed to buy one. We gave him the equivalent of about

$5 (about $40 in 2020) in Jordanian money, and he smiled as he walked away. The dress remains one of our prized possessions. I often wonder if I should donate it to a museum, but even now, despite being hung out for more than 50 years, it carries the musty smell of being packed away somewhere in Bethlehem.

12.

Desert and Disease—Iraq

On August 21st, we started out across the desert to Baghdad. We had more than 500 miles ahead of us. We were prepared: the van had had its checkup; we had stocked up on canned food and water; we had extra gas and oil and an extra tire. But we felt the enormity of this decision. Though we had bought our Iraq visas a month before, and we had been talking about this route for several months, we hadn't known until August 1 that the class in Peshawar, West Pakistan, was definitely on the schedule. Before then, there had always been the option of continuing our travel on a different route. In campgrounds we had talked to travelers who were planning to drive across North Africa toward Morocco. Others were going down the east coast of Africa. Still others were taking a boat back to Europe on the Mediterranean Sea. Up to this point, we could have chosen any of those. But now we were cutting off those options. After a year of traveling, we had made the huge decision to go east. Once on our way, we would not go back to Europe. We would probably continue until we reached the Pacific Ocean. As we started the drive toward Baghdad, we were sure that this was the right decision: head east.

Bedouins and Baghdad

THE DRIVE ACROSS THE Iraqi desert was hot and dry, the landscape was flat and barren, and the road went straight as far as we could see. There were rocks and dirt. Nothing green. Every now and then we saw a camel caravan, occasionally a nomadic camp. These were the only things that changed the landscape. I looked at Mick as he drove. There was sweat dripping down his neck, and his shirt looked like it could be wrung out. He was guzzling water from our blue plastic jug, water that I had boiled for 20 minutes and then dropped an iodine tablet in just for good measure. The red line on our thermometer was inching toward 125 degrees. We had the window partly open to get a bit of breeze, but it wasn't helping much. Of course, we had no air conditioning; we didn't know anyone who did. At about that time I was thinking, *Yikes! This is not how I pictured my honeymoon!* We had left Amman, Jordan, at 7 a.m., and by 4 p.m. we had driven over 300 miles, about halfway to Baghdad. We stopped in the town of Ar-Rutba, where we bought a juicy watermelon and some Coca-Colas that seemed to taste better than anything I could remember.

While we were wondering where to camp, we got out of the van near a small group of Bedouins and their camels. One of the men walked over to Mick and, without saying anything, hugged him. As Mick was reeling in surprise, the man took hold of Mick's hand, leading him down the dusty street. I watched them walk off, their hands swinging together like schoolgirls'. I wasn't worried, though I did wonder how far they would go. With Mick's American phobia about strolling while holding hands with men, I knew that he would be uncomfortable but would try to "go with the flow." As it turned out, they didn't go far. I watched as Mick and the other man turned around and walked back, still hand in hand. When I later asked Mick about it, he said he was astonished at the feel of the man's hand: it was extraordinarily strong and as rough as coarse sandpaper. I wonder what the other man felt about Mick. Did he tell his wife that he had strolled along the street with a foreigner? Had he ever done this before? Was he tickled to have gotten up the nerve to walk up and hug Mick? With even more than the usual barrage of unanswered questions in my mind, we pulled off the road to camp near the Bedouins. It cooled off that night a bit, at least enough for us to pull the sheet around us. We had another 282 miles of desert to go before reaching Baghdad.

Camels on the road between Amman and Baghdad

The next day, we crossed the Euphrates River at Ramadi, a town located on the fertile plain of central Iraq. At this point, we were in Mesopotamia. Again, I was hit by the power of a word and its historical significance. The simple act of saying "We are in Mesopotamia" was exciting, just as it was when we said "Let's stop in Jerusalem" or "Let's camp tonight in Bethlehem." Though I had academic knowledge of these places, this was different. Here we were, right there, right then.

We had not heard of Ramadi, though many years later, between 2003 and 2006, it became well-known as a focal point in the Iraq War and was occupied by the U.S. military. In 1966 there was no war, and to us it felt welcoming to be in a town, especially after the sparsely populated desert in western Iraq. As we approached the outskirts of Ramadi, we drove by a few soldiers who were standing by the road waving their arms. We didn't stop, as we had made it a practice not to pick up people. When we got into town, we stopped to buy some 7UPs and melon. Two soldiers approached us saying that we had driven across a police command post, and we must go back. They seemed upset or angry, and not very pleasant, so we turned around and went back.

We gave the police the papers we had, which seemed to satisfy them, and then drove on back through town to continue on our way to Baghdad. We got through town, but at the eastern edge of town, two policemen again stopped us. They had been contacted by the command post on the west side of town and were waiting for us. They repeated to us that we had to go back to the other command post so the police could check our documents. We said we had already shown our papers to them and had been allowed to go on. But these police either didn't believe us, didn't understand, or were under orders not to let us pass. One man called back to the other police command post to find out if we had really been given permission to leave. He gave the phone to Mick, who also reminded the men at the western police command post that we had been allowed to leave. Finally, the eastern command post police said OK, we could go.

Relieved, we were about to drive on but then remembered that, with all the confusion at police command posts, we had forgotten to fill up our gas tank. So, reluctantly we turned back, heading for a gas station. But even there, the attendants knew that we had "evaded" the police, and they told us we had to go back to the first police post on the west side of town. How did they ever get that information? Again—in limited language—we argued, saying that we had already passed all police posts and had been given the OK to leave Ramadi. We finally got our gas and drove off. I watched through the back window, relieved that no one came after us.

IN BAGHDAD WE FOUND a most welcome campground, a true oasis nestled under tall date palms and surrounded by green grass. The dates that dropped from the palms felt dry and crunchy under my feet, but the ones we ate were moist and sweet. The weather, though, was miserable. Instead of dry heat, it was now hot and humid. Despite that, we toured the city during the day, shopped in the souks (bazaars), took refuge from the heat in the YMCA lounge, and, in the evening, exchanged travel tales and tips with the other campers, mostly British, German, and Australian. The ones we spent the most time with were two Germans: Rolfe and Bernd. They were headed east, like us, as was another German camper, Andreas. The five of us got along well.

Campground in Baghdad

Mick's journal. Baghdad. August 22, 1966:

Damn but it's hot! That stretch across the desert was miserable, just a few Bedouins and soldiers occupy the area. Our first impression of Baghdad is that it . . . is hot, smelly (like garbage), and teeming with cars and people. . . . It's good that we have canned food. The meat here hangs in the sun and 120 degree heat and [it] bubbles. . . . [Many of the people in our campground] . . . have had articles stolen from them, including one man's entire back pocket. . . . We could also get taken too easily, as I know we have in the few dealings we've had thus far. [In] three out of the last five gas stops we've been cheated. Very little is marked for prices, so it's easy to cheat us.

Excerpt of letter to my parents. Baghdad. August 24, 1966:

Dear Daddy and Mom,
The heat here is almost unbearable. It gets up to 125 degrees F in the afternoon, and during the night it doesn't seem to get much cooler.

We seem to be drinking something constantly and neither of us feels like eating. Yesterday afternoon we tried to keep cool by staying at the campground, wearing bathing suits and ducking under the [campground] shower every fifteen minutes. Even so, my skin is sticky with perspiration.

The scariest thing about driving here is the possibility of hitting someone. People constantly walk right out into the road without looking. And pushcarts have as much right on a highway as we do. We never drive at night because many cars and carts have no lights or don't use their lights. The scary thing is that we are told that the driver who kills someone will be killed himself if he stops. We have heard this over and over again from many different people. If you hit something, you must never stop but go right to a police station or to an American Embassy, where someone will protect you. It is so against our training not to stop, but I'm sure we would keep going here after some of the stories we've heard. In many ways, this area is still an "eye-for-an-eye" area. Many of the travelers we meet carry guns or knives, but I'm certainly against that too. I don't think there is any danger as long as we use common sense—which we do, of course.

Love,
Patti

As I read this letter from the advantage of hindsight, and the fact of being more than 50 years older, I wonder what my parents thought when they read it. And I wonder about my last statement. Did I really think that using "common sense" could avert danger? Would I be so casual today? I doubt it.

ONE EVENING, WE WENT out for a drive around downtown Baghdad with Rolfe and Bernd in their old Mercedes. As usual it was hot; the stench from the open drainage system in the streets permeated our nostrils. As we were driving back to camp, we heard a flap-flap-flap noise. The car had a flat tire. We were in a downtown intersection with a place to pull over, so we stopped immediately. As soon as the car stopped, people began milling around us. Rolfe and Bernd got out, opened the trunk, and began to dig under their clothes and cooking items to get out the tools and the spare tire. There was no place to put anything, so we were all holding as much as we could. People continued to gather, pressing toward us and the car. I was afraid that someone might grab things from the open trunk or pick up the tools and run.

We locked the car doors and tried to shield the car from the people and keep our eyes on the jack, lug nuts, and hubcap. I had gotten out of the car but soon got back in, feeling vulnerable as more and more men edged in around us, closer and closer, not saying anything. I felt some relief when the police came and began to chase people away, but it didn't help much. Men kept pushing in, evidently to get a look at what was happening. The policemen had revolvers, and one policeman began beating a boy with his gun. The boy hit the policeman right back. There was little control. I felt that at any moment the situation could blow up.

As Mick was watching over the car, he heard a voice in his ear. In perfect English, the voice said, "Be careful. These people are dangerous. Leave quickly." Mick turned around but couldn't tell who had whispered to him. Maybe whoever it was had walked away. We didn't need anyone to convince us, though; as soon as the new tire was on, Mick, Rolfe, and Bernd jumped back in the car and we drove off. When we looked back, the mob at the street corner had dispersed. I was scared and shaking, but when we got back to the security of our campsite, I just felt relieved that nothing had been taken and that there had been no violence.

Our days in Baghdad were filled not only with trying to get cool or dealing with car issues. One day we met a teacher who invited us to his home. That pleasant evening was more than a change from daily life at the campground; it also gave us a view of life for the middle class in this city. Another eye-opener was a visit to the Baghdad Jesuit College, a school for teenage boys that seemed quite well-known in the area. The priests were dedicated in their goal of providing a strong secondary school education, but they said that the government hampered them at every turn. They were charged huge taxes. Their mail was searched. Money for school donations was taken. Sometimes they got their money back, but even then, a percentage would be deducted for "handling charges." Recently the priests had ordered tape recorders for language teaching, but the school was charged a customs fee of 100 percent. When the priests asked why, they were told that they should have bought the equipment in Iraq. They would have, the priests said, but there were no such tape recorders for sale in Baghdad. It was useless to argue with the authorities; often, the priests said, they ended up bribing the officials to bring the taxes down. Many years later I learned that, with Iraqi nationalization in 1969, the Jesuits were expelled. The school, however, continued as an elite secondary school.

On one of our last days in Baghdad, we drove out to see the Arch of Ctesiphon on the banks of the Tigris River. Built in the first century BCE, Ctesiphon later became the largest city in the world and is mentioned in the Book of Ezra in the Hebrew Bible. Though not much more than the arch of this magnificent city remains, it gave us an inkling of its grandeur.

Arch of Ctesiphon, Baghdad

We had planned to stay in Baghdad for a few more days before leaving for Tehran, Iran, but one morning our Jesuit friends came to the camp to bring the news: "All Borders Closed Due to Cholera Outbreak." We didn't pay much attention to it at first, since we had already had our cholera shots.

But we soon realized that this didn't matter. Our international immuni-
zation cards meant nothing. The Jesuits said that people were being given
shots, all from the same needle. And then we saw it ourselves: the military
officials were lining people up on the street, giving them shots one after
another. We didn't think the authorities would come to our campsite with
their needles, but we didn't want to test that theory. We knew we had to
get out. The borders were closed, though, and we had no information as to
how long this would be the case. A few days? A month? How long would
it take to contain the outbreak? We had no idea, but we knew we didn't
want to sit around and wait for some indeterminate time. Mick's class was
scheduled to begin in two weeks.

After sharing the news and getting updates with other travelers at the
campground, we went to the Iranian Embassy to see if anyone could tell
us more about the border situation. "The border?" the officer said. "No
problem. Of course, the borders are open." I was skeptical. We had learned
long ago to trust the news from other travelers more than from officers in
starched uniforms. We had already heard that a German traveler had been
turned back at the Iranian border. We had also heard from another couple
that there was a five-day quarantine at the Jordanian border. That meant we
were hemmed in from both sides. We decided to try for more information
at the U.S. Embassy.

"Everything is closed," the officer said. "The airports and all borders.
No one is allowed in or out of the country."

"For how long?" I asked.

"No idea. It could be days or weeks. No one knows."

After we pumped him for more information, the officer told us that if
we drove south to Basra, the southern port city next to the Tigris River, we
might be able to get across to Iran from there. The Iranian city of Khorramshahr was only a few kilometers from Basra. Or we might be able to drive
into Kuwait and from there somehow get into Iran. The officer suggested
that we go to the U.S. Consulate in Basra and see if they could help us. It
seemed to be worth a try, even though this meant adding more than 350
miles to our journey for an outcome that was by no means certain. With

the West Pakistan class deadline looming, though, we decided to go. Before leaving the U.S. Embassy, we were led to the nurses' station and given another cholera booster shot. "Can't hurt," the nurse said.

Basra and the Swamps

BACK AT THE BAGHDAD campground, we relayed our new information and our plan to our German friends, Rolfe and Bernd. They were itching to get moving too, so we decided to drive in tandem. It would be safer for all of us. The next day, we left in the morning and drove all the way to Basra, 368 miles, with barely a stop during the long, hot, humid drive. When we arrived in Basra, we couldn't find a campground, but we did see a park that looked shady and inviting, with palm trees loaded with dates. We stopped there and set up for the night. In the next morning, we were not surprised when the city police showed up. We thought they might kick us out, but after we explained that all we were doing was sleeping there until we could contact the consulate, they gave us permission.

Breakfast with Rolfe and Bernd in Basra

That day, we went to the American Consulate to see if there was any updated information on border closures. We spoke to Jim Bumpus, the vice consul, who was a few years older than Mick. Jim didn't have any additional news about the Iranian border, but he said that the border with Kuwait was closed, too, and that last year it had been closed for three months.

We had expected our visit to the consulate to be short, but Jim seemed eager to talk. Since there was nothing we could do about the border closure, we hung around the consulate, trading travel stories. We told Jim about Mick's upcoming job in Peshawar and our deadline for getting there, about our drive from Baghdad, and about our camping in the park downtown. I realized as we were talking that Jim and we had somewhat similar life-styles—that is, involving international travel—though his was full-time with the State Department and ours was a more loosely structured itinerant teaching life. Still, it seemed to be two sides of the same coin.

Jim went out of his way to help us. He knew how important it was for us to get to Peshawar and how anxious we were to get across the border to Iran, so he said he would contact the consulate in Khorramshahr, Iran, to see if they could do anything. He also let Mick use the consulate phone to call the Peshawar Air Station to let the Education Office know that we might be a few days late.

That night, Jim graciously invited us to his home for dinner. He even said we could take showers there. We accepted with pleasure, as the idea of a shower, a relaxing dinner, and a good conversation was unbelievably exciting. The evening didn't disappoint me. We learned much about how it was to live in Iraq as a State Department employee, we talked about the political situation in that region, and both Jim and his wife seemed intrigued to hear our travel stories.

The next day, we met more foreigners coming through Basra.

Excerpt of letter to my parents. Basra, Iraq. August 28, 1966:

> *Dear Daddy and Mom,*
>
> *Last evening, five people our age came through from Iran. (Iraq will let anyone in; it's everyone else who won't let us out.) Three were German boys traveling together and two were a darling Swiss couple—both teachers, same levels as us. We brought them all to our personal island "camp" and shared a big dinner. Everyone brought different*

cans which mixed well, and we had rice too. Quite fun—especially with our normal spectators (women in black veils, children, and men with the eyes popping out). We did normal things for Europeans and Americans, but unheard-of things for here. We brought out blankets and pillows to sit in the shade and talk and drink cool drinks. (Unheard of!) They really stared when we brought out different stoves and camping equipment, canned food, and laughingly put together a dinner for nine people. I wonder what they thought about our strange array of tents and mosquito netting that we set up for the night. It is also quite strange here for men to take their shirts off or wear shorts, and for Rosemarie (the Swiss girl) and me to be joking and fooling around with the men. We have certainly gotten used to doing everything with a crowd of 15 or 20 people staring gap-mouthed at us in silence.

I still remember my exuberance at our impromptu party that day. I felt so open and free just having fun and relaxing with other travelers so much like us. Though we were from three different countries, we shared a culture through our similar ways of speaking, dressing, eating, and playing. If we had all been in Europe, we might have been more aware of cultural differences between our countries, but in Iraq, the similarities were more apparent than the differences. The spontaneity and ease of togetherness was intoxicating!

My letter of August 28 continues:

This morning we went on a boat trip into the swampland near here (between the rivers). It's a fascinating place with a culture all its own. Many of the people way back in the swamps never—or rarely—come out. We were also told that it is a place where people go who are trying to hide (criminals mainly). There are no roads, of course. You must paddle in, in small boats. We took a three-hour trip in (six of us). We stopped at one mud and woven house area where the men were very nice but all women and children either ran away or were told to stay inside. Most of the children were naked. They live on carabao milk and cheese, and they grow rice. It's very tropical in the swamp area. I would

like to go further in but of course it's more expensive. It takes two or
three days to cross the swamps in a paddleboat.

Love,

Patti

Boat building in a swamp village with Bernd,
Rosemarie, Rolfe, Iraqi family, Patti

When I look again at photos from our swamp trip in Iraq, I am surprised to see what we were all wearing. I had forgotten that both of our German friends often wore shorts without a shirt. Though neither Mick nor I wore shorts, Rosemarie and I both wore sleeveless blouses with our knee-length skirts and dresses. At the time I felt it was fine. Now I think I should have been more conservative, more aware of the image I was projecting.

Years after we left southern Iraq, especially during the 1980s and 1990s, the marshlands were almost completely drained, and the people relocated. The area has now been partially restored and reinundated, though not without considerable environmental effects.

Traveling as a Woman

I ENJOYED BEING WITH Rosemarie. Finally, I had a woman to talk to. We shared our experiences with men, for one thing. I told her about the man in Adana who grabbed my bottom and the man in Beirut who tried to kiss me in the elevator. Even though most of the time in Iraq I had three men (Mick, Rolfe, and Bernd) who acted as my "bodyguards," I still seemed to be a target for men, especially when my three bodyguards were not surrounding me. I told Rosemarie that I found myself watching each man who came toward me, and if he didn't move out of my way, I'd walk out into the street to avoid him. If I didn't do that, I would invariably be brushed, patted, or stroked. It was more than annoying; I felt like I was an object that could be handled. I hated it. But I also hated the fact that I had begun to view all men as the enemy. Rosemarie said she had the same experiences. Now she carried a hatpin, holding it in her dangling hand with its sharp point facing out. If a man got too close, he would get a jab in the thigh. Perfect, I thought. Now, if only I could find a hatpin. I never did get one, but always thought this was an ingenious response.

One afternoon, I went to a bakery with Rolfe to buy bread. It was crowded with men, maybe up to 20 people at a small counter. Rolfe and I both had to elbow our way up to the counter, pushing against people to get ahead. At first, I didn't push enough, and people kept getting in front of me. As I got more forceful and wormed my way up, I lost sight of Rolfe. There were men on all sides of me, and they were bigger and taller than me. Finally, I got to the front, and as I was trying to get the attention of the bread seller, I felt a man lean up against my whole backside with his erect penis against my skirt. I felt sickened, but I couldn't turn around or yell at the guy since I was hemmed in. My immediate thought was that this man might be distracting me to steal my money, so I kept my head, holding my bag even tighter against me as I tried to get the attention of the seller. But this man wasn't after money. He just leaned harder into my whole backside. I was stuck in one spot. There was nothing I could do, and nobody else knew that the man was rubbing against me. I tried to call Rolfe, but he was in the process of buying his bread and didn't hear me with all the commotion of people yelling to get the attention of the seller. Besides, what could Rolfe do? In moments that seemed like hours, I bought my bread and squirmed out of the bakery as fast as I could. I started to cry when I told Mick what had happened; again, I was reminded of how relieved I was to have three men as my bodyguards.

A LITTLE LATER that day, when Mick, Rolfe, Bernd, and I were shopping in the souk, we saw some good-looking apples. That was "a find" for us, but when Mick gave the seller a coin for the apples, the man shouted out "Counterfeit!" and demanded more money. As the seller continued shouting at us, and the usual crowd was growing, I got worried. It was stiflingly hot in the souk, and I just wanted to get out. But then the police appeared. We tried to explain that we had given the man a perfectly good coin, but the policeman either did not understand, did not want to listen, or did not want to make a scene. He indicated that we had to come with him to the police station. The police station! This was a first for us, and not a good sign, but we followed, fearfully, as the crowd around us scattered. Would we be arrested? When we got to the station, the police chief was taking a nap, and he did not seem happy to be disturbed. He reluctantly looked us over and listened to the man who had brought us in. Then he took the coin, dropped it on the floor, and declared, in a tone of authority, that it was good. We had no idea what criteria he used to make his judgment. The way it bounced? The sound it made? At any rate, our coin was deemed good, and we were free to go.

Over the Pipeline

ON OUR THIRD MORNING camped in the Basra city park, as we were wondering how long we would need to wait to cross the border, we were surprised to see Jim driving up. "Quick," he said. "I've just arranged a border crossing for you. You must leave immediately. The U.S. Consular officer from Iran will meet you at 10:30 this morning at the border. You'll have your quarantine there." It was 10 minutes to 9, and we knew that the bridge over the Tigris River would close at 9 a.m. It took us two minutes to throw everything in the car. We raced to the bridge, getting there just in time. Rolfe and Bernd followed us, as we had decided that we would continue to drive in tandem through Iran. After we crossed the bridge, we were at the Iraqi guard station, but the guard wouldn't stamp our passports with the exit stamp because he said we couldn't get into Iran. "Yes, we can," Mick insisted. "We have an appointment with the U.S. Consular officer." After much arguing, the Iraqi border official finally stamped our passports, and we drove, as instructed, toward the Iranian border and quarantine station.

It was only 10 miles through the no-man's-land of desert between the border stations of Iran and Iraq, but the drive seemed to last forever. We had no problem finding the highway, but soon after we left Basra, it was hard to see where the road was. It had turned to sand, with only bare indications of where other cars had driven. Jim hadn't mentioned this to us; he had only told us to go east as far as we could until we reached the oil pipe. Then turn north until we found a place to drive over the pipeline. This sounded easy, but I thought we'd be on a real road, not just sand. The more we drove, the more worried I became. We didn't have a compass. What if we were going in the wrong direction? What if we didn't see the oil pipeline?

Desert track between Basra and the Iranian border.
Rolfe and Bernd's Mercedes in front.

With our anxiety mounting, we continued driving. Finally, unmistakably, the pipeline loomed into view. It was huge. It blocked our way, being much too high to drive over. As instructed, we turned left—north-ward—and drove alongside the pipeline for a few miles until we saw a dirt ramp that would allow cars to go over. We were so relieved that we shouted to each other, "Hooray!" "Yay, we made it!" Up and over we drove, and on the other side was the Iranian quarantine station. At least we assumed that it was the station. In an expanse of sand, under the burning sun, was a kiosk with a few people hanging around. No trees, no real buildings, no grass, no water. There was hardly anything there. We had been told that there would be a five-day quarantine and were dreading the thought of spending five days in the middle of nowhere in the hot sun. However, a few minutes after we got to the station, we saw a white U.S. Embassy van drive up. "Are you the Sullivans?" the man, whom I'll call Bill Phillips, asked us. "I'm from the American Consulate in Khorramshahr. I got a phone call from Jim in Basra asking me to help you through the border, and I've arranged for your quarantine in town." We couldn't believe our luck. Here was another U.S. Embassy official who was young, friendly, and unbelievably kind. After thanking him profusely, we followed the embassy car to Khorramshahr, now feeling relaxed. We left Rolfe and Bernd at the quarantine station, but they assured us that they would get through; we agreed to meet in Khorramshahr.

13.

Quarantine and Dusty Roads—Iran

I thought Bill would take us to some sort of consulate building, but he stopped the car in front of a two-story house that looked like a palace to me. "This is the home of one of our consular officers who's gone for a while. You can stay here for a few days. Just don't leave." Leave? Why would I ever leave? The house was air-conditioned, and it had a pool, a bed with clean sheets, a bathroom with a shower, a large living room, and a real kitchen. There were date palms and even a tennis court in the huge yard. I couldn't believe it. It seemed like heaven. Or Shangri-La. I jumped in the pool right away. Bill had told us that our quarantine would be only two days, not five, but at this point I was hoping for five. For the next two days we lazed around, feeling like VIPs as we rattled around in spacious rooms. By the end of the second day, I had been swimming in the pool six times. I had never imagined that quarantine could be so welcome.

I discovered a bathroom scale in this lovely house, so I gingerly stepped on it. I thought I might have lost a few pounds, and I was right—a bit thinner, but nothing drastic. Mick took his turn. The scale showed his weight at 145; he had lost almost 30 pounds! Both of us were down to our high school or junior high school weights. Since leaving Turkey, we hadn't had much to eat besides dates and our canned items, especially in Iraq. I hadn't bought any fresh meat there, since it smelled and looked horrible hanging in the heat, and there weren't many vegetables for sale. Now, though, in Khorramshahr, we were getting more food.

Bill dropped by to chat and to be sure we had enough to eat. He and his wife invited us to their house. Over dinner, they told us the story of how the arrangements had been made for our border crossing. I was amazed. Evidently Jim in Basra, Iraq, had called Bill in Khorramshahr, Iran, and had so strongly advocated for permission for us to cross that Bill had invited the Iranian officials to dinner that night and managed to persuade them to give us permission papers. Bill said that it was extremely unusual, and even he was surprised that the Iranian officials had agreed. He said we were the only people who had been given permission to cross from Basra into Iran since the cholera epidemic began.

Excerpt of letter to my parents. Khorramshahr, Iran. August 29, 1966:

Dear Daddy and Mom,

I must admit that a lot of this [border-crossing permission] is because of my dear husband. He is not one to sit around waiting for people to do things for him. He talks to people and pulls every possible angle to make things happen. He's just friendly and happy—so people do things for him. I am too shy to break the ice. Anyway, I'm glad I didn't marry someone who just sits and doesn't try anything.

Love,

Patti

The only downside of our quarantine was that we had to report to the Iranian health authorities each morning. On the first day, the young Iranian doctor apologized as he examined us rectally with a Q-tip to check for cholera. Then he gave us some kind of antibiotic pills, saying we had to take two each day. We were sure we didn't need them, but on the first day we took them. After that, we kept the pills, putting them away for some possible future need. The doctor didn't seem to care. After three days of this confinement, the health authorities said we didn't have cholera and were free to go. We profusely thanked Bill for his help, left our paradise, and headed out again in our camper home.

Cities, Bazaars, and Mosques

OUR RELUCTANCE TO LEAVE the confines of a comfortable house was overshadowed by the pressure of getting to Peshawar in time for Mick's class. We were so concerned that we drove 379 miles that day. As Mick wrote in his journal, "The road was fairly well paved halfway but then we encountered the dirt and rock road. What a miserable stretch. It is so dusty that now we're completely covered through and through with dust." We pulled over to sleep in the small town of Kazeroon, Iran, south of Shiraz, where we were kept awake by the heat and the mosquitoes buzzing around. The next day entailed another long drive over dirt roads. The Zagros mountains were so steep that we had to use first gear all the way up. We reached Shiraz and went right to our destination—Persepolis—where we spent the night. I had read about this ancient capital built during the reign of Darius the Great in 515 BCE, but I had no idea it would be so large and impressive.

Persepolis

Cooling off in southern Iran

Excerpt of journal entry. September 4, 1966:

The best things about [the Persepolis ruins] are the bas-reliefs and the carvings. Almost every remaining stone is delicately and completely filled with reliefs. The staircases are particularly nice. . . . Darius's tem-

ple must have been magnificent. All the doorways and windows are covered with life-sized reliefs of kings and lions. Evidently they used to be polished so highly that one could see his [sic] face in the marble. I wonder [what] the room furnishings were [like]? It seems that one person would feel mighty small walking into the huge reception room to meet Darius.

It was a 270-mile drive from Persepolis to Isfahan, and we were again traveling in tandem with Rolfe and Bernd. They had gotten through the quarantine quickly, so we had been able to meet up with them in Khorramshahr. We decided to stick together, at least from time to time. Not only was it safer; it was more fun. Usually, when Mick and I stopped for lunch, we would sit inside House or sprawl out on rocks somewhere. Rolfe and Bernd, though, would bring out their small folding table and chairs, as they had at the campground in Basra. It felt quite fancy and proper to sit at a table outside for lunch.

ISFAHAN! WHAT A CITY! The name is magical, and the bazaar was the biggest I'd ever seen. When we drove up to it, a smiling young boy attached himself to us. He led us through the many twists and turns as we exclaimed over the wealth of items for sale. Inside the bazaar and out, artisans were crafting their wares in the same way that had been done for hundreds of years. In an old mill, a camel wore blinders as it walked around a circle pulling a grindstone to make soap. On the rooftops of the mill, newly dyed wool was hanging out to dry.

There was no end of things I wanted to buy in this city, but I knew we had to keep extra money on hand in case of a car breakdown or some emergency. If we were lucky, there might be a check for us in Tehran, but we couldn't count on that. We did, though, dole out money for several items, including a small carpet. We were both getting caught up in the desire to know more about carpets. They were all so gorgeous, each with its own history.

Excerpt of letter to my parents. Isfahan, Iran. September 5, 1966:

Dear Daddy and Mom,

You must come to Isfahan. We have decided that if we were to live for a year in any Middle East city we've been in, this would be our first choice. The bazaar is unequaled as far as we're concerned. It's clean, airy, covers six kilometers (all covered), and is chock full of wonderful things. [We] can't resist buying some things. We have bought a beautiful hand-engraved brass pitcher, a delicate silver bracelet, a hand-printed tablecloth (with designs of Persepolis), a "miniature" showing a lion hunt in camel bone with a brass frame—all for about $9.50. Also today we really broke down and splurged. We bought a gorgeous carpet. It's old—maybe 70 or 80 years, but in a delightful way. It's quite large and cost us $70. I can't wait to see how it looks in the States. Here it looks wonderful. It's a deep rich red.

The mosques are also gorgeous. I think they are supposed to be the most beautiful mosques in the Middle East. The mosaic tiles are so intricate and colorful. We watched some men make more tiles for one mosque today. It sure is painstaking work.

Love,
Patti

Mosque in Isfahan

Excerpt from Mick's letter to his parents. Isfahan, Iran. September 6, 1966:

Hi,

I'm eating well again and my "runs" have finally quit after three straight weeks. In the 120-degree heat we only took in liquids and it got to me finally. I lost another five pounds—now 145. But here in Isfahan the weather has cooled, I have medication, and am eating good food—again. Fresh pasteurized milk, eggs, meat, fruit—all are rather plentiful here, much unlike Iraq, where fresh meat was next to impossible to obtain. It spoiled in the heat. So now I'll gain some weight back.

M

After three days, we left Isfahan. As we drove north toward Tehran, the van suddenly made sputtering noises, and the engine jerked and went out. Mick had always feared that something like this would happen, but it had not. Until now. He steered the car to the side of the road, and we got out. There was nothing around—no trees, no water, no tents, not even a donkey or camel. Immediately I began to worry. How long would we be stranded? Would Rolfe and Bernd come looking for us? If so, when? Mick said we might have to hitch a ride on a camel. I assumed he was joking, but there was some truth in it. More likely we'd be able to flag down a truck to haul us to the next town. But would one of us stay with the car alone? While we were both going over possible scenarios, Mick lifted the engine door at the back of House and peered inside. He is not a car repairman, nor is he an electrician, but he is resourceful and logical. One wire was dangling down; Mick thought it could have caused a short in the engine. He tucked the wire up and wrapped it with tape, hoping beyond hope that it would work. It did. The car started right up, and we never had that problem again. He still considers this simple action to be his most memorable car repair job!

WE CONTINUED OUR DRIVE to Tehran, a long 307 miles, where we found a place to camp by a swimming pool a few kilometers west of the airport. The city was the most modern we had been in since Beirut. Girls and women looked very smart in their Western-style dresses. The traffic, though, was the worst we had encountered. I wrote, "*It seems to be a game of 'chicken' to see who will stop first.*" It didn't seem to matter that there were traffic lights, stop signs, and policemen. If there were rules of the road, we didn't understand them, so we drove slowly and carefully.

Our first stop in Tehran was the post office. We were hoping that Mick's check from the class in Turkey had arrived in California and that Mick's mom had sent it to us at the poste restante address in Tehran. I stood at the counter, thumbing through the box of letters with return addresses from all over the world. And yes, there it was. She had sent part of his salary, as he had asked. Relieved, we went to the bank and bought traveler's checks to take us through to Peshawar. In his return letter to his mom, Mick wrote, "*We happily received the money—thanks much. Hold the remainder of the check, after deducting $114 for health insurance, and I'll ask you to send it to Pakistan. You should also receive a check for $35 from the University of Maryland. If you don't get it let me know.*"

Mick's class was supposed to begin on Monday, September 7, but since he had called the office from Khorramshahr, the department knew we would be about a week late. Even so, Mick wanted to contact Peshawar again to let them know we were on our way. We walked into the U.S. Embassy and spoke to the person at the desk, who was quite willing to help us out, and Mick was able to get a message to the Education Office at the Peshawar Air Station. What I remember most about entering the embassy was not the telephone call; it was seeing the sign "Women" and the spotlessly clean bathroom. I needed it! We later coined a term for the act of seeing a clean bathroom: the embassy syndrome. Seeing it and you've got to go! There's a clear connection between the mind and body.

This was not the first time we had entered a U.S. Embassy, but from the vantage point of the 21st century, it was surprisingly accessible. At that time, U.S. Embassies were often located near city centers where they were easily available, not only to Americans but to local people and visitors as well. After 2001, many of our embassies were rebuilt, sometimes farther away from downtown, surrounded by tall iron fences and gates. They became more secure, but not as welcoming, and certainly not as easy to enter, at least for people who are not employees.

Though Mick had gotten the message through to Peshawar, he was worried that the class would get canceled like the one in Spain. If that happened, we'd really be hard-pressed for money. But there was nothing we could do about that now, so we decided to spend two more days in Tehran. We visited the archaeological museum and Golestan Palace, dazzling with its cut glass, mirrors on the wall, jeweled throne, and magnificent carpets. The palace was still being used for official receptions, but it was mostly a museum. We also took the van to a shop for a checkup before the next long drive to Kabul, Afghanistan.

From Tehran, we expected it would take three days to get to Herat in western Afghanistan, and another three to get through Afghanistan and into Peshawar. We could arrive in a week, just in time for Mick's class. With that calculation, we decided to make a slight detour to the Caspian Sea, 166 miles north of Tehran. We crossed over high, rugged mountains, skirting the highest peak in Iran, Mount Damavand, and then down into the seaside town of Babolsar. After three weeks of dry, dusty roads, it was a relief to be in a sub-tropical climate. The houses were made of grass instead of mud. We camped right on the sea, feeling pleased with ourselves that we had taken this route.

The next day, back on our way to Mashhad, our route took us through lush green country on a paved road, and then, when the pavement ended, we were back in dirt, dust, and rocks. We were not surprised, since we had already heard that the road was rocky all the way to the Afghan border, but we were dismayed, knowing that these miles of washboard road would be terrible for the van as well as for us. We assumed that everything inside would be thick with dust. That was all true, but it was worse than we expected. Before we reached Mashhad, the car began jerking. *Oh no*, I thought. *Not again.* Mick feared that we might have some kind of electrical problem, and he was worried out of his mind. Since we didn't know if the car would keep going, we stopped for the night in the village of Bojnoord, Iran. We had already driven 334 miles that day but were still almost 300 miles from Mashhad. The next morning, I held my breath as Mick turned the key. The car didn't start. I was trying to stay calm as we waited silently for a few minutes. And then, after a few tries, the engine started up and thereafter ran well. Maybe it had gotten clogged with dust.

The countryside on the way to Mashhad was like what we had already been through—bare mountains and a dusty road—but we saw more and more beggars. Every time we stopped, someone would come up to us begging for money. We stayed with our policy of not giving money, but I felt conflicted about this. Compared with these people, we were rich. We owned a car; we had money for gas, food, and clothes; and we knew we would be paid for work. But still, we were watching our money every day, spending only about $30 a week for both of us for all our expenses. If we gave out money, whom would we give it to? Women? Children? People with obvious health needs? Where would we draw the line? People crowded around us with their hands out. There were so many people who needed money and food that I didn't know where to begin. I felt cruel and uncomfortable as we justified to ourselves our no-giving policy.

We hadn't seen Rolfe and Bernd since leaving Isfahan but had planned to meet them in Mashhad so that we could drive together through Afghanistan. When we reached Mashhad, we went to the post office as usual, hoping for mail. We parked, walked in, and headed for the open box on top of one of the counters labeled "Poste Restante." Again, as in Tehran, I thumbed through the box, which contained a pile of letters, but found nothing for us. I forgot my disappointment, though, as soon as we emerged from the post office. There, hanging around waiting for us, were Rolfe and Bernd. Relieved, we hugged as old friends.

I had not known that Mashhad was one of the holiest cities of the world, that it was a major pilgrimage center. While Rolfe and Bernd waited for us, they had learned a lot from a man outside the post office. As foreigners and infidels, we couldn't go into the mosque. Nor could we go alone to the bazaar, since it was near the great mosque. But this man would guide us. "Us," however, did not include me, as a woman. I felt fine waiting for the men and encouraged them all to go, but Rolfe said he would stay with me. He and I had a fine time poking around shops. When Mick and Bernd got back from their bazaar trip, Mick said he felt like we really were in a new part of the world now: Central Asia. Many of the men in the bazaar looked like pictures he had seen of people from Mongolia. He even felt that Genghis Khan might come galloping through. Mick and Bernd's guide said that many of the men in the bazaar had come as pilgrims from the mountains of Afghanistan, Pakistan, and parts of Russia, and that they were paying for their journeys by selling their rugs. We were clearly entering a new region.

Mashhad, entrance to bazaar

A country border is a line on a map. It is also a place where one's passport is stamped. But the border does not necessarily separate one culture from another. It is only one point within a cultural mix that extends out from both sides of the political boundary. When we left Mashhad and drove the next few hundred miles toward the border of Afghanistan, we began to see differences. Men's turbans were wrapped slightly differently. Many women wore black, but most women we saw did not cover their faces. Sometimes they held part of their cloak or veil over their faces, but maybe that was because I was a foreigner. As we got nearer to Afghanistan, we saw more women completely covered from head to toe.

In the town of Torbat-e Jam in Iran, we pulled over near some women who were washing clothes in a ditch by the street. As usual, people crowded around our van as we emerged; they looked friendly and welcoming. Some of the women were wearing black cloaks, but several were not. The women laughed and smiled as they asked us to take their pictures next to their sweetly dressed children.

Torbat-e Jam, Iran—people gathered around House, Patti inside

Women washing clothes at the drainage ditch

At the gas station in Torbat-e Jam, we got eight liters of gas. We had already filled up with 35 liters in Mashhad, but Mick, as usual, continued with his practice of keeping the gas tank full as much as possible, since we were never certain where the next gas station would be.

As we headed east, the road was terrible. Worse than terrible. At one point, the road leading up to a bridge had caved in, so we had to drive down the side of the riverbed and across the dry gulch. We had thought that it would take three days to get from Tehran, Iran, to Herat, Afghanistan, but we had misjudged it. We weren't even close to Herat, though we figured we'd be at the Afghan border in one more day. There were almost no cars or people on the road, but as we neared the border, we saw a large group of men putting up a banner next to the road. The surprising thing was that there was nothing around. Nothing. No houses or buildings, barely a road. We weren't sure what they were doing or why, but it was colorful, and the men and boys looked like they were having a good time. We stopped; they welcomed us and proudly posed for a few pictures. Then we drove away on the desolate, unpaved, dusty road, passing a few men on donkeys, on our way to the Iran-Afghanistan border.

Raising a banner near Iran-Afghanistan border

Donkey traffic on the highway

Bridge out near Iran-Afghanistan border

Part Four:

South Asia

September–December 1966

14.

The Border and Herat— Afghanistan

Though we had been crossing country borders for a year by now, I was still shocked at the Iran-Afghanistan border station. It consisted of a few low buildings in the desert, including a small hotel, a gas pump, and a restaurant. A few people were standing or sitting around, and we saw a couple of cars, but no one was moving. We were told that the border official was sleeping. We waited, along with Rolfe and Bernd and a few other travelers, in the dirty hotel restaurant, which served only warm Coca-Cola. It took two hours for the official to finish his nap and eat his lunch. Then he slowly began to stamp and sign our papers and passports.

Border station between Iran and Afghanistan

149

When we finally left the border station after topping our gas tank with five liters of gas, we still had about 80 miles to go to reach Herat. It took three hours. The road was like corrugated cardboard, with big dips and rises. Dust seeped into the car, covering everything we owned. I felt filthy through and through, but there was no place to wash. On the evening of September 11, we reached Herat. Though the third-largest city in Afghanistan, it was a small, dusty town with no paved roads.

Herat's main street.

Journal excerpt. Herat, Afghanistan. September 11, 1966:

This is our first night in Afghanistan and I'm really amazed. We arrived in Herat just about dusk today. It's much more primitive than I had imagined: mud homes, dirt roads. Every man had his turban on and his white skirt. There were few other cars. I saw about three jeeps (Russian and American makes) and one or two other old cars. Nobody has on western dress. There are virtually no women on the street. After looking for quite a while I saw one woman, but she was scarcely recognizable. Not one part of her body was visible. . . . Her face was so covered I wondered how she could see. It wasn't a veil but a face shroud the same material as the rest of her cloak.

We're parked in front of a hotel tonight because Rolfe and Bernd wanted to sleep in a hotel. I suppose this is one of the safest places. This town reminds me a little of old western movies with its dirt streets, its horse-carriage taxis, its old buildings. The main difference is that the men wear turbans and skirts.

We cooked dinner with Rolfe and Bernd that night on the street in front of their hotel. We had all become used to having a crowd of people staring at us at every moment, but sometimes it was more unpleasant than others. This was one of those times. We were tired of people watching our every move, so we parked our cars so close to each other that we could open the doors to shield our little cooking stove. It made for a relatively private dinner.

After Rolfe and Bernd left, I was setting up for the night when I caught a glimpse of a child walking up to us. He was facing away at first, but when he turned his head, I saw that his upper lip was open right up to his nose. He pointed to his face and put his hand out for money. After looking at us for a while, he slunk back into the shadows. Later another child limped up to us, pointing to his leg. The wound looked dirty but not infected, so I cleansed it with water, dabbed on some antibiotic and wrapped it with a clean bandage. It was such a small thing to do from my perspective, but for this child, who evidently had no access to first aid equipment, it was crucial. The boy smiled and seemed happy as he walked away. This was the first of several occasions in the months to come when we would see heartbreaking evidence of poverty and the lack of health care.

WE LEFT HERAT the next day. We needed to hurry because of Mick's upcoming class, so we gave Rolfe and Bernd our contact through the Education Department at the Peshawar Air Station, telling them to look us up when they got there. For us, it was now another long desert drive to Kandahar, 352 miles, but at least the highway was paved—as we were later told—by the Soviets. We were also told that the U.S. had built a large airport in Kandahar. We wondered why the U.S. would spend so much money on such an expensive project in such an out-of-the-way place. The local traffic certainly did not warrant it. Was the new Kandahar airport also built for some possible future strike against the Soviets? Maybe, I thought at the time, but I didn't think much about it. How could we know that at the end of the 1970s the Soviet Union would invade Afghanistan, and this road would be closed to travelers like us. And of course, we never imagined that the towns we were passing through would, 35 years later, become the site of the United States' longest war.

A Pharmacy in Kandahar

SINCE IT WAS the second-largest city in Afghanistan, we expected Kandahar to have the feel of a modern city. It did not. It looked like a dusty outpost, albeit bigger than Herat. We saw only a few women, and they were completely covered in *chadri*, the head-to-toe full-length burka with embroidered holes over the eyes.

Our goal in Kandahar was to look up a pharmacist. During the spring of 1965, when Mick was teaching at Santa Barbara City College in California, he had a student from Afghanistan named Nabi, whose father was a pharmacist in Kandahar. Mick was fascinated with Nabi's stories about his background, especially the ones about Nabi's father, who lived in a compound with his four wives and many children. Nabi told Mick that the wives would hang a flag outside one of the houses to indicate where Nabi's father would sleep that night. Evidently it was the women who made the decision. Mick later wrote to Nabi saying that we hoped to get to Afghanistan. Nabi wrote right back, giving Mick directions to the pharmacy and saying that he would write to his father about us. So here we were, looking for a particular pharmacy. We found one that fit the description and went in.

The pharmacy was probably fairly clean by Afghan standards, but it looked dirty to us. It was busy. Men sat on benches, most likely waiting their turn to see the doctor who was in the pharmacy. Women were sitting on the floor in the back. We introduced ourselves to the man behind the counter, who spoke enough English to let us know that he was Nabi's uncle. We were in the right pharmacy, at least, but Nabi's uncle didn't seem to understand who we were or why we were there. That was harder to explain. Maybe Nabi's letter had not gotten there, or maybe Nabi's father had not told his brother about us. Or maybe it was just too strange for this man to see two foreigners walking into his shop. At any rate, he didn't seem very welcoming, and he didn't try to find his brother. We didn't know what to do or what else to say, so we left after a few minutes. It was disappointing and uncomfortable. I wish I could have spoken Dari, a dialect of Persian Farsi and one of the two official languages of Afghanistan (Dari and Pashto). And I would have loved to know what Nabi's uncle told his brother later that day.

We learned later, by talking to an Afghan friend, how limited medical care was for women. The usual procedure, this friend said, was that the doctor would ask the man what was wrong with his wife. The man would then ask his wife and repeat the information to the doctor. The doctor would never see, touch, or talk directly to the woman. Our Afghan friend added that there were no female doctors, since the men would not let a woman examine them, nor would they let their wives go to a female doctor.

Kandahar

Kabul Gorge and Khyber Pass

MUCH AS I would have liked to stay longer in Kandahar, we couldn't because of our rush to get to Peshawar. The drive to Kabul was long—371 miles—but at least the road was paved. We were stopped twice between Kandahar and Kabul to pay a road fee. I didn't know who would be receiving the tolls, but I hoped they would be used for road upkeep. At least the drive was made more interesting because of the colorful painted trucks plying the route. Most of the trucks were jam-packed with people, often stacked one on top of another. How they held on was a mystery to me.

Trucks in Afghanistan

Journal excerpt. Kabul, Afghanistan. September 14, 1966:

Compared to other Afghani cities, this one is quite modern. There are many modern buildings and several women in western dress. Of course all the school children wear western clothes—black skirts and blouses and long black stockings and a white headscarf. I doubt that they will ever go into chaderi. In the villages, though, probably all the little girls will. It'll be a long time before the women are "emancipated" here.

Last night in Kabul we walked around a few of the stores. There are gorgeous carpet shops of course! Also there are many shops where men make sheep jackets and coats . . . very good-looking jackets for rough winter wear. We may come back and buy some. They also make fur slippers, karakul (newborn lamb) hats, gloves, and other yummies.

We parked in front of the Pakistani Embassy to eat and sleep last night, since there was no other place. One of the men who works in the embassy came out and invited us to sleep in his house. So we did. The bed was not as nice as ours, but it was very nice of him to invite us to his house. People are always trying to be nice to us by inviting us in to sleep because they think that sleeping in the car is a hardship. They don't realize that our bed is much more comfortable and cozier than theirs, and that it is not hardship at all, but that we love it!

Kabul animal market   Kabul Green Door Bazaar

We could spend only a day in Kabul, barely enough time to walk around a few shopping areas and see the animal market. That day, though, increased my desire to learn more about the country.

We left on September 13 for the last leg of this journey: 193 miles from Kabul to Peshawar. Soon after leaving Kabul, we passed through the Kabul Gorge, then continued on to the West Pakistani border. All this time during the past year, we had been driving "normally" on the right side of the road as in the U.S. But immediately after the border control, we had to cross over to the left, as in Britain. The move felt too sudden to me. I kept thinking that the trucks were headed right for us, especially as we rounded tight mountain bends. Mick managed fine, though, with no accidents. I didn't feel like Genghis Khan, but I was thrilled to be driving through the Khyber Pass, such an integral part of the ancient Silk Road.

Kabul Gorge

Khyber Pass, looking east toward Pakistan

15.

A Job, a House, and Visitors—West Pakistan

We arrived at the Peshawar Air Station, on Wednesday, September 14, after driving 916 miles in three days, including one night in Kandahar and one night in Kabul. Sergeant Tippet, the education officer at the base, greeted us warmly, but I wonder what we looked like. I know how I felt: tired, dirty, and ready to stop moving. We were at first dismayed when Sergeant Tippet said that the anthropology class hadn't filled, so he couldn't offer Mick two classes. But the good news was that the sociology class was a go, so at least we'd get the $450 that would keep us on the road. We thought we might even try to stay in Peshawar for the second term if Mick could get another class. That would mean that we could stay until the end in the middle of January, and we would definitely have enough money to arrange for boat passage from India around to Japan, and then across the Pacific. But now we needed to focus on where to live for the next two months. We were OK for that first night, though; we were offered beds in VIP quarters. I could hardly wait to get into the shower.

On Friday, the Tippets told us that they had found a place for us to rent for the next few months. The house was on the outer edge of Peshawar, in University Town near the beautiful campus of Peshawar University. It was quite far from the base, about 11 miles, but that seemed OK since

Mick only had to be on the base Tuesday and Friday evenings when he had a class to teach.

The house looked perfect. We had our own entrance to a large, sparsely furnished bedroom with a fireplace (surprisingly) and our own bathroom. There were no other houses on either side, and only a field in front. Our hosts, Sergeant and Mrs. Smith, said we could use their refrigerator. They didn't offer the use of their kitchen for cooking, but we didn't need it, nor did we want to intrude on their space. We were quite used to our breakfast of Nescafé with bread and jam, and fruit for lunch. We'd figure out dinners. We planned to travel as much as we could throughout the region anyway, so we wouldn't be there much. We immediately began moving a few things in.

Our house in Peshawar (left side room)

That evening, Mick taught his first class. It went well, and we were both pleased that enough students showed up. We'd be able to stay in Peshawar for two more months. Though we loved living in our own VW House, it felt luxurious to have a large bedroom where we could stand up, walk around the bed, and have our own bathroom with a toilet, sink, and shower. The next morning, though, I found out that there wasn't any hot water. We hadn't thought to ask about hot water, but I guess it was standard in Pakistani houses not to have any. There was a showerhead in the corner of the bathroom, but no enclosed shower stall. I didn't mind that the water sprayed the whole bathroom, but I balked at getting under cold water. As the days went on, I finally did get used to it, at least sort of. I never really enjoyed the showers, especially for washing my hair, but I accommodated. And the water wasn't icy cold as it came from the tap, just almost lukewarm.

We spent the whole day both Saturday and Sunday unpacking and cleaning out the van. We took everything out and scrubbed inside and out, going through mountains of dirt. On Monday morning we got a message from the education office at the base saying that we had visitors. Our friends Rolfe and Bernd had arrived in Peshawar the night before; we were so pleased they had found us. We met them in town, and since we had been given permission to use the commissary on the base, we offered to buy them a case of beer before taking them to our new house. Mick told Rolfe that he had some beer to put in the fridge. "Never mind," Rolfe said. "I'll drink it warm right now." They hadn't had beer in months!

That night, Rolfe and Bernd pitched their tent in our yard. It had been a week since we had left them in Herat, so we stayed up late, regaling each other with travel stories from Kandahar and Kabul. So much fun to compare adventures! The next day, Rolfe and Bernd washed and cleaned out their car, taking advantage of having a hose and driveway, just as we had done two days earlier. We got the distinct impression that the Smiths weren't so pleased with us having our friends come by, especially since again the yard was covered with items strewn around. The Smiths didn't say anything; they just glowered a bit as they looked over the yard. I didn't worry about it much, as I knew the mess was temporary. After lunch with us, Rolfe and Bernd left for India. We were all sad as we hugged goodbye, realizing that it was unlikely we'd meet again, since we were staying in Peshawar for the next two months. As it turned out, that was the case. Now, so many years later, I regret that we did not exchange some way of getting in touch.

Peshawar women in cart

Peshawar street

Guns in Kohat

WEDNESDAY, SEPTEMBER 21, the day after Mick's second night class, we took our first day trip out of Peshawar, heading south to the villages of Kohat and Darra. We invited a new friend, Peter, a University of Maryland instructor who was teaching philosophy at the base, to join us. The road was well paved, but as we drove south, we saw a sign saying that we were entering tribal territory and that if we left the road, we would be under tribal law, no longer under government protection. Duly warned, we stayed on the road.

Tribal area sign

Our first stop was at the village of Darra on Kohat Pass, well known for its production of firearms. Small factories, the size of single rooms, lined the dusty streets and alleys, each one crammed with rifles and guns of all types. The craftsmen were making replicas of American rifles, pistols, and mortars, even with the label "Made in the USA" and "original" serial numbers. We watched the men use primitive tools as they sanded and polished the wood. They would fit metal parts together by holding them over an open fire until they were red-hot and then pound the heated parts with heavy hammers. There were a few electrical-powered conveyor belts, but most of the work was done by hand. The finished guns looked exactly like the original machine-made models, at least to me.

While walking around the village, I felt like we were in a western movie set with men carrying rifles and wearing bandoliers. I was afraid, not because I thought we would be attacked in any way, but because the men were careless in the way they handled their guns. The rifles were slung over the men's shoulders casually, often with muzzles pointed toward people. Every now and then, I jumped as we heard a gun going off. We had heard that it was not unusual for people to be shot by mistake, often several a month, though we also heard it could be several a week. Either way, it was more than I wanted to think about.

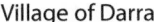

Village of Darra

Gun shops in Darra, Kohat District

After leaving Darra, we drove over the mountain pass to the ancient town of Kohat, also the home of a large Pakistani Air Force base. It was a pretty town with green trees and lovely houses, at least for the many people working on the base. As we walked around the Kohat bazaar, I looked for other Western-dressed women but didn't see any. There were only a few women in the bazaar, all of them well covered. I noticed one woman with glasses and only then realized that this was the first pair of glasses I had seen for a long time. We went back to Peshawar that afternoon, energized and excited about our first foray into the northwest region of West Pakistan.

Tribal Wedding

THE NEXT DAY, THURSDAY, we were invited to a tribal wedding by one of the Pakistani workers at the base. I was eagerly looking forward to the event, since it would give us a chance to see what local life was like, but we had no idea what the invitation entailed: what time should we get there, how long would it last, should we bring a gift, what should we wear? The man who had invited us hadn't given any details; it was just "Please come to our family wedding" as he gave us directions to the groom's house. We followed his directions, finally found the house, and hesitantly wandered toward it. We were relieved to see our friend. He said that we were an hour late and that everyone had been waiting for us. We had no idea that anyone would wait for us. Was this because we were foreigners? Or because Mick was a teacher? I was embarrassed, caught off guard as I realized once again how much I didn't know. And how much I had to learn.

The celebration was held in a dusty field where a tent had been set up. Under the canopy were two dancers—effeminate-looking men—with about a hundred people crowded around them. As we neared the tent, a large group of men left the circle and ran toward us. Then they stopped and stared. Even the dancers stopped spinning. We just smiled at them. Soon, though, the dancing began again, and people sauntered back to the tent. We were seated on a tied-rope bed (*charpoy*) near guests who were sprawled out to watch the dancers. The two men twirled around as the drums and accordions kept a beat.

One of the guests came up to me with paper money in his hand. He held it up against my cheek and the dancer gracefully twirled and danced over to me, picked up the money, gently pinched my cheek, and brushed his hand over my face. Then he twirled away, with his red and blue skirts flying outward in a cloud of dust. The process continued as more of the guests held money up to people's cheeks, eyes, chins, mouths, or heads. The male dancers had long hair that flew around their faces as they rhythmically tossed their heads from side to side. Some of the boys watching the dance had expressions of rapture as the music grew more intense. One of the people in the circle of dancers was a young boy of about 13, attired in a gold dress with a silky yellow scarf. He seemed shyer than the older men, as he slowly and provocatively rotated his delicate hands and arms. Later we were told that some men were taught these feminine actions from birth, while others adopted them later in life. Sometimes all the men in one family would become dancers. I assumed this was a paying job that would help the whole family.

After watching the dancers, we were ushered into a small room where a man brought in a huge plate with mounds of rice, both sweet and savory. Why were we the only ones being served? Was this food just for us? I didn't have much time to consider this, as we were gently but forcefully pushed into sitting down on the floor. This was my first time eating with my hands and I was sloppy; my skirt quickly filled up with bits of rice. We were soon told that the other guests had eaten an hour and a half ago and that the food had been saved for us. Once more, I was embarrassed, but our hosts didn't seem bothered; they just smiled and watched us. We had earlier been introduced to the groom, and while we were eating, he came in and out of our room several times. He asked if we were comfortable and added that he was nervous about seeing his prospective bride for the first time. When we finished eating, the groom left, and we were alone in the room. We didn't know what to do. Should we stay there? Would it be impolite to leave? Or impolite to stay? If we left, where should we go? My hands were greasy and sticky and there weren't any napkins, so I was glad when one of the men brought us bowls of water and soap for cleaning.

After what seemed like a long time, someone came in and told us to drive to the bride's village. One of the men gave us directions, but they were not very clear. Nor was it clear as to when we should get there. We saw some people leaving the tent area, but we didn't know if they were going to the bride's village or somewhere else. It was all confusing to us, even though the people we talked to were speaking English. We asked questions but got short, quick answers that didn't help enough. Maybe we didn't know the right questions to ask, or maybe the hosts thought we knew more about what was expected, since it was "common knowledge."

We left for the bride's village as instructed, following the minimal driving directions, and finally, after about 30 miles, were surprised to find that the bride's village was Darra, the gun village that we had visited the day before. We seemed to be late again, since several buses and two or three cars were already parked in front. A few men seemed to be waiting for us; they greeted us profusely, then took us to a room where we were served tea and biscuits. After that, we were led to another area of the village, where there was more music and dancing. The same dancers were there, along with a three-man band playing a box accordion, a flute, and a drum. Again, men crowded around the dancers. Mick noticed that the men had hung up their pistols on wall pegs, but they kept their rifles with them. Many of the men were shooting into the air.

Dancers and musicians

The main dancer

Dancing and shooting

There was another young American woman at the wedding. I asked her if she knew anything about Pakistani tribal weddings, but she didn't know any more than I did. What I really wanted to know was what the bride and other women were doing, since we hadn't seen any women at all. Tentatively I asked one of our hosts if I could see the bride. The man answered that the bride was in another part of the village, where only women were allowed, but that the other American woman and I could go there. He led us to two women who took us to another compound, where we were ushered into a yard jam-packed with gaily dressed women and girls. They crowded around us so tightly that our arms were pressed together; we could barely move. I asked one woman if I could congratulate the bride. She pushed us through the crowd across the dirt to a figure huddled on the ground, bent over with her face almost in the dirt. I assumed this was the bride, but she didn't look up, and the women kneeling around her immediately began covering her with silk scarves. I couldn't make sense of anything until I realized that the women around the bride were spreading a paste of henna dye in the part on top of her head. No wonder the bride was bent over! Now I understood why she didn't look up. I still didn't know why she was being covered with scarves. Was it to shield her from us, the foreign women? Or was it part of the dyeing process? Before I could think about much more, the women around the bride began pushing us away. Once again, I felt uncomfortable, like an intruder, and we left quickly. We heard later that the bride was 16 or 17 years old and the groom was 29 or 30.

After seeing the bride, I walked back to where the men were. We spent another half-hour listening to the music, watching the graceful dancers, and getting money snatched from around our faces. Then the pace quickened. More men joined the circle of dancers and began shooting their rifles. I worried about where the bullets might be coming down, but I didn't see anyone get hit with a falling bullet. Soon after, the headman came over to us and shook our hands, saying goodbye. Were we supposed to leave? Was the celebration over? I had expected the bride and groom to come in and a ceremony to take place. But this was the end of the day's celebration. The groom had still never seen his bride. Later we heard that the night before, an official had asked each one separately whether he and she agreed to marry the other. That was the official part. We were also told later that the groom and bride would each be taken separately to the groom's house in Peshawar. There they would see each other for the first time.

The day had been fascinating for us, but there was so much I now wanted to know about Pakistani tribal weddings, especially this one. The people had seemed genuinely pleased to have us there, but we must have caused inconveniences that we were not aware of. All in all, though, I felt honored to have been invited.

Kaghan Valley

AS WE WERE ANXIOUS to get in as much travel as we could, we planned our first weekend trip for the next day. Peter was ready to join us again, and we were glad to have another person with us. We had heard that the Kaghan Valley, up in the north on the Karakoram highway, was spectacular, so our destination was the town of Naran, high up in the mountains near Kashmir, in the shadow of the 26,000-foot-high mountain peak of Nanga Parbat. One problem, though, was that we were allowed to drive our own vehicle only part of the way, since we didn't have four-wheel drive. We were told we could rent a jeep and a driver in the town of Abbottabad, but we would have to be there first thing in the morning. Abbottabad! The name meant nothing to us then. Never could we have imagined that much of the world would later know this city as the place where Osama bin Laden was killed by American forces in May 2011. As for us in 1966, we were just wondering whether or not to make the trip. In the end, despite the distance and the potential issue of not finding a jeep, we decided to go, even though that meant leaving after Mick's Friday night class, driving all night, and getting back to Peshawar by Monday evening.

We kept ourselves awake that night by switching drivers and talking to each other, but by 4 a.m. we were so exhausted that we stopped for two hours to sleep in the car. When we reached Abbottabad, it was still early, so we decided to drive farther, up to the tiny village of Balakot, another town where we could hire a jeep. Located at about 4,000 feet, surrounded by mountains, Balakot was the beginning of Kaghan Valley. It was a small town, tucked into the edge of the mountains.

Us on the main bridge in
the village of Balakot

Balakot's main street

As it turned out, our decision to drive from Abbottabad up to Balakot wasn't such a good one. We arrived there at about 9 o'clock Saturday morning, only to hear that the last jeep had already left. There wouldn't be another one until 2 p.m. That meant five hours to wait, an annoying turn of events, since we had driven all night to get there in time (though we didn't know what "in time" meant). We hung around Balakot with not much to do until the afternoon. The hours passed slowly, but finally our jeep arrived; we parked House, hoped it would be safe, climbed into the jeep, and said goodbye to Balakot. Decades later, in 2005, we heard that this small town was completely destroyed by a major earthquake, resulting in a death toll of over 70,000. The town was later rebuilt in a nearby valley, but I doubt that it looked the same as in 1966.

Our jeep to the Kaghan Valley

We knew it would be 50 more miles to Naran, but I had no idea what we were in for. The trip took five hours, with the jeep inching along on the narrow, steep, and often slippery road. In those 50 miles we climbed from 4,000 feet to 8,500 feet, into spectacular snow-capped mountains. We had left Balakot on a very warm afternoon, but when we arrived at the Naran rest house at 7 p.m., I was shivering in the icy cold air. That night, though, we slept soundly while one of the staff kept a warm, crackling fire blazing in the fireplace.

Kaghan Valley

On Sunday morning, we took another jeep up the mountain and then hiked three miles to Lake Saif-ul-Muluk, a beautiful little lake at an altitude of over 10,000 feet. There were a few glaciers around; one of the peaks reached to 17,000 feet. It reminded me of Lake Solitude in the Teton Mountains in Wyoming, except that there were so many more mountains rising above us. Breathtaking! I shivered in the brisk air but loved it. We hiked back down to the rest house, ate a good Pakistani lunch, and then took another short trip in the afternoon.

Our second trip that day was also by jeep with three other travelers. We ended up at a rest house at Lulusar, perched on the top of a mountain, amid even higher mountain peaks. I was in awe, couldn't stop admiring the view. We five foreigners sat inside the rest house for a while having tea. It was one of those times when everybody gets along, everyone seems to have similar ideas, and the conversation flows. Dinner that night at the rest house was excellent. The cook produced tasty chicken and pilau along with another meat dish and pudding. That evening we continued talking nonstop. What a thoroughly satisfying evening it was, one that proceeded seamlessly among people who had just met.

Mick at Lake Saif-ul-Muluk   Near Lake Saif-ul-Muluk

After stopping for a second night at the Naran rest house, we began the descent back to Balakot in the jeep. Mick and I were in the back seat this time, which made the ride even bumpier and more uncomfortable than before. And it took much longer than we had thought. By the time we had retrieved our van in Balakot and arrived back to Peshawar, it was 6:30 p.m. We were dead tired and aching all over but thrilled to have made this 250-mile trip to such awe-inspiring mountain peaks.

Goodbye to the Van in Kabul

OUR BIG DECISION NOW was what to do about House. We had heard that it was impossible to sell a car or van in India. The Indian authorities had cracked down on the practice of people buying a car in Germany, driving it to India, selling it there for a profit, taking the bus back to Europe, and then repeating the whole process. Furthermore, we couldn't drive from India through East Pakistan (now Bangladesh) and Burma, so this seemed to be the end: we had driven as far east as we could. The only way out of India would be to turn around and go back west, or to put House on a ship. But even if we took a ship to Singapore, then what? Where could we drive? We would continually have to arrange for shipping our van, which would be expensive and complicated. The best thing was to go back to Kabul and try to sell House there. At least we knew that the Afghan government allowed cars to be bought and sold.

For the next few weeks we stayed in Peshawar, getting House ready to sell. It needed work on the differential, for one thing. We wanted to have the car in the best condition possible before putting it up for sale. Even as we contemplated traveling without House, Mick's excitement about traveling to new places had not lessened. In fact, traveling for the past year had only increased his desire for more.

Excerpt from Mick's letter to his parents. Peshawar, Pakistan. October 2, 1966:

> Hi,
>
> There is too much world to be seen on one trip. Had I the money and the time, I would continue at least for the next five years. I'd love to get up into tribal Russia near the city of Samarkand. Maybe China will open up in a few years and permission can be granted to drive through that western enigma. This is the only life, believe me. I don't plan to ever own a house or anything that will keep me in one place.
>
> M

From time to time, we checked the post office for general delivery/ poste restante mail, and one day we were surprised and pleased to get a letter from Dave and Kathy, the couple with the little girl whom we had met four months previous at the campground outside Istanbul. They would be coming through Peshawar in about a week. We had completely forgotten that we had given them the Peshawar post office address. We wrote right back to the post office address they had given us, giving directions to our house, hoping they'd get the letter in time. They did, and what fun it was to catch up on all our travel adventures! Dave and Kathy parked their camper at our place for a few days, happy to have a house to hang out in. Three-year-old Lizzie had grown a bit, but otherwise she was still the happy traveler she had been in Istanbul. I asked Kathy if she wanted any food that I could buy at the commissary, and she said it would be great if they could have about five boxes of macaroni and cheese, which Lizzie loved. I said sure, but when I returned with my groceries, I realized from the look on Kathy's face that I had made a huge mistake. I presented her with five large boxes of plain macaroni noodles and five big packages of cheddar cheese. I had not been aware of the small Kraft dinner-in-a-minute mac 'n' cheese boxes that kids like. Kathy was gracious, though, as she said that there would be enough macaroni to last them a long time. Dave and Kathy drove on toward India after a few days with us, which probably pleased the Smiths. Again, they seemed not too happy with us hosting more scroungy-looking traveler friends.

ON OCTOBER 12, AFTER being in Peshawar for a month, we traveled again up the Khyber Pass to Kabul, with the goal of selling House. This time it was even more thrilling to be crossing over this strategic gateway that has historical references going back to Cyrus the Great in 600 BCE. At the highest point of the pass, we stopped at the small market town of Landi Kotal, where we had heard that one could buy or sell almost anything. I was fascinated by the variety of items, especially those from China, which, at that time, was a country that Americans were not allowed to enter. I didn't buy anything. I was afraid of being accused of or arrested for bringing contraband items across the Afghan border.

It was 122 miles up to Jalalabad in Afghanistan, where we spent the night. We had our hubcaps painted there as a last measure before putting the car up for sale. The next day we drove another 114 miles up to Kabul.

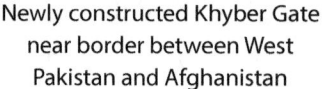
Newly constructed Khyber Gate
near border between West
Pakistan and Afghanistan

Village in Afghanistan

We had almost a week to sell the car before having to be back in Pesha-war for Mick's class. Since we had no idea how to go about it, we decided to park in the middle of the downtown area in front of the Khyber Restaurant with my sign, <FOR SALE>, in the back window. We hung out there all day, reading, talking, making lunch and dinner, and then sleeping. It was a good place to be—a central visible spot in the city where we could get food and use the washroom in the restaurant. A lot of people came by and stopped to talk, but they only wanted to pay $500 or $600. We knew the camper was worth more than that, so we waited. The next few days were like the first day. For the most part, we lolled about in front of the Khyber Restaurant, but when we got really bored, we'd take off for a while.

LUCKILY FOR US, WE heard that a *buzkashi* game was being held in honor of King Zahir Shah's birthday. We had never heard of the game, so of course we went. It was by far the most interesting thing we did during those five waiting days in Kabul. We drove outside the city to the large open field, where there was visible excitement in the air: men hanging around, ani-matedly talking and gesturing as they waited for the game to begin. The king and his entourage sat in a special section under a canopy. Suddenly we heard horns bellowing and saw men on horses lining up. The game began. I described it in my journal.

Journal excerpt. October 21, 1966:

First a headless calf (or goat) is brought onto the field. Then the players, on their gorgeous horses, try to carry the calf around the field and drop it into a shallow sandy pit. While a man on one team is carrying the calf, the other team members ride furiously alongside him, beating him with a whip as they try to wrest the dead animal from him. Sometimes two opposing men both grab the goat/calf, pulling and wrestling it between them. Then someone breaks away, dragging the calf. To carry it, they put one of the calf's legs through their stirrup and step on it, the rest of the carcass dragging in the dust alongside the horse.

There are many dangers in this game. We heard that a man is killed or seriously injured in almost every game. This one was no exception. I happened to be watching through our binoculars when two players and horses collided and went down. One man lay briefly in one position, then fell flat. I thought he may have gone unconscious but found out later that he had been killed. The ambulance rushed onto the field, and four men brusquely grabbed his four limbs and threw him onto a stretcher. Then the game went on. At another point, a horse and man stumbled, and the horse rolled completely over the man. They both got up immediately. What a game.

A few of the players (*chapandaz*)

The game underway: goat carcass carried by men on brown horses at left.

After the *buzkashi* game, we went back to our parking space by the Khyber Restaurant, and what a surprise: there was Andreas driving up in his VW camper van! We had met Andreas back in the Baghdad campground about two months previous when we were all stuck there because of the cholera outbreak. How exciting to see him again! We told him that we were trying to sell our camper and would be traveling to India fairly soon. Andreas said he was heading to Kathmandu and would be traveling through India for a few weeks or a month. He said he had plenty of room in his van, and would we like to continue on to India with him? We could sleep in his small tent, and since we would be cooking all our meals, we would all save money. The deal was made; it was perfect for all of us. We agreed to pay for half the gas, and we would have all the advantages of traveling by car. Andreas said he would hang out in Afghanistan and Pakistan until we were ready to go. It was another of those spontaneous meetings that worked out well for everyone.

After five days of being parked in Kabul, just when I was getting exceptionally discouraged, a local businessman and government official, Dr. Rassoul, appeared. He took one look at the car and said, "I'll buy it. I'll give you $975." That was still less than we wanted to sell it for, but we were desperate. Dr. Rassoul explained that the Afghan government required him to pay a tax of the equivalent of U.S. $2,000, so he was, in fact, paying almost $3,000 for the car. He agreed to buy our Jet Gaz camping stove and some other gear for another $25, so we would end up with $1,000. Since we had originally bought the car in Germany for almost $2,000, it seemed reasonable to sell the car at half of what we had paid. We agreed to the deal but said that even though we had to go back to Peshawar for Mick's class, we would return the next weekend to complete the sale. In the meantime, Dr. Rassoul said he would get all the necessary papers and permissions from the government.

We drove back to Peshawar for Mick's upcoming Tuesday and Friday classes feeling relieved but sad. House had been our home for more than a year. It had seen us through 27 countries and more than 30,000 miles, but we knew this was the best decision.

THE NEXT WEEK, on October 22, we drove back up to Kabul, taking only what we could carry back by hand. We both worried that the car deal wouldn't go through or that we wouldn't be able to find Dr. Rassoul, but no, that didn't happen. When we got to his house, there he was, waiting for us. He introduced us to his Swiss wife and their small daughter. Dr. Rassoul explained that he hadn't had time to complete the paperwork, but the good news for him was that the Afghan government had reduced his cost by half. He only had to pay $1,000 in transfer fees. For us, though, the bad news was that the paperwork would take a few more days. Mick sent a telegram back to Peshawar saying that he had to cancel his next class.

We slept in House the first night, but the second night the Rassouls invited us to sleep in their guest room. We agreed, mainly because we wanted to keep House clean and ready to sell. In the end, we spent four nights with them before the paperwork was finished.

The longer we were in Kabul, the more fascinated we became by the strength and pride of the people, emanating from the country's rich tribal history. People were open and welcoming to us. I felt comfortable walking around, not fearful. The country seemed on the brink of change, mainly because of the liberal policies of King Zahir Shah. It was common to see women at universities and in businesses. They were not required to wear the long cloaks, called chador, *chadari*, or burqa, that covered them from head to toe, though many of the older women still did.

Rug cleaning and stretching   Kabul bus

On October 27, after five long days waiting in Kabul, the paperwork was done, and our car was sold. We hooked up with Andreas for our trip back to Peshawar. Though it was sad to leave House, we felt good about the decision to travel with Andreas. He had not only waited for us for a week in Kabul but also said he would stay in Peshawar for the next 10 days until Mick's class was over and we could set out to India together.

Back in Peshawar, while waiting for Mick's teaching term to end, Andreas camped outside our Peshawar home. I'm sure the Smiths did not realize what they were getting themselves in for when they decided to rent out their room to us. We didn't either. But our traveler friends—first Rolfe and Bernd; then Dave, Kathy, and Lizzie; and lastly Andreas—all enjoyed our room and the yard. Everyone needed to wash clothes and vehicles, and our shower was quite well used. But since we, as renters, were clean, polite, and friendly, I felt that it was OK to welcome our itinerant friends to the Smiths' yard.

Dir and Swat

OUR FINAL WEEKEND in Peshawar was coming up, so Andreas suggested that we take a trip up to Dir and Swat. At that time, both were independent princely states in the northwest of the region, but a few years later, in 1969, they merged with West Pakistan, which in 1971 became Pakistan. Dir and Swat were closer to Peshawar than our previous mountain foray up Kaghan Valley, but we had heard that the mountains and lakes around Swat were just as gorgeous. This time there were five of us going: Mick and me, Andreas, and Peter and his friend Violet. I was impressed with Violet. She was from Alice Springs in Australia, and she was traveling alone. This was the first time I had met any woman who was traveling alone in this part of the world. Violet seemed able to take care of anything she came across in her travels. She was self-assured and tough, as well as a lot of fun. Still, this was the first time for us to travel as a group, without our own vehicle. The trip would involve negotiation and consideration of others when making decisions such as which route to take, where to camp, and how often to stop.

THE ROAD TO DIR and Swat branched off to the north not far from Peshawar. What began as a paved highway became a narrow, bumpy dirt road as we drove farther up into Dir. It was getting late in the afternoon, and we wanted to set up camp before we reached the town, so we began looking for a place to pull over for the night. The first flat spot we saw was only a small area where the road widened. It was not ideal, being right by the road, but we didn't know how much farther it was to the town or where else we might prepare dinner and set up the tent. As it turned out, we had stopped in the middle of a thoroughfare: a steady stream of tribal people and their donkeys trotted right by us. They didn't seem to be fazed, however, or very interested as we set up for dinner and the night.

We had a deal: Andreas would sleep in his own VW camper, and the four of us would crowd into Andreas's small tent. Both Mick and I slept just fine, but Peter and Violet didn't. In the morning they both complained that they didn't have enough space. It's true that the tent was way too small for four people and that the two of them were taller and bigger than the two of us. But they had made the decision to go with us knowing that there was only one tent. Clearly, these two people, having recently met, hadn't had a year of cuddling in the back of a van or making do with odd sleeping arrangements.

That day (whether because of the complaints or the donkeys) we all decided not to continue the drive up to Dir but instead to drive back to the fork in the road, and from there into Swat. Peter and Violet opted to stay in the town of Saidu Sharif (the capital of Swat) for the night as Andreas and the two of us went on northward to the town of Kalam. The mountains were breathtakingly beautiful, as we had expected, but it was cold. We found a beautiful spot in the woods, just below the snow level. Andreas slept in his car again, while Mick and I pitched his tent. In the morning it was 36 degrees; even my lined goat-hair Afghan coat didn't keep me warm. We ate a quick breakfast outside and left.

Camping in Andreas's tent
near Kalam, Swat

Driving to Swat

Final Days in Peshawar

BACK IN PESHAWAR, WE were invited to another Pakistani wedding. This one was smaller than the tribal wedding we had been to earlier. It was held in town and didn't involve music, dancing, or food, at least during the time we were there. I was invited to greet the women and was even able take a picture of the bride. I felt lucky to have been able to see these two ways of celebrating weddings in Peshawar.

The bride

Dressed up for the wedding

WE WERE GETTING READY to move on. Mick's sociology class was ending, and I had to agree with him that it was relaxing to be around other Americans and foreign travelers: people with whom we shared a culture. I was also especially thankful that we had access to the medical clinic on the base. We both had caught up on vaccinations, replenished malaria pills, and visited the dentist. I even had an impacted wisdom tooth pulled. Peshawar was a respite for us—a time to relax a bit, to take stock of what we had, and to prepare for what we might need. Now I was ready to travel again, ready to see more of South Asia.

As we pared down our belongings so that we could carry everything we owned, I thought about how much baggage we had jettisoned over the past 14 months. We had arrived in Europe not only with several suitcases, but also with a steamer trunk. At this point, I couldn't even remember what had been in the trunk and why those things had been so important to me. Eight months later we emptied that steamer trunk and left it in Greece. Over the next year, we sent home several boxes of things we didn't need, but now we were still carrying too much. It was easy, though, to pare down our belongings to one duffel bag, one attaché case, and the small green "weekend" suitcase that I had originally brought with me from the States. With these, we had room for teaching materials as well as all our clothes, two sleeping bags, our tiny benzene stove, two cooking pots, two plastic bowls, two plastic plates, two sets of eating utensils, and one serving/cooking spoon. We were traveling light, equipped to sleep anywhere and cook our own food. We were ready.

It may seem strange, at least in retrospect, that we were traveling with suitcases and a heavy duffel bag rather than backpacks, but when we left the U.S. in 1965, hikers were commonly using military-type rucksacks made of canvas. Without padded waist belts and straps, they were awkward to carry—and sometimes painful—as they hung heavily from one's shoulders. It would be a few more years before lightweight backpacks were readily available.

We were leaving Peshawar with enough money (we hoped) to get to Japan. There was a chance of Mick getting another class with the University of Maryland, probably in Bangkok, but as usual we couldn't count on it.

We were both somewhat cavalier about the vagueness of our upcoming travel; in fact, we didn't want to be tied down to any schedule. We did keep in touch with our parents; we regularly wrote letters. At the time, I felt like I was keeping in close touch, but looking back now, as a parent and grandparent, in an age when communication is quick, even instantaneous, I realize how difficult it must have been for our parents during the many weeks when they didn't know where we were or have any way to contact us. How worried they must have been!

Excerpt from Mick's letter to his parents. Peshawar, Pakistan. October 27, 1966:

> Hi,
> We will leave Peshawar next week and travel with a German to Delhi and Nepal. From there we plan to travel through India and eventually take a freighter across to Penang and down to Singapore. Our next address, then, will be in Singapore, but where and when haven't been decided yet.
>
> Mick

Excerpt from letter to my parents. Peshawar, Pakistan. November 2, 1966:

> Dear Daddy and Mom,
> We are leaving in three days. . . . We are pretty excited about our new way of traveling in this part of our journey. . . . Since our plans are so indefinite and since the mails take so long, we'll give you a Singapore address. You can use that until (probably) the end of November. We'll probably get there at the beginning of December. Send mail to: Thos. Cook and Son, Rotterdam Building, 39 Robinson Road, Singapore 1.
>
> Love,
> Patti

16.

On the Road—West Pakistan to India

O n November 8, after almost two months living in Peshawar, we piled everything into Andreas's VW van, including a store of canned and dried food. Despite being sad to leave House—our home for the past 14 months—I was ready to start traveling anew. It might be more difficult, since there would now be three people to agree on such daily questions as how far to drive, when to stop, where to camp, when to leave in the morning, and how to share costs, but we all felt that we could get along easily enough to live together in close quarters. Our plan was to be together for a month or two as we made our way through West Pakistan, then northern India and into Nepal.

We could have driven east to the Indian border near Lahore in one day, but we wanted to see some of the ancient Indus Valley civilizations, including Mohenjo-Daro and Harappa (both dating to about 3000 BCE), so we decided to drive south on the west side of the Indus River and then back up north on the east side of the river. The round trip was about 2,000 miles, with the midpoint being Karachi, Pakistan's main port city on the Arabian Sea.

Lunch stop with Andreas   Filling up our jugs at a local well

A Palace for Us

ON THE THIRD DAY after leaving Peshawar, when we were just south of the
town of Taunsa, we decided to veer off the main road and drive east toward
the Indus River just because we wanted to see it. According to our map,
there was a road going directly that way, toward a village by the river. We
were in good spirits as we left the main highway, but soon we saw a detour
sign: the road was under construction. We tried to follow the detour, but we
didn't see any more signs, and the road got narrower and narrower. Soon we
were driving on a dirt path, then on faint tracks, and finally we were slowly
making our way across a dusty field. "Where's the road?" I said, mostly to
myself. Our map didn't help us at all, but we kept going, hoping to reach
the village and camp there for the night. But how far was it? We were going
east, and the Indus River was east of us, so we couldn't go too far out of the
way. Still, I was getting a bit anxious. Maybe we all were. None of us were
saying anything; we just stared ahead looking for faint marks of a road.

Suddenly we saw children, shouting and laughing as they ran through
the fields and alongside us, thumping on the sides of the van. We smiled
and waved to them out the window, relieved that a village would soon be
in sight. And it was. We found out later that it was the village of Rojhan.
As we slowly drove our dusty van down the street, more people emerged,
probably wondering as much about us as we were about them. We pulled
up at what seemed to be a good place to camp, got out to stretch our legs,
and looked around. Curious people sauntered up, looking at and inside

our camper. We smiled at them and began unloading our tent and other supplies when a kind-looking man dressed in white with a starched white turban approached us. In very clear English he introduced himself as Sham Suddin Mazari. We told him that we were on our way to Karachi and would like to camp there. He listened and said, "You must come with me."

We put everything away and got back in the car. Mr. Mazari walked ahead of our camper, proudly erect, as we slowly followed, children scampering all about. Soon, ahead of us sitting on a slight rise of a hill, we saw a large pink-hued building that was shuttered and looked vacant. As we drove up, a man, probably the caretaker, appeared on the steps. Mr. Mazari spoke briefly to him, whereupon this man straightened up and saluted us. *What?* I thought. *Why is he saluting? This isn't the Raj; the British left 19 years ago.* As though answering my thoughts, Mr. Mazari explained that this was the palace of the chieftain of the Mazari tribe, one of the oldest Baluch tribes in West Pakistan. The palace was 100 years old and had been used for visiting dignitaries. He said that the chieftain was not there now but we should be his guests and sleep inside the palace. I felt like we were interlopers, since it was clear that we were not dignitaries, but Mr. Mazari didn't seem bothered by this. Maybe he was pleased that we were so effusive about the palace and appreciative of the hospitality.

We walked up the grand veranda as the caretaker took out his keys and slowly opened the large front door. We stepped in. Light began to stream in as the caretaker proceeded to open all the shutters, one by one. As it got brighter inside, we began to see walls and ceilings that were completely covered with delicately painted vines, flowers, and arabesques. The carved wooden doors were inlaid with ivory, and plush red Persian and Afghan carpets covered the floors from wall to wall. One of the rooms had seating along the wall, and another had rolled pillows with decorative shams that clearly called out to be reclined upon. There was nothing else in the palace: no furniture, no lights, no running water.

We wandered from room to room, speechless, admiring the painted walls, the wooden shutters, the carved doors. Soon several men appeared with basins of hot water for baths. After that, more men arrived with trays of tea and sweets. They bowed respectfully and left. We sat and looked at one another for a while, not knowing what to say or what to do. Everyone had left, even the children. It was quiet.

The palace in Rojhan

Mr. Mazari

Rojhan Palace entrance

We drank our tea and brought in a few items for the night, but we felt too messy and dirty and dusty to be lounging in this palace. It would have been delightful to take full baths but there wasn't enough water for the three of us, so we ended up taking turns dousing ourselves from the basins that had been put in a back room. The water wasn't hot anymore, but at least we were able to clean off the dust. Then we sat around, luxuriating in our surroundings and taking some photos. We wondered what we should do about dinner. We didn't want to leave the palace to look for a restaurant or a food store, so we brought in our benzene camping stoves to heat up some cans of food. This seemed even more incongruous than bringing in our old clothes, but no one had a better plan.

Adjoining the main carpeted room was a smaller room with a tiled floor where the men had put the basins of water. It didn't look like a kitchen, but it seemed like the appropriate place for us to cook. There were no counters or shelves, so we squatted on the floor to light our stoves and heat up our dinner. Just as we finished eating and cleaning up, we heard someone coming. And there again was Mr. Mazari, along with several men bringing in trays of food. Dinner!

The men laid the food trays carefully on the rug and left. We were taken aback as we looked over the large trays of various meats and several kinds of vegetables. There were no plates, no utensils, and no napkins. We used our hands in the best way we could to bring the food to our mouths. As each of us took a bite, we gasped! It was far and away the spiciest food any of us had ever eaten. We alternately laughed and wiped away tears as our mouths burned. We didn't want to be impolite, but when we had eaten all we could, the trays were still loaded with food. Soon the men returned. I don't know if they were surprised at how much food was left, but they silently picked up the trays and went into the back room. Mick glanced through the door and saw them quickly scooping up the rest of our food. At first, I was glad that they ate it, but then I wondered about the people who had cooked our dinner. Would they get any of the food? Several people, probably women, had gone to an enormous amount of trouble to prepare our dinner and would now probably have the job of cleaning up. I would have liked to thank them.

We were thrilled to be such honored guests, but why were they so kind and generous to us? We were kids in our mid-20s; we were travelers just passing through. We didn't deserve this honor. Even so, that night we spread our sleeping bags out on the beautiful carpets and had a quiet, peaceful sleep. The next morning, the sun streamed into the room, and men arrived again with steaming trays of food for breakfast. It was delicious, not spicy. We ate every bit. As we drove out the next morning, we waved goodbye to our hosts, telling them that we would never forget the kindness they showered upon us. I never have.

Dak Bungalows

ON OUR JOURNEY SOUTH to Karachi, we planned to camp out every night, sleeping in Andreas's tent, but it didn't always work out that way. When we first tried camping, we stopped in a place at the side of the road that seemed to be somewhat secluded, but immediately after getting out of the car we were surrounded by people. They stood around us in a semicircle, silently staring at us. We continued setting up the tent and getting out our dinner supplies. Someone held up a lantern near us. I wasn't sure if it was for our benefit or so that they could see us better. Regardless, we ate dinner in front of rows of faces silently glowing in the lamplight. I was wondering how long they would stay after we climbed into bed, but before that happened, a policeman drove up and insisted that we move to the police station. We said we felt fine where we were, but he said that the people were dangerous. I didn't agree about the danger, and I didn't think we would be more comfortable in the police station, but we all did agree that it would be more private. In fact, we couldn't disagree with a policeman's commands anyway, so we took down the tent and followed him to a nearby station, where we put our sleeping bags on the floor. As I had thought, it was not very comfortable.

From then on, for the next several weeks, the pattern continued. Though we tried to camp, we usually ended up being guided to a dak bungalow. These dak bungalows, also called inspection bungalows or tourist rest houses, had been built during the time of the British Raj for government or military travelers. They were common in almost every town but were rarely used at the time we were there. They were basic, often with no electricity or running water, and usually with little more inside than a *charpoy* (knotted rope) bed. Generally, we weren't charged anything, but if we were, it was usually between 10 cents and 40 cents. One time we were charged only 2 cents. We used our camp stoves and candles for light. In one bungalow there was a well in the yard, so we could draw water and bathe. Usually, the only person around was a watchman or guard (*chowkidar*), though one time a policeman sent two armed guards to protect us. I was quite surprised, as I didn't think we were in danger, but there they were. I don't know if the guards stayed awake all night with their guns ready or if they went to sleep like we did, but they left in the morning.

Some of the dak bungalows had a separate room for washing. Mick remembers one wash area that consisted of plain mud walls with a water pipe above and a small depression for water to run out through a hole in the corner of the wall. The *chowkidar* told Mick to keep a lookout for snakes, as they sometimes crawled in through the holes. From that moment on, Mick never went into a wash area without peering into the dark corners, always keeping an eye on the holes. Maybe he scared them off, because he never did see a snake.

For me, having a room for washing was not as important as having a toilet. At one dak bungalow, when I asked the watchman for a bathroom, I was shown to a small concrete room with a packed mud floor. Besides the four walls there was nothing else in it. When the watchman brought in cans of water, presumably to douse myself with, I thought I had been misunderstood, that "bathroom" was not the appropriate word. I tried using other words: toilet, toilette, loo, WC, but the man kept assuring me that this was the correct room. I was mystified, confused. Was I supposed to squat and use the floor? Would someone come in and clean up after me? I didn't know what was appropriate, but it did not feel right to me to use a floor as a toilet, so I didn't. I went outside and wandered about until I found a spot that seemed better to me. In reflecting, though, I think that he had shown me the correct room for the toilet. I was the one who didn't understand. That watchman may have wondered why I would go outdoors instead of relieving myself in the privacy of a room.

FINDING A PLACE to sleep or wash was not our only daily issue. Every time we stopped the van, people would appear seemingly from nowhere. Both young and old would surround us. Most of the time, people did not say anything or do anything. They just looked at us. I reasoned to myself that they were only interested in what we looked like and how we were living, but the whole situation became more and more irritating to all of us.

Andreas's camper, barely visible behind the crowd

Advice in Karachi

AFTER ABOUT A WEEK of traveling south, we reached Karachi, a large, bustling city that looked beautiful to me. We were ready to stop for a while but did not expect to be so lucky. Andreas went into the Goethe Institute to meet a friend, and the outcome was that we were invited by the German director of the Goethe Institute to stay at his home. It was delightful! The director and his wife were as eager to hear about our travels as we were to get a sense of their lives in Karachi. We ended up staying with them for four days, mainly because Andreas's van was in the shop getting repaired.

In addition to learning about life in Karachi, we gained a wealth of information about traveling onward. One evening, our hosts brought out maps of Southeast Asia, unfolding them carefully on the dining room table, smoothing out the creases. We focused intently on the landmasses and seas, as they suggested that we fly from Calcutta (now Kolkata) or Chittagong to Bangkok, rather than go from India straight to Singapore, as many travelers in Karachi were doing. They also said we shouldn't miss Indonesia, that we could get a freighter quite cheaply from Singapore to Djakarta. I loved talking about pros and cons of various routes, especially since our plans for travel after India were not yet set. Just knowing that we could go anywhere was what made the map reading so compelling. Talking to this couple, planning where to go next, and getting useful travel advice was not the only plus. These kind people also gave us breakfast and dinner and even asked their servant to wash our clothes. Once more in our travels, we felt incredibly fortunate to meet such people.

WHILE IN KARACHI, WE wrote again to our parents about our further travel plans.

Excerpt of letter to my parents. Karachi, Pakistan. November 15, 1966:

Dear Daddy and Mom,

You'll have to send our Christmas presents before we can tell you whether we'll be in Bangkok or Singapore. So, send them to Singapore. There is no American Express office or Thos. Cook in Bangkok. We'll just have to be in Singapore in time to get them. If you write right away and if this letter doesn't take too long to reach you, you could write us in Calcutta. We probably won't be there before December 6th or 7th, and possibly a few days later. From Calcutta we'll either take a boat or go to Chittagong and fly. So I hope you can write there—c/o American Express.... Next year for sure we'll be with you for Christmas and maybe Thanksgiving too....

Mick is quite upset about the elections in California. The Democrats seem to have lost everywhere. How do you feel about Reagan as Governor? Were many of your friends backing him?

P.S. We have changed our minds since I began this letter. We will almost for sure be flying from Chittagong or Calcutta to Bangkok. This is the cheapest thing. So don't mail anything to Singapore unless you have already. Send things for Christmas to Bangkok, Thailand c/o American Embassy. The Embassy will hold mail for a month or two.

Love,

Patti

On November 19, we left Karachi for our trip back up to Lahore, this time on the east side of the Indus River. The route north was quicker than our drive south, and it was easy to find places to sleep, though now the government bungalows were not free. One night we were invited to stay in a German club guest room, thanks to Andreas's contacts. We had hot running water, clean sheets, and comfortable beds, and we could drink the water from the tap. We had almost forgotten what it was like not to put iodine tablets in our drinking water. And the German club didn't charge us for the room.

The Self-Sufficient Mardens

ONE OF THE HIGHLIGHTS on the trip north was meeting—by chance—the Mardens. We had been trying to visit the elegant Sadiq Garh palace, built in 1882, in the town of Dera Nawab Sahib, Bahawalpur, but the gate was locked. As we looked for someone who could give us information about it, up walked General Marden, a former British army general. He invited us to meet his wife and have lunch with them, and of course we leapt at the chance to hear more about their lives in Pakistan.

Both the general and his wife were gracious hosts who seemed eager to talk. They had lived in Dera Nawab Sahib since 1931. For the first several years, they lived in the king's palace, but in 1938 they built their own house. As they led us around, both inside and outside the house, I found myself increasingly amazed at their self-sufficiency. The general had not only built all their furniture but also designed an air-conditioning system for the house by filling an open window with bricks and arranging for water to drip down over the bricks. On the inside he had set up a fan to pull the air in from outside, cooling it as it came through the dripping water.

The Mardens' self-sufficiency was even more evident outside their home. Over the years, they had turned land that had been desert into a fertile garden with hundreds of trees where, despite the day's heat, it was cool and pleasant. Water for irrigation may have come from ancient wells or canals from the Indus River, but whatever the source, they were now able to grow everything they needed: fruits, vegetables, and even wheat. They kept cows for meat, butter, milk, and cream, and other animals for food. Lunch with the Mardens was delicious. Along with their own fresh-picked vegetables, they served goose curry, prepared from their own geese.

As we ate lunch, they continued to regale us with tales of their lives. General Marden talked about the latter years of the British Raj. He said that—at that time—the king had thousands of jewels that he kept in gunnysacks, as well as a 100-place solid silver service set and two other sets of utensils with gold and silver inlays. There were thousands of bodyguards and servants back then. Now everything had been reduced significantly, but the present king—though now a figurehead—still owned many of those items.

In bringing us more up to date, Mrs. Marden said that shortly before we arrived that day, she had been walking in their garden next to a bush when a nest of young cobras popped out. She whacked them all quickly with a golf club. Mick was aghast at the idea of almost stepping on a writhing mass of snakes. I, on the other hand, wondered about the golf club. Did she always carry it around when she walked outside? And did she kill those snakes all at once, or did some slither away? It was hard to imagine the scene.

After lunch, Mrs. Marden asked if we would like to go see her women's clinic. Of course, we said. We didn't know she had a clinic. I described it in my journal.

Journal excerpt. Lohdran, Pakistan. November 22, 1966:

As we came to her place of work, we saw hundreds of women silently sitting in very neat rows, completely covered with their burkas. It was

an astonishing sight. In the past thirty years, this woman (Mrs. Marden)
has built up a wonderful welfare program. At different set intervals
(daily, weekly, monthly, etc.), the needy women from all around come
and receive milk, food, clothes, health care, etc. Mrs. Marden gets the
material from different societies the world over: e.g., Church World
Service, Catholic Relief Society, UNICEF. She distributes it according
to need. She knows every woman and her particular situation as to
money, number of children, husband's job (if any). The women all have
cards by which she keeps track of them. She has more work and is
doing more good than some similar organizations with ten times the
number of people working. She only has three people working with
her. One woman is in charge of disseminating birth control informa-
tion. This is extremely difficult because they are so uninformed and
superstitious and they say it is wrong because of religion. However,
the women need this and they know they need it. They know that
they need and want to control the number of children because they
can't afford them. However, [Mrs. Marden said] the job of teaching the
women and men family planning is extremely difficult.

Besides the clinic for women, Mrs. Marden has a small library, an
animal welfare hospital, and an animal preservation society. What
an amazing woman!

Mrs. Marden followed strict procedures at the clinic. When she
handed out the milk powder, she made the women mix it with water
immediately and give it to the children. She told us that if she gave
them the dried milk alone, some would trade it for opium. I had the
clear feeling that the women respected and trusted Mrs. Marden for her
clarity and consistency.

A few days later, we stayed in a guesthouse that had a kitchen, so
we decided to splurge and cook a chicken for dinner. As we were looking
for chicken meat at the market, a local man guided us to the part of the
market with live chickens in baskets. The man helped us pick the perfect
one, whereupon the seller quickly cut its throat and put it in a box until

it stopped thumping. Then he plucked it, wrapped it in newspaper, and handed it to us. Our dinner was quite tough that night, but certainly fresh.

WE HAD ONE MORE day of driving before getting to Lahore, our last city in West Pakistan. We had settled into a nice routine with Andreas and had gotten along well. Usually at lunchtime we would carefully set out our picnic food on Andreas's little table with his tablecloth, small plates, and sets of utensils. We washed our fruit and vegetables in potassium permanganate, a disinfectant that caused the water to turn purple. How curious we must have seemed to the constant crowds that silently appeared.

In general, we ignored the crowds around us, and usually they kept their distance. But still, being a constant object of attention continued to take its toll on us. One day while we were getting gas, a crowd of people inched forward to the van, some of them standing right in front of the windshield with their hands on the glass. Others were putting their hands in the car window, peering in, watching our every movement. It felt eerie and, more than that, invasive. Andreas had filled the tank and was ready to go, but the people didn't move away from the van. This wasn't the first time this had happened, but it was one too many for Andreas. He yelled at the people, getting more and more upset as no one moved back from the windshield. Suddenly he took his foot off the clutch, and the van lurched forward. Fortunately, no one was hit, and no one fell. Slowly people backed away.

I was sitting in the front passenger seat and was immediately frightened, not only at seeing Andreas's anger, but also at the fact that he made the car jump. Mostly, though, I was surprised that I myself shared similar feelings. Though I didn't want to hurt anyone, part of me also wanted to run right into the people. If they had moved away, or if they had smiled and talked, if they had been animated in any way, I think I would have felt different. But being stared at in such close proximity had finally gotten to me. I was shocked at myself, worried that I could actually have those feelings. My intellectual side was telling me that I was under stress, that I needed to put myself in another frame of mind. Of course, I said to myself, we were an oddity, so it was natural that people would stare, would want to look inside the van. I should try to imagine seeing ourselves from their perspective. At that moment, though, these rational thoughts were eclipsed by my frustration and aggravation.

ON NOVEMBER 24, 16 days after leaving Peshawar, we were in Lahore, close to the Indian border. We spent the night at the YMCA, leaving early in the morning, since we didn't know how long it would take to get through the border. We hadn't eaten breakfast, so we looked for a place where we could pull over, fire up our benzene stove, and spread out our food. There was nothing even close to being suitable. The best place we found was the empty parking lot in front of Grindlays Bank in Lahore. It hadn't opened yet, and there were no crowds around. Andreas didn't set up his small table, but there were some shelf-like places in the wall of the bank where we could set out food. At least here, in this early hour when the sun was just peeking out, we were able to have a few quiet moments to ourselves while we ate an early breakfast. Afterward Mick and I went shopping while Andreas took the car in for a quick repair, and we soon set off toward the Indian border, a few miles to the east.

Breakfast outside Grindlays Bank in Lahore

17.

Highs and Lows in India and Nepal

Crossing the border into India entailed the usual wait, but we didn't mind hanging out for a few hours. What surprised us was the amount of militarization. It seemed like either policemen or army people were everywhere, on both sides of the border. Apparently, no trucks were allowed to drive between the countries at that time, but we saw people carrying goods from one side to the other, openly exchanging them. I wondered what the military patrols were looking for and why the trucks weren't going through.

We passed the time at the border by talking to other travelers. Mostly they were European men traveling alone or in small groups, but I did talk briefly to one woman from Switzerland who was traveling with her husband. The person we talked to the most, though, was Per, from Norway. We all three immediately liked him, so when he said he was looking for a ride to India, we asked him if he'd like to join us. I don't remember how Per had gotten to Pakistan, but at that point he was alone. We had plenty of room for one more person, and he could help with gas and other expenses. We knew he'd be a great addition to our little group.

On our second day in India, our food supplies were running low, so we stopped at a small market. For more than a year, Mick and I had been shopping in local markets. We couldn't always buy exactly what we had planned, but there was always something that would do. This day was different. "Sorry, no rice," the vendor said, as we were looking right at a bin of rice in front of us. Surprised, we went to another store and were told the same thing. A young man noticed our confusion and explained that we needed a ration card to buy rice or wheat. He kindly let us use his, so we were able to buy three kilos of rice. For the moment we were fine, but we wondered how we would be able to travel in India if we couldn't buy basic staples. We had yet to learn that chapatis and dahl from street vendors and small restaurants would be our daily sustenance.

AS WE DROVE THROUGH rural India, stopping in Sikar, Jaipur, Bharatpur, and Agra, we were continually struck by extremes. On one hand, temples, forts, and palaces were more impressive than any of us had imagined. On the other hand, we were uncomfortable seeing so many people lined up in front of palaces begging for food. I realized that it was a cultural practice to give to the poor, but it was still hard for me to walk by so many people with their hands out. I felt overwhelmed and yet so inspired at the same time.

Procession in Sikar

In the town of Sikar, we happened upon a festival. The streets were jam-packed with people dressed in red, yellow, and orange; men with red jackets were playing musical instruments; and horses were drawing a tall structure of a temple. I loved the pageantry. In Jaipur, the palaces were magnificent, an example of the luxury that once was India. The observatory, built in 1728 by a maharaja, amazed us. In Alwar, the palace seemed to be built right out of the rocks. I had no idea that I would be so mesmerized by the beauty and serenity in these cities.

Festival in Jaipur

One afternoon, we were ambling down the street in Jaipur eating bananas when suddenly Per felt a little tug on his hand. "Hey," he said, and we all looked up. A monkey was contentedly munching on Per's banana. It had cleverly torn one banana off the whole bunch so quickly that none of us saw anything. In fact, we hadn't even noticed all the monkeys around us. After that, we furtively hid our bananas from these street-smart pesky critters.

A Maharaja

IN THE TOWN of Bharatpur, we were camping on the front lawn of a tourist bungalow when a young Indian army doctor and his wife came over to us, started up a conversation, and then invited us to their home. To get ready for the evening, we washed up outside: put on bathing suits, pumped water from the outside well, heated up the water on our tiny camp stove, and then poured it over each other. Clean and ready for anything!

When we got to our hosts' home, they told us that they had been invited to go to the palace of the maharaja of Bharatpur that evening, and would we like to accompany them? Of course! Here was another unexpected special invitation—a chance to experience local life, a chance to meet a maharaja. The doctor explained that several village and tribal leaders had been invited to the palace, but he didn't know when the maharaja would arrive or even if he would arrive. Sometimes, he said, the maharaja didn't feel well and didn't show up. We didn't mind. Either way would be fascinating. As we drove to the palace, the doctor told us that we should greet the maharaja with the words "Your Excellency" and that it was important to sit with our heads lower than the maharaja's. I kept those things in mind.

The palace, with its expansive garden grounds, looked sumptuous as we drove up. We waited by the large entrance door, enjoying the garden and the warm evening air while the doctor went in to find out if the maharaja would be coming and to make sure that we would be allowed inside. Fairly quickly, the doctor returned, saying that the maharaja wasn't feeling too well but would probably arrive soon, and we had permission to go in.

Our host escorted us into the palace. Though its once-opulent quarters had looked impressive from the garden, it appeared dated and a bit neglected as we entered. Paint was peeling off the walls, and piles of dirt peeked out behind brooms stacked in corners. We quietly entered a room where several men were already sitting on the floor. In front of them, against one wall, was the not-yet-occupied low couch, clearly well-worn. Its arms were smoothed with age. We sat down near the others on floor pillows. The maharaja was not there yet, but we were told he would be coming soon. We waited and waited, and finally, after what seemed like an hour but was probably much less, he entered.

He was not at all what I expected, not the image I had as to what a maharaja would look like. He was a short, portly man wearing a sport shirt, and he stumbled a bit as he came into the room. It didn't take us long to realize that the problem was not that the maharaja was "not feeling well" but that he was drunk! He perfunctorily greeted everyone and tried to sit down on the couch, but he slouched and began slowly sliding down. Immediately all the men in the room slumped down, as did we. The maharaja slid down more, and the people in the room followed suit. Finally, he had slumped so much that he was on the floor. There we were, all the people in the room, practically lying on the floor. I was having a hard time holding my reclining position. It was uncomfortable, and also I felt a little silly. I would have giggled, but the atmosphere seemed quite serious. The maharaja didn't talk much, and it was hard to understand him because of the slurring, but he did mention the upcoming elections. At the close of the audience, he stood up and handed out money to each of the village leaders as they left.

The evening was fascinating to me, partly because it was not what I had expected. The more I thought about it, the more questions I had. Luckily, our doctor friend gave us some background about what we had just been a part of. He said that this was an election period, and the maharaja was entertaining village leaders to secure their votes. As he was passing out the money, he was saying (or implying), "You'll vote for me; you'll vote for me." The important matter at hand was that the Indian government was in the process of phasing out stipends that had been given to maharajas in India. Apparently, each successive generation would receive only half the amount of their elders. Our friend said that this maharaja's father had been given a stipend that allowed him to own 86 cars and solid-gold tableware. Those days were gone, but the current maharaja of Bharatpur was adapting to the change. Rather than cling to the old system, he wanted to be a duly elected official. To that end, he was running for parliament. The whole evening was quite an eye-opener. This was the end of an era. It had been 20 years since 1947, the end of British rule.

FROM BHARATPUR IT WAS a short drive to Agra, where we spent two days. Of course, I had heard of and seen pictures of the Taj Mahal, but I had no idea that it would affect me so much. It was the most impressive building I had ever seen. We walked around for about an hour and a half in the afternoon and then went back in the evening for an enchanting moonlit walk. The next day, we spent all morning at the Agra fort with its three palaces. Fascinated with the history, I began reading as much as I could about the Mughal Empire. My schooling had not taught me anything about South Asian history.

Being Guests in Delhi

IN DELHI WE STOPPED to get our bearings and decide where to go, when a young man who seemed a few years younger than us walked up to our van. With a smile and a friendly look, he asked us where we were from, where we had been, where we were going. We asked him about Delhi, about places to visit and places to stay. After so many weeks of being stared at, it was exciting to have an engaging conversation. He said his name was Ravi and that he lived with his family not far from where we were parked. He invited all four of us to his home, saying that his parents would love to meet us. We hesitated, wondering if it would be appropriate for us all to show up, since he hadn't asked his family. But he kept insisting, so we accepted his invitation. Ravi's family welcomed us with open arms and insisted that we stay in their guest quarters. We ended up spending six days in this lovely quiet space that looked out onto flowers and bushes. We didn't have a shower, but in the garden outside was a low faucet where we could throw water over ourselves with a small bucket. And to top it off, the family gave us breakfast and dinner, took us sightseeing, and explained local traditions.

In my borrowed sari

A few days after arriving in Delhi, we were invited to have dinner with an American family from my hometown in California. When I told Ravi's mother, she graciously asked, "Would you like to wear one of my saris?" I was floored and thrilled. Later that afternoon, she appeared with a beautiful silk cloth draped over her arms. I stood still as she dressed me: wrapping the material around me, folding it snugly at my waist, tucking it in firmly, then draping the remainder across my shoulder. I had never worn a sari and was surprised to find it so comfortable. Our dinner with friends that night was delicious, but I would have been more relaxed if I hadn't worried the whole time that I would spill food on the silk.

Ravi's aunt enlightened us with her work at a birth control clinic in Delhi. The most common birth control method at the time was the IUD ("the loop," as she called it). There was a vigorous campaign in India to reduce the birth rate. Radio commentaries, newspaper articles, billboards, and public lectures helped spread the word, but it was difficult to counteract tradition. Too many people still viewed the idea of having many children as important for their own care in old age. Some religious leaders were also teaching against the use of birth control.

As we got ready to leave Delhi, we struggled with how to repay this family. In the end, we bought them a small outdoor table for their garden, hoping it would be appreciated and appropriate. We had loved learning about their lives and had felt honored to make friends with them, especially since, as low-budget travelers, we had met few people in India who had international experience, were educated, and had relatives in the U.S. Being guests of Ravi's family made me realize that I had never been as open, hospitable, and generous with travelers in the U.S. as this family had been with us. I hoped I would be a more welcoming person once I got back to the States. We kept in contact with Ravi's family for many years after that, and, in fact, my sister and her two children visited them in Delhi nine years later. Even after all those years, my sister said she was treated like family.

WHILE IN DELHI, WE had gotten visas for Nepal and permission to go to Darjeeling in northern India, where we thought we might spend Christmas. We had also filled out the paperwork that would allow as, as foreigners, to get a 50 percent reduction on Indian trains. At the time, even though we thought the policy was unfair to Indians, we still applied for it. Now, however, I think we should have paid the full fare. It wasn't very much.

It took us seven days to get from Delhi to Nepal, driving all day, cooking our own food, and bathing from time to time with well water. We slept in dak bungalows like we had in West Pakistan. I wrote about these in a letter to my parents.

Excerpt of letter to my parents. Delhi, India. December 2, 1966:

We've been sleeping in bungalows and rest houses that were built by the British. They are supposed to be used by military personnel, but foreigners are welcomed. Many are completely free, but for one we paid an extremely high price of 50 cents. These rooms are not fancy in the least. They have no running water and usually no electricity. In fact, all they have are tied-rope Indian beds on which we lay our sleeping bags. But they always have a pump where we can get water, and sometimes a man brings us a kerosene lantern. . . . We are almost always the only people in these bungalows, and they are in every town. I don't know why other tourists don't use them.

It was easy to find places to stay in India, but getting food continued to be a problem. Either we couldn't find what we needed in shops, or we couldn't buy anything because we didn't have a ration card, or what we found in restaurants was so spicy that we couldn't eat it. Our mainstay was eating chapatis and dahl at roadside stands. That was always available.

Chapati makers

Mick's journal comment about food. December 6, 1966:

> *Indian food has a tendency to be rather spicy. We went to a restaurant and soon my eyes were watering, and my nose was running. I was perspiring and trying in general to put the fire out. It's quite good, though.*

As much as possible during our travels, we had kept to our rule of driving only during daylight, but the day after leaving Delhi, we were late in getting to our planned stop in Mauranipur, and it got dark. All four of us were on the lookout, straining to see through the windows to avoid hitting people who were walking down the middle of the road or riding their bicycles without lights. We suddenly had to veer to keep from running into cows, buffaloes, dogs, chickens, and goats in the road, not to mention children. Trucks often drove without headlights or parked in the road without lights, so it was hard to see them until we were almost upon them. We were all tense, exhausted, and relieved when we finally got to the dak bungalow without an incident.

Temples and the Ganges

ONE OF THE MOST interesting towns we saw on the way to Nepal was Khajuraho. We spent about five hours there, wandering through the lovely gardens, gazing at the thousand-year-old temples. Only 20 of the once-85 different temples still existed, their surfaces still covered with carvings of people and animals, many of them detailed and explicit erotic art.

At one of the temple gardens in Khajuraho I asked where the toilet was. The caretaker looked out across a field, made a sweeping movement with his hand, and said, "Over there." There wasn't much cover, but I didn't have any choice. I wandered around a bit looking for some bushes or at least a tree, and finally chose a spot with a few slim trees around. My bowels were telling me that I couldn't wait. As I was squatting down, I heard a noise behind me. I glanced around and saw a man, not too far away, just standing and looking at me. I was in no position to move, and I didn't. In fact, as a testimony to how inured I had become to being stared at, I just turned around and ignored him. He stood still. I finished, pulled up my pants, and walked away. But as I left, I felt disgusted, angry, and embarrassed. Why did that man just stand there staring at me? Was this acceptable in his culture? Was he astonished at seeing a foreigner defecating behind a tree? Or was he getting some kind of sexual pleasure? Whatever it was, I felt numb as I told myself that he was not seeing anything new. And what choice did I have, anyway?

IN BENARES, WE GOT up at a chilly 5:45 a.m. to go down to the Ganges River (the Ganga). The sun was just peeking out, but already the *ghats* (steps leading to the river) were crowded and busy, lined with people begging. By 8 a.m., a colorful array of people covered the steps, many of them shivering and shaking as they plunged into the sacred waters quickly, sometimes ducking completely under the water. Women's saris clung to their wet bodies. Nobody seemed interested in anyone else as they dressed and undressed on the steps. Even we were not stared at much. We took a small rowboat up and down the river, fascinated by all the activity along the banks. One body, lying on a pile of wood, was about to be cremated. Two men were covering it with more wood.

Dawn on the Ganges River

The *ghats* in Benares

Giving alms in Benares

AFTER LEAVING THE GANGES we walked to some of the temples in the city. The crowds were so thick that we could hardly make our way up the narrow streets. At one point, a cow came directly for me with prominent horns on its lowered head. I stepped quickly aside, but the cow almost knocked another woman over. Nobody else paid any attention to it.

It was not only cows and the bathers that astonished us. On one corner in town we saw a woman sitting on the sidewalk holding a very young child. It looked like the child did not have legs or arms, though it was hard to make out more than a deformed lump. The shocking thing was not seeing a malformed child but the fact that the child's body was painted white and covered with pink dots. Was this to get the attention of passersby? It seemed inhumane and cruel to me. I tried to rationalize that maybe the decoration led to a better chance of survival for the child, but it was still hard to accept. I struggled to understand this particular incident, as well as the larger culture. At one point, I felt upset and confused, and the next moment I was filled with awe and wonder. I needed to put these daily experiences into a broader perspective, but it wasn't easy. In my journal that day, after describing the horrendous experience of seeing this small child, I wrote, "Though I feel that I've become almost 'immune' to these sights, still at times they get me down." In that same journal entry, I focused on a more positive aspect of that day.

Journal entry. Benares, India. December 12, 1966:

We also visited a silk weaver today. He was weaving in gold and silver threads in flowers on a purple saree. What tedious work! He has a cardboard pattern which pulls up the right combination of threads, but still he has to put each gold or silver thread through the silk thread for each cross thread. It takes a long time. The threads look so silky and shiny and the finished sarees are magnificent.

On the way to the city of Patna, the largest city in Bihar state, Andreas decided to take a shortcut. He was anxious to get to Kathmandu, as we were behind our schedule. With the regular route, we probably would have gotten to Patna at about noon, but instead our "shortcut" ended up taking much longer. We had to ford streams and climb out of ditches. When we finally reached Patna in the late afternoon, hungry and tired, the first thing we all noticed was a store with a sign over the door: "Soda Fountain and Milk Bar."

With surprise and great anticipation, we stopped and went in. It sounded too good to be true. And it was. There was no ice cream, but there was a jug of uncovered milk sitting on the counter, surrounded by fried chili peppers. The shopkeeper said that he had three kinds of milk: chocolate, vanilla, and pasteurized. We didn't try it. But we did buy some pancake things that were rolled around potatoes. They were quite good, once we had purged from our minds the image of a soda fountain.

We were again delayed as we drove from Patna to Raxaul, the border town just before entering Nepal. The road was good, but we couldn't find a boat that would take us across the Ganges, so we had to detour 70 miles to get to a bridge. We had trouble finding food in Raxaul; a few stores were open, but they didn't have much for sale. We stopped in a restaurant, but the server said that they weren't cooking anything because of the famine. Famine? We hadn't realized that there was a famine in Bihar state, but now, as we cooked up our remaining *souji*, our "cream of wheat" staple, at least we understood why we couldn't buy more food.

Lunch with Andreas and Per, and our group of onlookers

That night in Raxaul was the last time for us to be traveling with Andreas and Per. After Kathmandu, Mick and I would be on our own, traveling by bus and train. Since the two of us would be returning to Raxaul to get the train to Calcutta (now Kolkata) in two days, we decided to buy our tickets ahead of time. And with that, we got our first inkling of the hassle of traveling on Indian third-class trains. The station was so filled with people that we couldn't walk right up to the ticket window. We had to step over people who were sleeping or sitting on the floor. And even then, it wasn't easy to get to the small window for ticket sales. People were pushing, shoving, and grabbing at us. I didn't know if they were afraid that they wouldn't be able to buy tickets for some reason or if this was standard practice, but there seemed to be no order, no line, just chaos. Even as I was leaning in, trying to talk with the ticket seller through the tiny window, people were pushing against me. I finally did manage to buy two tickets on a third-class train to Kolkata, leaving in two days. The cost was only $1.90 for two, for the distance of 744 kilometers. We didn't have seat assignments but figured it wouldn't matter. With tickets in hand, I just wanted to get out of the station. I was not looking forward to negotiating train travel, if this was what we would have to deal with.

Camaraderie in Kathmandu

AS WE NEARED KATHMANDU, I was thrilled to see the whole Himalayan range, with Annapurna to our left and Everest to our right. The air was clear. The sun was shining. The sky was bright blue. It felt fantastic, refreshing. I would have liked to hike, go climbing in the mountains, or take a plane across the peaks to small villages. But we didn't. We could stay for only two days, since we needed to get to Bangkok by early January to find out if Mick would have a teaching job.

In Kathmandu, we rented bikes and pedaled about two miles out of town to a Buddhist temple. The monkeys seemed to be having as much fun as we were, as they slid down the banisters on a long stairway that went up the mountains. But the most exciting thing that day was talking to other travelers.

Journal excerpt. Kathmandu, Nepal. December 16, 1966:

> *We found out that the Globe Restaurant (a little scroungy place) was the center for tourists. It sure was. It was taken over tonight by all nationalities of travelers, usually between ages 22–30. These are people who are trying to sell their car or their motorcycle or are just hitchhiking (trying to sell anything to keep traveling). It's fun to meet these people, though there are usually a few "nuts" in the crowd. I seem to always be the only female in the groupings.*
>
> *It's interesting to talk with these travelers because we all have very similar experiences. Practically all were caught in Iraq during the quarantine, and each person has his own little story of how he got through the border. Most of us have taken similar routes across Iran and Afghanistan. Everyone has been to Kabul, and half the people are wearing "Kabul coats." Some of these people we have met off and on at unexpected places from all across the Middle East to India and Nepal. What a life!*

That night, I just wanted to talk and talk and talk. We were with like-minded people, laughing and almost crying at the same experiences, with everyone excitedly adding to everyone else's stories. We didn't know then that Kathmandu would soon be *the* place where so many travelers would be heading. In a few years, the route from Europe to India and Nepal would become known as "the hippie trail." It would be populated by young people looking for excitement, for hashish, for nirvana. In 1966, these travelers were few, and if some were trying out drugs, we were not aware of it. In fact, I had not yet heard the word *hashish*, though the drug must have been around.

Buses and Trains

AS WE PACKED UP to leave Kathmandu, we were especially sad to leave Andreas and Per. We had been traveling in Andreas's VW camper for the past 36 days and would miss the camaraderie. Andreas wanted to stay in Kathmandu until he sold his camper. Per would stay in Nepal until he felt like leaving. As for us, we were now beginning a new stage of travel. The first stage had been our 14 months of living and camping in House. The second was with Andreas and Per in Andreas's VW camper van. Now we were going off with no vehicle and no tent. We would be relying on public transportation and hotel rooms. We were somewhat nervous about what lay ahead and were not looking forward to taking the bus back to India. Though it was less than a hundred miles back to the border town of Raxaul, we were told that it would take about eight or nine hours to get there.

December 17, 1966, had to go down as our worst travel day of the previous 15 months. We got up early, had breakfast, and hurried to the Kathmandu bus station. The bus was an hour late in coming, but when it arrived, we said goodbye to Andreas and Per, climbed aboard, and rumbled off. The first part of the trip was through the jungle, and then, as we zigzagged up from the valley, we had our final view through murky windows of the spectacular Himalayan range. That was the best part of the day.

We had been riding for two hours when a tire blew out. It took two and a half hours before the tire was repaired and the bus started up again. At 2 p.m., we stopped for lunch. Everyone piled out and stormed into a little shack. Some of the people, those who looked somewhat well off, went upstairs, but we followed the others into a large room with an earthen floor and cooking pots at one end. Narrow boards lined the wall along a long low table. I assumed that this was a bench, so I sat down on it before realizing that everyone else was squatting on the board. I tried to squat, but the board teetered, and I slipped right off. Completely embarrassed, I decided I'd better sit. Mick had already decided that. We both felt a little silly, sitting with our bums on the bench rather than our feet, but neither of us thought we could manage squatting on the bench, balancing while eating. Soon we heard the clatter of plates being passed out, and then came men with scoops of food for each plate. Lunch was quickly and efficiently served. There was plenty for everyone: rice, dahl, radishes, and bits of liver (which I pushed aside). We had gotten much better at eating with our hands, so we dug right in.

After lunch, we got on the bus again, behind schedule because of the flat tire. We lumbered on through the long afternoon until we were only about seven or eight miles outside the town of Birganj, our stop for the night on the Nepalese side of the border. In the gathering darkness, we were both worried about—in fact, scared to death of—driving in the dark. Our fears were not unfounded. Before we reached Birganj, the bus stopped. The road was blocked because of a truck and cart that had collided on the bridge. We learned later that the vehicles had been there for four hours waiting for help. Our bus driver couldn't pass the truck and cart, so he decided to drive through the river. It wasn't deep, but in a few minutes the bus was stuck. We sat there in the riverbed, along with everyone else, while the driver spun the tires, which just sank deeper into the wet sand. The driver got up, told everyone that his "assistant" would stay with the bus, and walked off, wading through the muck. This assistant (his son?) was a boy who looked no more than 14 years old.

After what seemed like hours, two tractors arrived. Our driver was still not back, so the boy sat up at the wheel, ready to steer the bus out of the muck. He could barely see over the steering wheel and didn't seem to know much about driving this bus. Mick, who was practically tearing his hair out with the events so far, squirmed as he watched the boy put the gear into reverse while the tractors were trying to pull the bus forward. Mick was beside himself. He wanted to jump into the driver's seat, but he held back. I'm sure he would have done a better job than the boy, but he didn't take over. Instead, he stood by the driver's seat and watched the boy's every move. The boy soon realized that he was in the wrong gear, the bus finally lurched out of the watery sand, and the boy started driving. While everyone else on the bus merely sat, Mick continued to stand right beside the front seat, ready to grab the wheel in a second. Trying to be calm, he told the boy to go no faster than 5 miles per hour. The boy seemed serious as he drove slowly down the darkened highway. In a few miles, our original driver appeared. He got in the bus and drove us the rest of the way into town. We began to relax, but not for long.

Before we reached the bus stop in Birganj, people all around us started to get up and grab their belongings from the overhead rack. We stayed seated, thinking it would be easier to get out after the rush. The bus stopped and people began pushing and shoving in their dash to get out of the bus. We took our time, picked up Mick's duffel bag and my small suitcase, got out, and began looking for a place to sleep. We went to the first hotel we saw. "Sorry," the proprietor said. "We have no more rooms." We went to two more hotels, only to get the same story. Now we understood why people had been in such a hurry to get out. They must have known that there were not enough rooms in this small town, especially since we were hours late in arriving. We stood in the road, tired and hungry, with me fighting back tears, when a policeman came up to us. We asked him if there were any more hotels in town or any other place to stay. "No," he said. "All taken. There is nothing else." It was night, it was dark, and we were dumbfounded. This had never happened to us before; we had always had a camper or at least a tent with us. The policemen, maybe feeling sorry for us, offered the police station as a place to sleep. Relieved, we followed him for a few blocks.

The station was dark, but the policeman turned on a dim light in the office and I could make out a desk, a fan, and a few papers taped to the walls. The floor and walls were concrete. There was nothing else there. The policemen left, and we spread our sleeping bags out flat on the cold concrete floor. I went outside to look for a secluded place to pee. There was none. Next to the police station was a concrete ditch with a bit of dirty water running through it. I squatted over the ditch as I had seen many people do. It was dark enough to feel private.

That night was horrible, as hard and cold and uncomfortable as a concrete floor could be. In the morning, I got up early since I knew there would be no privacy for peeing. There wasn't. I squatted over the same ditch, but this time a few people were walking by. They didn't look at me, but I felt exposed.

That morning, we got on the bus again to complete the journey to Raxaul. When we crossed the Nepalese border, the official simply waved the whole busload through. I guess officially we never left Nepal. We hopped on a pedicab in Raxaul to go to the train station. The driver was ornery, as was I. He asked for way more money than we had been paying for pedicabs. I was bargaining with him when Mick, somewhat annoyed at me, pointed out that I was arguing over the equivalent of about one penny. The driver wanted 6 anna, and I wanted to pay him 5. We got our 5-anna ride, and then Mick tipped him 4 piasas (there are 6 piasas in 1 anna, so it came to less than half a cent). At the time, I felt adamant about those annas and piasas. In retrospect, I had sunk to a new low by dickering over pennies with a pedicab driver who probably lived on little else.

THOUGH DECEMBER 17 HAD been our worst travel day, the next few were not much better. On December 18, we got on our first Indian third-class train in Raxaul. We were in the waiting area at 7:45 a.m. for our 8 a.m. train. It arrived at 10:30. Once we'd boarded, we sat on wooden benches along with the masses of people. We were supposed to change trains at 9:15 but obviously had missed our connection. We were told that there would be another train at 1:30, so we had a lunch of rice, dahl, and curry (eaten with fingers, of course) in a dirty little mud-walled restaurant. The stationmaster, maybe surprised that we were eating there, invited us to his room for tea and betel nut. I didn't chew any betel nut, but I did enjoy the tea. He told us that 60 to 70 percent of the people bought tickets for the trains. The rest just got on free. The authorities didn't do anything about it because the people might fight, and, after all, there were more people riding free than there were people to police them.

Our 1:30 train was surprisingly only 15 minutes late, and it was a bit nicer. We sat in a compartment with a group of friendly Chinese people from Sikkim who had been on the bus with us from Kathmandu. Even with our limited language skills, we had good talks and a relaxing afternoon.

Riding on third-class trains in India was not always comfortable, but it was never boring. There were people to talk to, of course, and constant activity. Vendors hopped on and off to peddle their wares. Young boys rode from station to station, often singing while sitting on the floor, holding their hands out for coins. Sometimes, when they wanted to go from one car to the next, the peddlers or young boys would climb outside one moving car and leap to the next one. I could hardly look.

Our last train change that day was in Samastipur. We pulled into the station at 7:45 p.m., relieved that we were in time for the 8:40 p.m. train to Calcutta. We had already bought tickets for a reserved sleeper on that train, so we thought there would be no problem. Again, we were mistaken. When we got off in Samastipur, we didn't know where to find the train to Calcutta. It was hard to run around with the duffel bag and suitcase, so I stayed with our gear while Mick went to find the right platform. The first man he asked told him that there was no 8:40 train. But when Mick showed him that we had tickets, he said that the train was too full so we couldn't get on. Then Mick went to the ticket office and again showed our tickets. The ticket agent said that there was an 8:40 train; he explained which platform to go to, adding that we could get on because we had a reserved sleeper.

This had taken quite a bit of time, so Mick came running back to me, harried and insistent: "Hurry, we need to run." We raced over to the right platform, where throngs of people were trying to push onto that one train. It seemed that "reserved" meant nothing. Rather, it seemed to be "first come—first served." Discouraged, hungry, sleepy, dirty, and mad, we gave up. We didn't get on. It was too much to deal with and not worth the hassle. We got a room in the railway retiring area for 50 cents. The room was about as basic as it could be, but we were both sound asleep in a matter of minutes.

The next day, we were told that we couldn't get a train until 4:30 p.m. We bought a reserved sleeper compartment and decided that we would go to the station at 3:30 to wait for it and be ready to jump on. But at least that morning we had time to wash up. I had never felt so grimy in such a short time. It had been only two days since leaving the Tourist Center in Kathmandu, but since then, we had been on buses and trains constantly, with one night on the cold concrete floor of a police station.

We now had a day's wait in Samastipur. We walked around town, not seeing much, but we did buy more *souji* and sugar for later breakfasts. We also struck up a conversation with an American Jesuit priest who had been in Samastipur for 34 years, never having gone back to the States. He took us to his church, gave us a good lunch, and proudly showed us the plants and trees he had cultivated: coconuts, mangos, papayas, dahl, litchi, grapes, onions, potatoes, bamboo. He added, however, that much of their fruit was either stolen or ruined from insect damage.

The 4:30 p.m. train to Calcutta arrived, and we got settled into our reserved sleeper compartment. This time the system had worked for us, and even though it was a third-class train, it was comfortable. We relaxed, glad to be on the final portion of this trip. We had decided to stay in Calcutta only one night so that we could spend more time in Darjeeling, but we knew it would be a rush to make all the arrangements in such a short time. We would need to find out how best to get up north (bus? train? plane?), find out where to buy the tickets, and of course find a place to sleep that night. There was no one around to ask, there were no guidebooks to help us, and we weren't used to having a deadline like this. For most of our travel of the past year, we had taken our time, changing our schedule whenever needed. These next two days would try our patience, but we didn't know that yet.

Very early that next morning, December 20, our train pulled into Howrah station. Hordes of people were sitting and sleeping on the station floor. Seeing this mass of humanity, I craved quiet and space. I just wanted to find a place where we could cook and eat our breakfast apart from the crowds. We saw a staircase going up to a balcony overlooking the main floor of the station, but there was a rope across the bottom steps and a sign: "First-class passengers." We ignored the sign, ducked under the rope, and went up. I thought a guard would stop us, but no one did. In retrospect, I realize that we had the advantage and privilege of being white foreigners, something that didn't occur to me at the time. Even if it had, though, I doubt that we would have done anything differently.

The upstairs was surprisingly quiet. Hardly anyone was around, and we even spied an empty bench. We fired up our tiny stove and cooked up a pot of *souji*. The few people around us didn't pay any attention; some were changing their clothes; others were snoring on benches or the floor. We ate a leisurely breakfast, cleaned up our bowls and utensils, and packed everything away. Since we knew we would be in Calcutta for only one night, we left most of our gear in storage at Howrah station. It would be much easier to manage local buses in town without the duffel bag.

Cooking *souji* for breakfast upstairs in Howrah station, Kolkata

Outside Howrah station, we got on a bus heading to the center of town. It was a good thing we didn't have much to carry, since the bus was packed—in fact, overpacked—with people. After the bus crossed Howrah Bridge and we were on the main street heading toward downtown, Mick heard a loud *crack* and the bus suddenly stopped. I had no idea what the noise was, but Mick said he thought that the U bolt on the drive shaft had shattered. I guess that was it. So here we were again, in a broken-down bus. We were not surprised. No one else seemed surprised either. People just gathered their belongings and filed out of the bus. The driver stood outside and gave us our bus fare back. He said that another bus would arrive "soon," but we decided to walk the rest of the way into town.

Our immediate destination was the American Express office, which we found without too much trouble. We hadn't been in touch with our parents or had any mail since leaving Peshawar on November 7, almost six weeks earlier. Now we hoped for, hungered for, news. The American Express office was still closed when we arrived, but next door was a store with English-language magazines. Relieved that we wouldn't have to stand on the sidewalk, we went in and happily passed the time reading. But the best reading came when the American Express office opened. We had a packet of letters; it was like getting candy.

It was still early in the day when we set out to get tickets for Darjeeling, as well as make reservations for our upcoming travel to Bangkok. We heard that we could fly to Darjeeling on India Air, and while we were walking to the airline office, we saw the Swiss couple whom we had met at the West Pakistan–India border. They were also going to the India Airlines office for tickets to Darjeeling. We walked together, making plans to meet again in Darjeeling. At the airline office, though, we were surprised at the cost; it was way too expensive. Not only that, but the agent said our permission to travel to Darjeeling had expired. The agent was able to renew our permission, but while we waited for it, we changed our minds about flying. We decided to take the train to Darjeeling instead. That meant that we would have to reapply for a new rail discount, since it had also expired, and for that we had to go to another office. All this was taking a lot more time than we had planned, but the idea of taking the train to Darjeeling sounded better all the time. Even though it would entail a long overnight train ride, it was cheap and would include riding on the narrow-gauge "toy train" for the final part of the trip. By the time we had received our renewed rail passes, however, it was too late to buy the train tickets. We were told we could buy them at the station the next day before the train left at about noon.

During that first day in Calcutta, we also made the decision to fly to Bangkok by way of Rangoon (now Yangon) on Union of Burma Airways. Since this airline wasn't a member of the International Air Traffic Association (IATA), we worried about safety, but it was much cheaper than other airlines, so we opted for it. We could leave in one week, on December 27. We were all ready to buy the Bangkok air tickets when we realized that we didn't have enough money in rupees to pay for them. We would have to find a place that would change traveler's checks into rupees, but that was neither easy nor quick. It could take an hour or more at a bank, and we didn't have that much time.

The day was getting more frustrating each hour. We needed rupees not only for our plane tickets to Bangkok but also to pay for visas for Burma (which became Myanmar in 1989). We went to two banks, but both said they couldn't do it because it was too late; they would be closing soon.

Everything seemed too complicated at this point, and the day was almost over. We would have to wait until the next day to buy our train tickets at the station (not at Howrah station, where our luggage was stored), get our air tickets to Bangkok, and get our Burmese visas: all this between 10:00 a.m., when the offices opened, and 12:45 p.m., when the train to Darjeeling left. The task seemed almost insurmountable.

At the end of the day, both of us were tired, angry, and frustrated. After running around from office to office to office and waiting in line after line after line, I felt that nothing worked in this city and no one cared. Time didn't seem to matter to anyone, or at least my concept of time: how to get things done efficiently. I realized that I was viewing all this from my American perspective, but that didn't stop my frustration. I was practically in tears. I was mad at everything and everyone I saw. And it seemed to me that no one had anything to do other than stare.

And it wasn't only us that people were staring at. At a pond in town, we saw a man sitting with a drop line, fishing. It looked like he was half asleep, waiting for a fish to bite; his eyes were half closed. That wasn't too strange, but around him was a huge crowd ("hundreds," Mick says in his journal) of people just looking at him. Maybe they were engaged in something I didn't understand, but in my frazzled state of mind, I just thought, *Don't they have anything better to do?*

When the stores and offices were all closed and we didn't have tickets for anywhere, I felt that the day had been wasted. Dinner revived me to some extent. We had decided to splurge on a Chinese meal. It tasted wonderful, such a welcome change after eating chapatis, rice, and dahl for the past month. After dinner, feeling energized again, we went to Spence's Hotel, hoping that the hotel bank would change our money. Amazingly they did. We were so tired by then that we got a room at Spence's. We bargained for the price and ended up paying $5. That was much more than we had been used to paying, but we took the room. At least it had hot running water, clean sheets, and breakfast in the morning. That night, even though tired, we went to a movie: *Those Magnificent Men in Their Flying Machines*, a relief from the trials of the day.

On the way back to the hotel that evening, we took a man-pulled rickshaw, something we didn't like to do because we felt guilty having a man pull us. But that was the only vehicle we saw, and the man really wanted to get a fare. We rationalized that we were helping him. As we rode back to Spence's Hotel, we passed bodies lying on the sidewalk and in front of shops. I assumed they were sleeping, though we had been told that often in the morning a cart would pick up people who had died in the night.

That evening, knowing that we had a precious few hours the next morning to accomplish our tasks, we worked out a detailed plan. We had already decided that we didn't need to take all our luggage to Darjeeling, but unfortunately, we did need some of our things. We'd have to take the bus back to Howrah station to get what we needed from our stored luggage. After that, I would take the bags with me to the Burmese Embassy to get our visas and wait there while Mick went to buy our plane tickets to Bangkok. We hadn't split up like this since leaving Peshawar about six weeks before, but I felt renewed and ready to attack the laid-back approach I knew I'd face.

The next morning began easily. We got up early, got to Howrah station quickly, and retrieved what we needed from our luggage. Then, while Mick went to the airline office, I went to the Burmese Embassy, where I filled out the papers, turned in our passport, and waited. And waited some more. No one seemed to be working, including the embassy personnel. For two hours I sat there with our luggage, anxiously looking at my watch, knowing that the train was scheduled to leave at 12:45, wondering if Mick was making more progress than I was.

Suddenly there was Mick, running in breathlessly with his news. He said that he had gotten to the airline office in what he thought was plenty of time. The sign on the door said it would open at 10 a.m., but no one was around to sell tickets. The watchman told him to sit and have tea. There were a few others there who were sitting and waiting. Not Mick. He said he was pacing the floor like a caged bull. Finally, at 11:15 an agent arrived. Mick was able to buy our tickets and then run all the way back to the Burmese Embassy, where I, of course, had accomplished nothing. We continued waiting up to what we thought was the last minute, when finally, a man behind the desk told us that there wasn't time to get our visas. We would have to get them after returning from Darjeeling. Too anxious about getting the train to be frustrated or angry, we left in an instant, arriving at the station barely in time to buy two reserved seats in the third-class compartment. Yes! We were able to get on the train.

It took us all afternoon to get up to the Ganges River, and when we got there that evening, the train stopped. There was no railway bridge, so everyone had to get out to cross on a ferry. We followed everyone in our third-class compartment and ended up on the lower deck of the ferry. It was crowded and dirty, so we snuck upstairs to first class and ordered dinner there. When we landed on the other side of the river, we thought we would just walk onto a new train, but no, it was half a mile away, and everyone began pushing and shoving as they ran to the train.

We had already reserved a sleeping compartment when we bought our tickets, but having had the experience in which "reserved" didn't seem to matter, Mick was energized. He wanted to get there first, so he dashed on ahead, pushing through the crowd with his large duffel bag over his shoulder. I ran to keep up with him but couldn't get through all the people as well as he could. It wasn't hard to see him, though, as he was a head taller than everyone else and the only one with a duffel bag. His fevered exuberance paid off, and we managed to get our reserved sleeper that night. And what a surprise to see the compartment! It was beautiful—all paneled in wood. We relaxed that night to the gentle sway of the train.

The Hills of Darjeeling

THE NEXT MORNING in New Jalpaiguri, we got off the regular train in order to board the "toy train" to Darjeeling. The train ran on a two-foot-wide track and had a steam engine about the size of a large Land Rover. It took us about seven hours to cover 58 miles. Chugging up the mountain, we zigzagged through switchbacks to gain altitude. At times the track ran directly through small towns, so close that we could almost touch the storefronts. We wound through teak forests and lush gardens on our way from an elevation of 323 feet up to 7,218 feet.

The toy train to Darjeeling

Darjeeling was refreshing, so nicely cool after the plains of India. We stayed three nights at the Tourist Lodge and had two dinners at Glenary's Restaurant, where we found not only good food, but a delightful exchange of tales with other travelers. I thoroughly enjoyed the Himalayan Mountaineering Institute, run by Tenzing Norgay. The Tibetan Refugee Self-Help Centre, which provided Tibetan refugees with a new life, was run impressively, with everyone contributing skills in whatever way they could, usually by painting, weaving, or woodworking. In turn, the refugees received free meals, rooms, childcare, and medical care. People we saw there looked happy and healthy. It was at the Centre that we were served yak butter tea, which was . . . pretty awful.

I loved walking up and down the hilly streets in the high-mountain air of Darjeeling. It was almost Christmas, and I felt like celebrating. Even though there were probably more Hindus and Buddhists there than Christians, there was a Christmassy feeling in town. A few decorations dangled above us, and now and then we heard Christmas carols playing. On our first day (December 22), we came across a bakery that was selling plum pudding and some fancy decorated fruitcake. We splurged and bought some of both. We also saw a holly bush, picked up a branch, took it into our room, and decorated it with a few bits of colored paper. It made a fine Christmas tree. I had bought Mick a Gurkha knife that I wrapped and put under our "tree" with a couple of other presents. To celebrate even more, we decided to invite a few other travelers to a Christmas Eve party.

On December 24, we got up at 3:30 a.m. to take a jeep up Tiger Hill to see the sunrise over Kanchenjunga. Spectacular! But freezing. The fireplace in the rest house did little besides bring smoke into the room. For me, the sunrise made everything worth it, but that was not Mick's reaction. In his journal he wrote that it was "no more impressive than others I have seen." I was surprised at his response, especially since the sunrise was such a go-to event. Later I realized that Mick's red-green colorblindness would of course affect what he saw: the colors were muted to him. I knew that he was color-blind, but since he rarely mentioned the effects, I had forgotten about it. After more than a year of marriage, I was still learning new things about this man.

Sunrise over Kanchenjunga

That evening, we invited five people to our Christmas Eve party: one American couple, the Swiss couple we had seen in Calcutta, and one Austrian. Our room had a fireplace, so we built a fire, but the flue didn't work, so the room quickly filled up with smoke. We served plum pudding, fruitcake, and tea but didn't do much else that night, since we had to get up at 3:30 a.m. the next morning (Christmas) to start our journey back to Calcutta. Before we went to bed, we hung stockings, and then, in the wee hours of the morning, we opened the stockings and the little pile of presents.

OUR FLIGHT BACK to Calcutta was cheap, the equivalent of only $7 each, but since there was no airport in Darjeeling, we had a long ride down the mountain to get to the airport. When we finally reached the airport, there was the plane: an old DC-3 cargo plane. I had never been in a plane like this. Instead of rows of seats, there were benches running along the sides of the plane. It was a scary, awful trip. The plane bounced up and down like crazy. Passengers around me were throwing up; I barely managed not to be one of them.

In Calcutta again, we spent our last two nights in India at the Salvation Army Hostel. It turned out to be a welcome break. The hostel restaurant served breakfast, lunch, and dinner, and they offered more than chapatis and dahl. After getting our room that first day, we decided to go out to a museum, but once we got there, we turned around and went right back to the hostel. We were tired of the jostling crowds. It all seemed like too much. We wanted the quiet of our room at the hostel.

As soon as we got to the hostel, Mick went to bed, exhausted. I felt his head; he had a fever and his temperature was soaring. He stayed in bed that day and the next, while I brought him soup and drinks from the hostel restaurant, and fruit from a nearby market. Our room was on the second floor, up a small circular metal staircase, almost like a ladder. I went up and down that staircase repeatedly during the next two days. While Mick stayed in bed, I got our visas for Burma and went back to Howrah station to retrieve our luggage. Mick started to feel better the second day, but he looked thin.

Though Mick's bout of sickness may have been caused by a virus, the stress we had been under since leaving Nepal certainly could have exacerbated it. It had not been easy to negotiate public transportation in India, to be calm when a train or a bus did not arrive, to relax even when we didn't understand the system. In all our travels between Europe and Nepal, we had not needed to depend on local transport, since we had been living either in our own camper van or Andreas's. As such, we could make our own decisions about where to go, what time to leave, and when to stop. And we always had our own bed. We didn't need to buy tickets on buses or trains or be constrained by someone else's time frame. Having our own vehicle also entailed stress, but it didn't compare to the frustration of relying on local transportation. I hadn't realized the luxury of this when living in our camper van.

It would be a short plane ride on Union of Burma Airways to Rangoon (now called Yangon). As we packed up our bags to go to the airport, I felt a renewal of energy. We were ready to move on. We needed a change.

Part Five:

Southeast and East Asia

January–July 1967

18.

A Teacher's Story—Burma

It had been only five years since the 1962 military coup in Burma, so we were not even sure that we could get a visa, but in fact, we were allowed 24 hours in the country. We'd have one afternoon and evening to see as much of Rangoon (Yangon) as possible. On the plane, Mick sat by a Japanese airline mechanic for Burmese Air who was on his way back to Rangoon to continue working. He told Mick that he, like us, could only get a very short visa. The mechanics would work as quickly as they could within their time frame and then would have to leave whether the plane was fixed or not. Yikes! Really? This did not give us much confidence in the airline, but in fact we had no trouble.

While we were on the plane, my neck started to ache and feel stiff. It became painful just to sit in the seat. I tried to get comfortable, but I couldn't turn my head and could hardly move at all. When we arrived in Rangoon, I slowly inched my body into a standing position and managed to carry my small suitcase. We got a room at the YMCA, and by then I was feeling much better, so we went out to walk around the downtown area. After a bit of walking around town, my neck started really hurting again, so reluctantly I went back to the hotel. I spent much of the afternoon in bed propped up with a pillow, mad that that was how I was spending my only time in this city.

WHILE I WAS NURSING a stiff neck, Mick, now feeling better, was raring to go. He spent all afternoon walking around, talking to people, and exploring the town. One of the people he met was a teacher who said he was too busy to talk right then, but he'd have time later. Mick gave him our hotel information, encouraging him to come by. We didn't know if he really would come, but he did. And I was feeling well enough to sit up and talk. The teacher seemed quite serious as he spoke in a whispered voice.

Mick's journal. Written in Bangkok about Rangoon, January 2, 1967:

> *Late that evening a teacher I had met earlier came to our room. He described what a repressive regime it was. All mail is censored, people can't travel between towns, there are military guards at all town entrances. People can't speak freely, and should they flee the country, reprisals will be taken against their relatives. . . . All Western representatives, [including] some diplomats, have been asked to leave, while Russian and Chinese technicians and other workers are increasing in number. Apparently, Burma's official policy of neutrality is simply a farce covering a leftist core.*

I didn't write a letter in Rangoon, but I did the next day after we had left Burma.

Letter excerpt. Written in Bangkok. December 28, 1966:

> *Dear Daddy and Mom,*
>
> *The people [in Rangoon] we talked to were unhappy with the present government. They said it was too repressive, but they didn't think it would change. In the past months most foreigners have been expelled—all missionaries, and people like USIS and the British Information Agency. All stores and companies have been nationalized, and the people are quite restricted in their personal lives. English has been switched to Burmese as the mandatory language and main language of the schools. However, Rangoon is a beautiful large clean*

city. We saw no beggars and no poor, sick, or malformed people (as in India). There was plenty of food for sale in the markets, but we were told that this was only the case in Rangoon. The outlying areas apparently need food. We stayed at the YMCA, and some of the people there spoke quite freely with us. They were all quite unhappy with this new regime but didn't think that it would change.

Love,

Patti

That night after the teacher left, my neck and back hurt so much that I barely slept. The only possible way to be somewhat comfortable was to arrange a pillow so that I was half-sitting. I couldn't move. I hated it. The next morning, December 28, stiff neck in tow, we got up at 4 a.m. to leave for the airport. By 9 a.m. we had landed in Bangkok. My neck and back had recovered; I had left the stiffness in Burma.

19.

A Job, a House, and Breakfast—Thailand

Excerpt of letter to my parents. Bangkok. December 28, 1966:

Dear Daddy and Mom,

We arrived in Bangkok this morning and it's terribly exciting. It's such a big, modern city, and, after India, it's soooo refreshing. Everybody looks clean and fresh and smiley. All the men have on clean, ironed white shirts, and the people look happy and healthy. After leaving India I feel like a big burden has been lifted off me. It's something that we didn't realize while we were in India, only after leaving. When one is in something, one sort of accepts it and lives it, but after getting out, you see what you were in.

In the same letter, I continue:

I felt horrible as we flew into the airport this morning. Just after we had touched down, three American fighter jets came in. They were all camouflaged and looked very scary. When we walked into the airport, the waiting room was crowded with American military men. Then a huge American passenger jet came in and hundreds more military men came in. They may have been just from the States. I felt as near to a war situation as I ever have. It's horrible! The things we've been

reading in the papers make the U.S. sound like a horrible pusher and
escalator of the war. Everything we read is anti-American.

Love,

Patti

Military Presence and Hotels

I HAD NOT EXPECTED to feel so close to, and so aware of, the American troop buildup in nearby Vietnam. The effect was evident throughout the city. Since there was not enough military housing in Bangkok, the U.S. military had taken over seven or eight large hotels, including King's Hotel. This large influx of Americans had affected the economy: prices had gone up and new products and services were available. As for us, we were delighted to find Wimpy hamburgers, ice cream parlors, and even pasteurized Foremost milk.

ON THE DAY WE arrived, Mick went to the military compound to find out whether he would be able to teach. As he was entering the building, he saw an announcement about the University of Maryland classes, and to his surprise, his name was listed for a Sociology 1 class. Mick asked the first man he saw where the education office was, and that man turned out to be the education director. They had set up a class for him without even knowing if he'd be there. It was a relief to know that we could count on staying in Bangkok for at least the next two months. We both felt great— ready for tropical weather, fresh fruit, and Thai food. Since Mick's class wouldn't begin until January 30, we had a month to find an apartment and see some of the countryside.

We had a contact to look up in Bangkok: the Prachuab family. My mother had sent us their name, as their daughter was a high school exchange student in my hometown in California. I was a bit hesitant to show up unannounced at their house, but they welcomed us warmly. Mr. Prachuab spoke English quite well and was able to translate to his wife. They seemed quite thrilled at this unexpected visit from us; they wanted to know all about my hometown. The conversation was fun for me, and probably relieving to them. We told them about Mick's teaching position, that we would be in Bangkok for two months, and that we had just arrived and were looking for a place to rent.

That day, they helped us way more than we could have imagined. They not only took us out to lunch at a fancy restaurant but also drove us around in a taxi trying to find the address we had of a house for rent. That rental wasn't available, but they insisted that we keep looking, so we spent most of that afternoon riding around town with them. I became increasingly embarrassed at all the time they were spending with us. Finally, we convinced them that they had done enough for us. My mistake then was that I asked if they knew of a cheap hotel. They ended up taking us to a large fancy downtown tourist hotel: the Empire. We protested that we couldn't stay there, but they insisted, telling us to wait in the cab while Mr. Prachuab spoke to the hotel manager. When he returned, he said that we must stay there for the next four days—all expenses paid. I was dumbfounded, but it was useless to argue. Mr. Prachuab said that his wife was a friend of the manager's wife, so he was able to make a deal. He kept telling us not worry about anything. I didn't know what to say or what to do. They had given us way too much. Was this expected in Thai culture? Should we repay them in some way? We were again confronted with the uncomfortable issue of not knowing how to act appropriately in a new culture.

WE CHECKED OUT OF the YMCA and took a taxi back to the Empire Hotel. As we entered the clean, spacious lobby with Mick's scruffy duffel bag and his attaché case, my travel-worn suitcase, and a few assorted handbags, we both felt conspicuous. In India and Nepal, our belongings seemed appropriate, even somewhat fancy, but here all our things looked dirty. Despite that, we were thrilled to be in the hotel. We unpacked, luxuriating in the plush room. The next day, we took some flowers over to the Prachuabs to thank them and then took ourselves out for a steak dinner at Mizu's Kitchen. We couldn't remember the last time we had eaten steak, and it tasted great.

That night, as Mick lay in our large, comfortable hotel bed under clean white sheets, he began shivering, sick again with a fever. The next morning, I found some fruit for sale outside the hotel, but he didn't want anything to eat. Later that day, I suggested a bowl of *souji*, the cream of wheat cereal that we had practically lived on in India. It would be tasty, filling, and easy to digest, like comfort food, I thought. We still had one small bag of *souji* that we had been carrying around in India, so I unpacked our trusty little benzene stove from the duffel bag, set it down on the hotel floor, squatted by it, and fired it up.

As I think about it these many years later, I wonder why I didn't at least set the stove on top of something. But I didn't. Maybe there was not enough space on the desk or countertop. At any rate, squatting by the stove was what I had been doing for months. It seemed normal, if somewhat strange in this setting. When the water came to a boil, I added a handful of *souji*. I cooked it well and stirred it carefully, but I couldn't get all the lumps out. This wasn't too surprising, since we often ate lumpy cereal, but I did my best to smash the lumps. I ladled out two bowls of *souji*, and we both ate everything. It tasted wonderful: warm and satisfying. But as I was putting the sack of raw *souji* away, I noticed more lumps that were stuck to the inside of the bag. The pieces were clumping together, and then I saw . . . oh no . . . the lumps were moving: they were wriggling worms. Out went the last of our *souji*, the whole bag thrown in the garbage. At least, I rationalized, the *souji* (and the critters) had been well cooked.

Mick stayed in bed only a few days, and I found places outside to buy food and bring it to our room. During these few days, the possibility of ordering room service never occurred to me, mainly because I had never done such a thing. I didn't even entertain the idea of buying food from the hotel restaurant and bringing it to our room. To my mind, buying anything in a fancy hotel would be way too expensive: that was what other

people did, those with more money. In the end, though, our four days at
the Empire Hotel turned out to be a welcome respite. Mick recovered. I
read, got our clothes washed at the hotel, and enjoyed the quietude. Many
years later, when Mick had a similar bout of chills and sweats, we found
out that, whatever he had, it was not malaria.

Now, with Mick up and around again, we did some shopping and
walked around the city. We bought delicious creamy milkshakes, a whole
pie, and a *Newsweek* magazine. We got visas for Laos. We saw a movie in
English: *Dr. Zhivago*. We were ready to take some short trips in Thailand.
Life seemed good, despite the inescapable presence of the U.S. military,
reminding me that my country was at war in Vietnam.

AFTER FOUR NIGHTS OF respite in the plush Empire Hotel, we returned to
our regular type of lodging. We spent two nights in the Station Hotel, but
it was quite run-down, so we decided to try the Thai Song Greet Hotel.
We had already had dinner there one night and found that for people like
us who were traveling as cheaply as possible, it was *the* place to go. Scruffy-
looking travelers sat around worn, coffee-splattered wooden tables regaling one another with their stories while chomping on tasty noodles. The
restaurant was perfect. It was where we could find out how to get around
in Thailand, where to eat, and where to sleep.

Sleeping in the hotel, though, was another story. Mick wrote in his
journal that it was "a cheap hotel, but a clean one," but I remember it as
being awful. It was dark inside, and the bathroom down the hall was so dirty
that I didn't want to touch anything. The upside was that it was extremely
cheap (the equivalent of $1.75 a night), and of course the draw was being
able to meet and talk to other like-minded travelers. We were again hearing
people refer to themselves as WTs, part of a loosely knit community of
low-budget travelers for whom a journey had become a way of life. One
American couple, Clark and Mardi, were planning to go to Laos and take
a riverboat down the Mekong River; others were talking about hiking in

the hill country up north or going to the beaches in the south. I wanted to do all of it, but we couldn't leave until we found a place to rent.

While hanging around the Thai Song Greet Hotel, we were astonished that we continued to see people that we had met along our route over the past year. The most surprising was seeing the Swiss couple that we had first met at the India–West Pakistan border back in November when we were all waiting to cross into India. They had also been in Kathmandu at the same time as us (though we didn't see them there). And we had met them by chance in Calcutta when we were all going to the Burmese Airlines office to buy tickets to Thailand. After that, we met them in Darjeeling, where we invited them to our Christmas Eve party. Now it seemed unbelievable that we were seeing them in Bangkok. They said they would probably go up to Chiang Mai in a few weeks, and we said we were planning to do the same. As usual, we laughingly said that we'd probably be running into them again.

After two nights in the Thai Song Greet Hotel, we heard about a room we could rent for two months. It was on the street called Soi Ruam Rudi, and it cost the equivalent of $83 a month, an excellent price, since most of the places we looked at were $200 or $300 a month. We moved in immediately. Our upstairs room overlooked a garden with banana trees, coconut palms, and colorful flowers. Everything smelled sweet and fresh. We had our own entrance, our own bathroom, and access to a telephone. Breakfast and laundry were included, and we were told that tea and cookies would sometimes be brought up to our room in the afternoon. The best part of the day was breakfast in the garden: fresh fruit (papaya, pomelo, pineapple, mango, or banana), two eggs, toast, tea or coffee. Every day it was a joy just to go down for breakfast. In fact, to this day Mick contends that those breakfasts saved his life!

The weather was hot, but I didn't mind the heat or humidity. I loved the gentle breeze coming through the screens on the windows. I loved the feel and the smell of the wooden walls and floors. I even loved the sound of the little geckos scooting up and down the walls. Our table fan gave us a comforting whirring sound all night.

Our room in Bangkok; Patti on deck

We found that we had many connections with our landlady. She had a son and daughter in California, and she herself had been at UC Berkeley for a year. The daughter, 17 years old, was in high school in Los Angeles. We became friends as well as renters. Once she took me to her seamstress, where I had some clothes made. The landlady was also renting out another room, this one to a military man. He was from San Luis Obispo and had two daughters going to Cal Poly (California Polytechnic State University, San Luis Obispo), where my father was a professor. In fact, this man's home was on the same street as the one I grew up on. Another surprising small-world connection.

SINCE WE HAD MORE than two weeks before Mick's class would begin on January 10, we packed up a few things and left on the bus for Laos. It took a whole day to get to the Thai border town of Nong Khai, and all was fine except that the man next to us kept vomiting. I did my best to block out the sound and smell, barely managing not to get sick myself. In fact, I was pleased that I was able to eat. There were vendors at each stop selling fruit, fried chicken on bamboo skewers, and other treats. Our bus trip took us right through the middle of Thailand, along fields and small houses on wooden stilts. We also passed three U.S. military bases, a jarring sight with American aircraft, runways, hangars, and housing spread out over the countryside. Again, I thought about this infusion of American military on the people and economy of Thailand. I could not fathom all the ways it would affect the country.

Laos and the Mekong River

IT WAS ALREADY LATE—about 9 p.m.—when we arrived in Nong Khai, but there were pedicabs at the station, so we managed with a few words and sign language to explain that we wanted a hotel. The pedicab driver took us to one that was bare and basic; at $1.50 it was fine for one short night. The next morning, we walked to the Mekong River, cleared customs, and boarded a ferryboat for Laos. On the Laotian side we shared a taxi for the 22-kilometer ride to Vientiane. The city didn't look much like the administrative capital of a country. The streets were narrow, and there was little vehicle traffic, most of which consisted of pedicabs. Some of the buildings were reminiscent of those built by the French colonists. We walked to the post office in hopes of getting a note from Clark and Mardi, the Americans we had met in Bangkok. And, not surprisingly, there they were, just leaving the post office as we arrived. We made plans to get together later that day.

That afternoon, we wandered into the United States Information Service (USIS) to see if we could get some information about the city and country. There we met a man named Don who was working with USAID in Vientiane. He and his wife, Carol, were at USIS that day doing some reading and research at the library. We asked them about their lives and work in Laos, and they asked us about our travels, and then they invited us to lunch at their house. I was excited to go, since I didn't want to end this conversation, and I also wanted to see their house.

It was a short walk to their large colonial French–style home with a lovely wrap-around veranda. We sat outside in the shade sipping cool drinks as Don continued talking about his work and their impressions of Vientiane. They had been there for six months and were very happy with their life. They had come from Texas with their two little boys. Don's job was to work on a project of dropping food and other necessities to the Hmong refugees who were in camps in northern Laos. Don explained that these tribespeople, who supported the Royal Lao government, had been left homeless after fighting either the Pathet Lao (anti-Lao-government Communist Laotians) or the Viet Minh (communist Vietnamese).

Don told us that there was an excellent communication system between the pro-government Laotians working in northern Laos and the USAID workers. He said that when a Laotian general found out that a family or group had been driven from their homes, he communicated the information to Vientiane, and immediately an American plane flew over one of the drop zones or landed near the people to bring food. Don said that the Laotian government was not very strong and could be taken over easily by the Pathet Lao communists and the North Vietnamese, probably in as little as a week.

The Laotian government knew this. The U.S. knew this. But the Pathet Lao didn't want to take over Laos, he said. All that would do would be to make a bigger war, since the U.S. would then put American troops in Laos to fight back. Don said that everyone hoped that when the Vietnam War was over, the Viet Minh would simply go back to Vietnam. That would be the end of the trouble in Laos, since the Pathet Lao by themselves wouldn't be able to take over the Royal Lao government. The Pathet Lao were only figureheads for the Viet Minh, he said. Without the backing from North Vietnam, they were nothing.[1]

On our first night in Vientiane, we stayed at the Hotel Saya in a room that was hot and noisy. The walls between the rooms went up about three-quarters of the way to the ceiling, with a wire mesh going the rest of the way up. This did allow for air circulation, but of course we could hear everyone around us. There was a shared toilet at the end of the hall on our floor. The sheets on the bed had probably not been changed for some time.

---

1   In fact, in 1975, two years after the U.S. pulled out of Laos and Vietnam, the North Vietnamese and the Pathet Lao forces did attack in Laos. The Lao national government accepted the Pathet Lao in order to avert complete destruction. They made a deal that gave some power to the Pathet Lao, but on May 1 of that year, the Pathet Lao took over the government completely.

Late in the night, Mick woke up and couldn't get back to sleep because of the noise in the room next to us, so he started writing in his journal. But the noise was getting louder, and he was getting more upset by the minute. Finally, he was so angry that he got up and knocked on the door, planning to go in and ask the people to tone it down. But he was taken aback when he saw three or four young guys holding AK-47 rifles, staring unsmilingly right at him. *Oh shit*, he thought. *Maybe they're Pathet Lao.* He made a quick decision not to ask them to quiet down as he slowly backed out the door and returned to our room, where he managed to get back to sleep. I didn't know about our neighbors with the AK-47s until morning. That day, we moved to the Hotel Phonsvan for two nights. Though it was even cheaper, there were actual walls between the rooms, the sheets were clean enough, and we didn't see anyone with a gun.

There wasn't much for us to do in Vientiane except walk through the busy morning market, a place where it seemed that anything could be bought. Spread out on blankets or cloths on packed dirt were clothes of all kinds, pills for eliminating tapeworms, armadillos in cages, and bunches of dried greenery.

As we were strolling through the market, we met an American couple who were new travelers to Asia, just coming from California. This was the first time we had met any travelers from that direction—that is, westward from the U.S. to Asia rather than eastward from Europe to Asia. These two looked quite different from the Californians we remembered. He had a long beard. She had long straight hair and was wearing a long skirt. They looked a bit unkempt and ragged to us. They were both exclaiming about everything, especially the green stuff that I had hardly noticed. "Wow!" the woman said. "That's pot! Do you know how much people would pay for that in San Francisco? They would die for it! At home, we stick our heads in paper bags to get a whiff from a tiny bit." I was surprised. California seemed very far away and long ago to us. If this couple represented the new California culture, things had obviously changed a lot since 1965.

In the market, we also met a man wearing civilian clothes who said he was in the U.S. military. He told Mick that the official position was that there were no U.S. military in Laos, but he smiled as he said this. Did he mean that there actually *were* U.S. military there? We knew about the USAID folks and about the dropping of food to Hmong people, but we hadn't seen any evidence of U.S. troops. We found out later that the "secret war" in Laos had begun in 1965, two years before we were there, and had lasted until 1973. Despite the term "secret," the U.S. presence in Laos was known, at least to Laotians and Thais and to people who read articles about it in the *New York Times*, the *Bangkok Post*, and other newspapers at the time. Also, the U.S. Congress was regularly briefed about the military operations, and they approved the financing. The U.S. policy of using Lao Hmong tribesmen to fight against the Viet Minh, however, wasn't fully explained to the American public until many years later.

LATER THAT AFTERNOON, we met Clark and Mardi again. They said they would be taking a riverboat down the Mekong River the next day, along with two other Americans and two Swiss travelers. The boats, they told us, were not made for passengers; they were transport barges that brought food and supplies to people up and down the river. It was intriguing and sounded like fun, but because the barges would be so close to the war zone, we first checked it out with an official at the USIS office. We were told that the barge trip should be safe, and with that as assurance, we decided to go.

THE MEKONG RIVER BEGINS in the mountains of southern China, runs south to become the border between Thailand and Laos, and then veers off through the middle of Cambodia before it ends up in the delta in southern Vietnam. We would be on the riverboat through a portion of the Mekong along the Laos-Thai border. The trip would take about three days, and several riverboats would be lashed together. There weren't any beds on the boats, nor was there any food, water, tables, or chairs, but we were told we'd be welcome to come if we wanted to sleep on the floor and bring our own food. With that information, we went back to the open market. Since we had nothing to sleep on, we bought a large blue-and-white-checked cotton sheet, one big enough to wrap all around both of us. We had no idea how much food we'd need, but we ended up buying two dozen bananas, one dozen rolls, one kilo of tomatoes, one can of paté, one box of raisins, and one bottle of wine. And one *Newsweek* magazine.

The next day, January 14, after three nights in Vientiane, we arrived at the boat dock at 8 a.m. as we had been advised to do. Several people were hanging around, waiting for the boats to leave. Though we had been told that these were not passenger boats, one of them was filled with women and children. I wondered who these women were and where they were going. The men kept saying the boats would be leaving "soon," but by 12:30 p.m. they still were not moving. Soon after that, though, the motors started up, and the eight of us foreigners split up to go on different boats. Mick and I went with Clark and Mardi on the barge *VT 173*, which was lashed behind the one with women and children. No other passengers were on our barge.

Waiting for our Mekong River barge; Clark, Mardi, Patti on left

Patti standing on top of barge VT 173

There was not much choice as to where to go on the barge. We could sit outside on the low roof, or we could go to a more private space below deck, separate from Clark and Mardi as well as from the crew. Mick and I climbed down the short ladder to check out a space. It was cool down there, a little dark, and a bit musty. It was separated from other parts of the boat by flimsy blue walls. Most of the area was piled high with boxes labeled "Omo," a brand of powdered detergent. There was also a car stashed there among the piles of boxes. I had no idea how a car could have been put into that area. Maybe the roof could be removed, or maybe the walls were movable. We set down our few items of food and clothes on a small bamboo mat between the car and the boxes of detergent, left them there, and went up back up to the low roof, where there was clear air and plenty of room.

It was much nicer outside. As the boat pulled out to the middle of the river, it gathered speed, bringing about a gentle breeze. For the next three days and two nights, we spent most of our time sitting on the rooftop, reading, eating, and watching the shore. The banks on both sides of the river were covered with tropical vegetation. We could see scattered villages from time to time. I never got bored. We had a few books plus our copy of *Newsweek*. We tore the magazine in half so that we could both read at the same time, something we had never done before, but which seemed ingenious, though I felt it was a bit disrespectful to tear the pages apart. The river was calm, beautiful, and relaxing despite the smell of exhaust and the chug-chugging of the diesel engine.

On the Mekong barge: Patti (lying down), Clark (reading), Mardi (sitting)

Lunch on the barge between Omo boxes and stowed car

On our first evening, the boat pulled over at a river tributary on the Laotian side to tie up for the night. We were able to get off and walk around the village, but the captain told us not to go beyond the first huts. Maybe he was afraid we'd get lost. Or maybe he thought the Pathet Lao villagers might be hostile to us. We were about 235 miles from Hanoi at that point, and about five miles from the Ho Chi Minh trail. It seemed peaceful to me, with small houses made of bamboo slats, perched up on stilts. People seemed interested in us, though not terribly. They didn't stare at us but continued their work as we slowly made our way around the village. One man had finished weaving some cloth; he showed us his loom, demonstrating the way he used it. After a short walk, it was getting dark, so we reluctantly went back to the boat. We snacked on a bit more of our food and then squeezed down in between the boxes on the wood planks in the hold. It had gotten chilly, and I felt a bit sunburned. We wrapped our one sheet around us, huddled together, and tried unsuccessfully to get comfortable on the thin bamboo mat and wood floor, shivering all night.

The second day was a repeat of the first day. The river was calm; the sun was warm. Our food, however, was dwindling. I wrote in my journal, "We're getting a bit hungry. . . . We're down to two of our twelve rolls, a half can of paté, a half bottle of wine, a half box of raisins, and a few bananas. After lunch today, we'll probably have a few raisins left. Dinner is going to be skimpy unless we can stop at Pakxan and buy some rice." In the afternoon of that second day, we did stop in the Laotian town of Pakxan, and we did find fried rice and cookies. Later that afternoon, the men on the boat put their nets into the water and filled up a bucket with fish. They chopped off the fish heads to make soup and ground the remainder of the fish into a mash to which they added some herbs. They invited us to share their dinner, which we did. Though it wasn't cooked, the fish mash tasted pretty good with sticky rice and vegetables.

While lounging on the roof that day, we saw American B-52 bombers flying overhead in the direction of Vietnam. We didn't know which air base they had left from, but since we had heard that there weren't any U.S. military airplanes based in Laos, we assumed they were coming from Thailand.[2] From our reading of newspapers and magazines, though, it seemed that the U.S. military was not sending bombers over northern Vietnam. Why,

---

2   Apparently, there were no regular American ground troops involved in Laos in 1967, but the CIA under the direction of U.S. Ambassador William Sullivan was conducting military operations. President Lyndon Johnson had authorized the ambassador to manage and conduct military operations that included U.S. military aircraft and personnel, but no U.S. military could be involved in decisions about their use. According to the CIA, Ambassador Sullivan insisted on an efficient, closely controlled country team. The *Washington Post*, in an October 22, 2013, article reporting on Sullivan's death, quotes former Assistant Secretary of State William Bundy as saying, "There wasn't a bag of rice dropped in Laos that he didn't know about." Our talk with Don about the USAID effort to drop food to Hmong tribes was consistent with this report.

then, were they over our heads at that point where we were on the border of Laos and close to the northern part of Vietnam? It was disturbing, to say the least. It was clear that we didn't know what was going on with the military in Vietnam or in Laos: what we were seeing from the Mekong River did not coincide with what we were reading.

The second night on our riverboat, we again docked at a small village. And again, Mick and I got off the boat and wandered around. We walked up to a small bamboo hut where a family was sitting outside. They gave us friendly, welcoming smiles, but we didn't share a language, so we wandered on a bit. I wanted to go farther into the jungle, since it looked cool and inviting, but we had been warned that there were tigers and snakes in the area. We didn't see any, and I didn't really think we'd see a tiger, but we decided not to risk it.

Laotian house on Mekong River bank

Laotian family on the bank
of the Mekong River

That night, Mick suggested that we sleep on top of the Omo soap boxes instead of on the floor, as they might be warmer and softer, so we began rearranging the piles of boxes. As we were heaving boxes on top of each other, we found some gunnysacks tucked in between the boxes. It was a perfect find. We spread them out under our sheet for a tiny bit of softness and more warmth. That night, with Omo soap boxes piled under and around us, over the gunnysacks, under the sheet, next to the stowed car, I wasn't cold.

On the morning of the third day, we finished the rest of our food: a few bananas, some raisins, cookies from the village, and a few sips of wine. The men on the boat offered us more of the fish mash and vegetables from the night before. It still tasted surprisingly good, but then again it may have been because our growling stomachs were ready for anything.

ON THE EVENING of January 16, we got off in Thakhet on the Lao side and said goodbye to our American and Swiss friends on the other boats. They were continuing down the river to Savannakhet, where they would make their way to Angkor Wat in Cambodia. At that time, Thailand had closed its border with Cambodia, so the only way to get to Angkor Wat was through Laos. We were tempted to go with them but had already made plans to go back to Bangkok and take one more trip: up north to Chiang Mai. Angkor Wat would have to wait for another time.

SINCE WE WERE LEAVING the barge on the Laotian side, we had to take a small ferry across the river to the town of Nakhon Phanom in Thailand. There we were immediately thrown into a bustling, noisy scene. What a change from the quiet, lazy river! Nakhon Phanom was the site of a large U.S. Air Force base, and the streets were filled with Americans and lined with an assortment of shops catering to them. Some of the shops even displayed prices written in U.S. dollars. Women who looked like prostitutes hung out on the street. We saw two women hustling two young Americans, who followed them into a house in front of us. I was uncomfortable and angry at seeing the effects of this U.S. military base on the town. We found out later that the military installation in Nakhon Phanom was a major air base for the secret war in Laos. The U.S. Air Force, along with Air America, operated out of this base, using it for strikes in Laos and North Vietnam.[3]

---

3   Robert Kaylor, writing in the *Washington Post* on September 25, 1968 ("The Secret Is Out: The U.S. Base Isn't Secret Anymore"), states that the U.S. base at Nakhon Phanom was the only one of the seven U.S. bases in Thailand that was "cloaked in secrecy." He reports that a U.S. official, when asked about the mission, responded, "No comment," but that some U.S. officials did say that American pilots would fly armed missions over Laos when the Laotian government requested it. The pilots were allowed to shoot back if they were fired upon. However, there had never been any official admission that U.S. planes were providing support for ground troops in Laos.

We spent one night at a hotel in Nakhon Phanom and the next day got on an early bus back to Bangkok. We were lucky to get the two front seats so that we could see the road ahead. For the first several hours, to the town of Ban Phai, we were on a dusty dirt road. From there to Bangkok the road was paved; we were told it was called "Friendship Highway," as it was paid for by U.S. funds. As soon as we hit the paved highway, our bus driver sped up. He roared up to another bus and tried to pass, then continued this "game" all the way back to Bangkok. He would attempt to pass another bus or truck. The other driver would also speed up, and the two vehicles would be barreling down the highway at up to 80 miles per hour, neck and neck, even around curves. Sometimes we passed the other vehicle, and sometimes our driver pulled back. I held on to my seat, fearful the whole time.

Once in Bangkok, it was a relief to have our own apartment to go to. We lolled around, washed clothes, read, and wrote letters, and most of all relished our garden breakfasts with fresh fruit and our afternoon tea and sweets. But we didn't stay long. After two nights, we left for Chiang Mai, since we had only one more week before the start of the new class term. We knew we wouldn't be able to travel much again for the next two months.

Chiang Mai and the Karen Hill Tribe

ON JANUARY 19, WE caught the 4 a.m. bus north to Chiang Mai. This driver was just like the one who drove from Nakhon Phanom. He wove in and out of traffic, passing cars and buses on narrow curves. Again, I held my breath.

At the Friendship Hotel in Chiang Mai, we were somewhat—but not too—surprised to meet the same Swiss couple that we had seen in Pakistan, in India, and at the Thai Song Greet Hotel in Bangkok. Of course, we decided to travel together in the area. The next day, at the Hill Tribe Center at Chiang Mai University, we talked to a man named Mr. Hinton who told us about a trail up to the Karen tribal village of Ban Falong near the town of Chom Thom. It wasn't far, he said. We could stay overnight there.

Two days later, we four left early in the morning on the bus for Chom Thom. Once there, at 9:30 a.m., we began our hike up the trail. After three hours of hiking and a refreshing half-hour stop by a cool flowing stream for a pomelo and rolls, we arrived at the mission run by Father Suigonette, a French missionary. He invited us to spend the night, since the next tribal village was farther than we had expected. I slept soundly that night in his bamboo hut, lulled by a light rustle of wind on the thatched roof, feeling the softness of bamboo slats under me.

House on the hike to a Karen village

Father Suigonette told us that he had come there 15 years earlier after having spent three years in China. He started the missionary school with about 10 boys from the Karen hill tribe, but now he had 150 boys and girls in the school. Some of them came from five or six days' walk away. They would stay at the school for four months, go home for two months to help with planting, and then return for another four months. A few of them would come back for another year, but rarely did they stay more than two years. The priest said that they had few visitors, maybe only once every six months, so they were very excited to see us. Most of the children had never seen any foreigners besides the priest and nuns.

We learned that the children were usually around 10 years old when they first came to school. The priest said that they would come with no discipline, but very quickly they adapted to the strict schedule enforced by the three Spanish sisters, the Karen teachers, and him. There was no written Karen language, so he was teaching the children to read and write using a Romanized alphabet version that he had devised. Besides school subjects, the girls were taught to sew. They also had to cut and comb their hair and keep their white dresses clean. He didn't say whether the boys had similar housekeeping tasks. He told us that the boys were often named for whatever significant event happened at their birth. Some of their names were "Father in the Woods," "Uncle Came to Visit," and "Rice Supply Is Low." The girls were more likely named after the moon or flowers.

On the weekends, the children had free time for several hours, so most of the boys would go into the woods to fish or catch frogs and crabs. The priest said they often brought in snakes, and once, a gibbon. Usually, the animals in the woods were not dangerous, he said, but recently a girl who had been bitten by a snake died. The family had reverently placed her body in a chair so that people could say goodbye to her.

On the day we were there, the children came back from the woods with sacks full of little frogs and fish. Some of the frogs were as small as about one inch, but most were bigger. Immediately the boys killed the frogs by either pressing their thumbs into the frogs until the skin broke with a *pop* or by twisting the frogs until they died. The children didn't seem to be doing this as play or as torture; it just seemed to be the easiest way to kill the animals. Once the frogs were dead, the boys cut into their stomachs, pulled out the innards, and pounded the frogs between two rocks to crush the bones. Then they cooked the little animals in tin cans over the fire. When lunch was called, the boys brought their whole cooked frogs to mix with their rice. All quite interesting! The priest said that the children gained a lot of weight quickly at the mission, and their health improved considerably. Before coming there, they had rarely eaten more than rice and chili peppers.

At the Karen mission, women wove their traditional blouses: black cotton with red embroidery. They said they would sell their blouses for $3, so I chose one that was beautifully designed: flowers of red and yellow, each one encircled by tiny white oblong shells. While I was with the women, the men took Mick aside to show him the flintlock rifles they used for shooting small birds and mammals. They said he could try shooting, so he aimed for some little animal but missed. That was the first (and last) time that he used a flintlock rifle.

Karen family

Karen woman weaving, with child

The next day, we decided not to hike up to the next village but instead hike back to Chom Thom and return to Chiang Mai, where we stayed for two more nights. Being in Chiang Mai was delightful, like being in a mountain resort with its fertile valley surrounded by jungles and mountains. Before leaving the area, we spent a night at the sacred temple of Wat Suthep.

DURING THESE TRIPS in Thailand, we reminded ourselves about how much we were enjoying taking short trips such as this. We would begin with an end goal or a general direction, but without much of a plan as to how to get there. We didn't have to worry about missing a bus or being late, since we didn't make any reservations. That left us flexible enough to take advantage of new information about local sites and places to go. Of course, in Thailand, part of the enjoyment came because we knew we had an apartment to go back to between short trips. It was a low-key, comfortable, inexpensive, and easy way to travel, and after almost two years on the road, we had honed our travel skills to a T.

Bangkok International School

BACK IN BANGKOK on January 25, I contacted the International School. They already had my California state teaching credential, since I had signed up as a substitute teacher before leaving for Vientiane. The school had an enrollment of 3,500 kids, grades 1–12, comprising about 75 different nationalities. Since English was the medium of instruction, I had told them that I could teach any subject or level, as well as academic classes for English as a foreign language. Our apartment was only about a 15-minute walk away, so it would be quick to get to the school. Mick also signed up for substitute teaching, as his University of Maryland class was only on Monday and Wednesday evenings, and his junior college credential included high school teaching. After signing up as substitutes, we bought an alarm clock. We didn't have a telephone in our room, but the landlady said that she would let us know if we had any calls. For the next several days, we woke up early, waiting for a phone call, but none came. It was both a disappointment and a relief.

ONE MORNING, WE WENT to a performance on the lawn of the Orient Hotel. I was looking forward to this production, as well as seeing the hotel. When we got there, I enjoyed wandering around the lobby, gawking at the décor. But while watching the lawn show, something felt amiss. The sweet aroma of tropical flowers was intoxicating, and the colorful costumes, dances, Thai boxing, fencing, and music were all fascinating and beautifully performed. But I felt removed from Thailand. The show seemed canned, and many people in the audience seemed more interested in taking pictures than watching the performers. I also realized this was the first time in our travels that we had attended a truly tourist event, one designed for the guests of this expensive hotel. Clearly, it was the opposite of the Thai Song Greet Hotel, and though I didn't like sleeping at the Thai Song Greet, I was much more comfortable being there than on the lawn of the Orient Hotel.

MICK BEGAN HIS UNIVERSITY of Maryland sociology class at the Air Force base on Monday, January 30, and the next Thursday, February 2, I was finally called in to substitute-teach. It was for high school trigonometry and algebra classes at the International High School. Since I had never taken trig and couldn't remember much about algebra, I walked to the school with some trepidation. My fears were not ungrounded: it turned out to be much worse than I had thought. The teachers had not left much in the way of lesson plans, and the kids reminded me of the high school students portrayed in the 1955 film *Blackboard Jungle*. In the trig class, I began by calling the roll, but the students kept laughing, calling themselves different names and making smart aleck remarks. I had to ask them what page they were on in the book, and they gave me different answers. Finally, I called on one of the boys who seemed to be listening to me, asking him to put some problems on the board. Then I asked the students to critique the math. That seemed to work. I managed to get through the morning.

At the break that first day, I saw one of the math teachers in the teachers' room and asked him if he could help me explain some of the math problems. This teacher, Clem Crow, had been teaching math for a while there. He laughed but calmly and clearly answered my questions, and was casual and fun to talk to. He said that I should let the kids figure out the problems themselves. That sounded fine, especially since I couldn't do all the problems myself anyway, but I knew that the students needed a lot of help. Many were quite confused about how to do the math. I think they had had too many substitute teachers, and maybe many of them were like me: not math teachers. That afternoon, though, my algebra classes went much better, and by the last period of the day, I was actually enjoying it. The principal asked me to come back the next day. The unexpected positive aspect of that day was meeting Clem. We continued to develop a strong friendship with Clem and his wife, Evelyn, during our stay in Thailand.

When I got home after that first day of teaching, I was surprised to hear Mick say that I had been called that afternoon to substitute in a fifth-grade class for the next day, but since I was already teaching, they asked Mick if he would come. He agreed, so the next day, I went back to the high school to teach math again, and Mick set out to teach fifth grade. It was quite a reversal, since I had had experience teaching elementary school and Mick had a credential for high school. But both of us got through the day without major problems.

After those first two days of teaching, we didn't get any more calls for a week. Since the telephone was downstairs in the landlady's part of the house, someone else would have to answer the phone. I woke up every day waiting for the landlady to tell us we had a call.

Excerpt of letter to my parents. Bangkok, Thailand. February 6, 1967:

Dear Daddy and Mom,

I have had my name in on the substitute list for a week—and no calls. Today I found out that the elementary school secretary had called me twice and no one has answered the phone. Really disconcerting. I guess I'll have to speak to the landlady again and explain how important it is for the servants to answer the phone. Or else we'll have to get up at 6 a.m. and sit by the phone.

Love,

Patti

After I explained our situation to our landlady, we both continued to get called almost every day. In the morning, the phone would ring, and the school secretary would ask one of us to come in, so either Mick or I would leave, not knowing whether the other person would be called. Generally, though, I taught in the elementary school (grades 3, 4, 5, and 6) and high school English. After teaching for about six weeks, I found that I liked fifth-grade English the best. Mick usually taught in the high school (history, social studies, science, geometry, English, U.S. government).

It was hard to deal with the students in the International High School; they were under a lot of pressure. Since Bangkok was the "rest and relaxation" (R and R) site for the U.S. military in Southeast Asia, most of the students, as well as many of the teachers, were from military families. When I went into one of my first classes in the elementary school and called a name on the roll sheet, one of the kids answered, "She's not here. Her dad got shot and she left." Similar responses continued as I called the roll. In fact, I had been called in as a substitute for that class because the regular teacher's husband had just been killed. The students knew that. They lived with it every day.

Though I was affected by the nearness of death that pervaded the atmosphere of the school, our time in the classrooms was not completely upsetting for either of us. We did have some fun and some surprises. One morning when I was in a third-grade class teaching arithmetic, Mick walked in with a big grin on his face and sat down quietly in one of the little chairs at the back. He stayed for about 20 minutes, just watching me. I was surprised and pleased, but it was hard to keep my mind on my teaching; I felt like I was performing for him. We didn't talk, but we exchanged glances, as though we had some secret between us. Later that afternoon, he told me that he had been on his break from teaching a high school class, so he thought he'd surprise me. He did. It was playful and fun.

On another day, a second-grade teacher was needed, but I had already been called to teach seventh grade. Mick said he would go to the second grade instead of me, even though he had never taught primary grades. At my break I walked into his class to see how he was doing. I found him sitting on a tiny chair, struggling with how to handle this classroom of little kids. They were crowded around him. He told me later that when he was trying to teach one group in a reading circle, a little girl came up to him and asked to go to the bathroom. He told her to wait. She stood there, and few minutes later she pulled on his shirt, saying that she didn't need to go to the bathroom anymore. He looked up and saw a little puddle on the floor where she was standing. Mick felt miserable but probably not as bad as the little girl felt. In a letter describing this day, he wrote, "All I saw were little people moving around the room, having to go to the bathroom, needing their pencils sharpened, crying, and always getting in my way. I felt like Gulliver." After this day of substituting in elementary school, Mick was more and more convinced that community college teaching was the career for him.

AS I WAS WALKING home from teaching one day, I noticed a man sitting by the side of the road with some items for sale spread out in front of him on a blanket. He motioned for me to come over, so I crossed the street to see what he had for sale. I was standing above him, looking down over the items, when I noticed his crossed legs. My eyes were glued to his rough-looking feet and toes, and I wondered if he had ever worn shoes, as his feet were so splayed out. In the middle of my reverie about his feet, I suddenly realized that the man had not been pointing to his toes; he was pointing to his penis, sticking right up near his toes. I hadn't even noticed it. But as I realized that he thought I was staring at—or maybe even admiring—his penis, I was thoroughly embarrassed. I quickly left and continued my walk home, upset at myself and feeling used. How could I not have realized what he was doing?

MICK HAD HIS 28TH birthday on February 7. I had a pair of pants and a tailored shirt made for him. All his other clothes were either too worn out or too big, given how much weight he had lost. He looked pretty snazzy in these new clothes. His mom sent him a much-appreciated gift of $20, so we went out to dinner at Nick's Number One restaurant, purported to be the best restaurant in Bangkok. It was housed in a gorgeous old wooden building that was supposed to be haunted. We thoroughly enjoyed the food and the atmosphere. No ghosts appeared.

BANGKOK TURNED OUT to be an R and R place for us as well as for the U.S. military. Despite being busy with teaching, we visited all the major wats, took a *klong* (canal) trip to the floating market in Thonburi, and bought souvenirs. We took advantage of nightlife activities by going to movies, concerts, and plays. We also got caught up on health issues by getting cholera shots, malaria tablets, and birth control pills. I was enjoying reading the new book *Tales from Siam*. We prepared for upcoming travel by getting visas for Hong Kong, and books and maps for East Asia. And we took care of personal feel-good items: I got my hair cut, we had clothes made, and we bought special treats such as ice cream and instant brownie mix. We also continued to meet other travelers, including a woman whom we had first met in Turkey six months before. We often went out to dinners and parties. It was a satisfying feeling over those three months in Thailand to have so many friends and to be socially as well as professionally active.

Along the *klong* in Thonburi, Bangkok.

ONE AFTERNOON, I HAD a serendipitous call from Clarke Straughan, another itinerant traveler who was then working as a hotel manager in Bangkok. He had been asked to pose for a *Sunset* magazine advertisement but also needed a woman in the photographs. I agreed to be that person, so on the designated afternoon a photographer took about 60 black-and-white photos of Clarke and me at one of the temples, posing as tourists while "nonchalantly" holding a copy of the magazine. We were each paid

Posing for the magazine ad

$15, given copies of the photos, and told that the advertisement would be in the October edition. The next fall, I looked for it for several months, as did my parents, but we never saw it.

We took only one more trip outside of Bangkok, a three-hour bus ride south to the beach at Pattaya. That night we spread our sheets out on the sand and slept peacefully under the stars. The next day we joined a group of scuba divers on a trip to an island about an hour out into the Bay of Siam. Snorkeling in that warm, clear water was like swimming in a tropical aquarium with spectacular coral and fish of all sizes and colors. I was entranced!

AT THE END OF our three months in Bangkok, the money we had made by teaching added up nicely. By the end of March, we had about a thousand dollars, $600 of which was from substitute teaching. We now had enough to buy boat tickets for upcoming travel, pay our Bangkok rent, buy a bronze teak flatware set, and still have enough money for the rest of our travel throughout Asia.

As we began to pack, we knew that we still had too much to carry. We would need to be as light as possible, as we'd be moving between ships, buses, and trains from now on. Fortunately, because of Mick's teaching, we again were able to use the military APO system. We sent almost everything we were carrying back to the U.S., including Mick's duffel bag, his attaché case, my little green suitcase, and even our sleeping bags and other camping gear. To take their place, I bought a cheap plastic hand satchel with a zipper top that was small and easy to carry. We were now down to this small satchel, my shoulder bag, and two open-topped basket-bags between us, a far cry from the trunk and assortment of suitcases that we had started with in 1965. We were traveling with only a few changes of clothes that we could wash out each night. It felt good.

From the travelers' grapevine we had heard that the French shipping line Messageries Maritimes was the cheapest way to get around Southeast Asia and that one of their ships, the SS *Vietnam,* would be sailing from

Singapore on April 13. The tickets were only $67 each for the 11-day trip from Singapore to Hong Kong, but for this price we would have to sleep in different four-berth cabins. Neither of us liked this idea of splitting up, but the low cost won out over our desire to sleep together. We also bought tickets from Hong Kong to Taiwan on the China Navigation Line. From there we were sure we'd find another ship to Japan. The final leg of our two-year journey would be on either the SS *President Cleveland* or the SS *President Wilson* from Japan to San Francisco. One of these sister ships would set sail on July 5, arriving in S.F. on July 17. It felt both strange and exciting to have a final date for our return to the U.S. We wrote to our parents, giving them our next mail pickup address: Thomas Cook & Son in Hong Kong.

AS WE WERE ARRANGING to leave Bangkok, we were delighted to find out that Clem and Evelyn Crow were also planning to leave at about the same time and that they, like us, were heading south through Malaysia to Singapore. We all decided that it would be great fun to meet again, so we agreed to go to the White House Hotel in Singapore and look for each other there some time after a week or two. Of course, there was no way to get in touch with each other while traveling, and the chances of being there at the same time were slim.

20.

Hitchhiking in Malaysia

When we bought our third-class train tickets from Bangkok to the Malaysian border, we didn't know that we'd be sitting on a wooden bench all day and night. The bench was hard, and it seemed to become harder as the day went on. The night was worse. We tried to lean on each other to get comfortable, but sleep was impossible. The straight-up bench back left no possible way to curl up. And then, when the train finally stopped at our destination, we weren't even at the Malaysian border. We had to get off the train in the town of Haad Yai in Thailand and buy another ticket to the border. From then on, though, things looked up. The Malaysian train had soft reclining seats and was not crowded. As we traveled south, we noticed the countryside beginning to change. We passed lush green cultivated fields; we saw more cars and paved roads than we had seen in Thailand.

Penang Island, then a member state of Malaysia and a free port, was the place to hang out. It was easily accessible by ferry, and we had heard that it had perfect weather with white sand beaches, palm trees, and local people who accepted travelers wandering through. We could hardly wait to get there. A Malay teacher we met on the train, who was also going to Penang, was friendly and talkative. He said that Malaysia was a diverse country, with Malays, Chinese, and Indians making up most of the population. Families could choose either an English, Malay, Chinese, or Islamic school for their children; the schools were all free. This teacher said he would like to show us around his home island of Penang, and he suggested we stay at the Singapore Hotel.

We followed the teacher's suggestion. The Singapore Hotel was perfect, not fancy but clean (though noisy) and cheap. It was only late afternoon, but we were exhausted from lack of sleep on the train. We had barely enough energy to check into the room and eat dinner. But we did manage to wash our clothes in the way that soon became a nightly ritual. The process was easy: get into the shower with dirty clothes in hand, stomp on them while soaping up, rinse them while showering, then wring out the clothes thoroughly and drape them over the clothesline that we had strung across the room. The joy that night was being able to stretch out fully on a bed, despite lying under drying clothes that swung like flags hanging overhead. We stayed in Penang for four nights, happy to be in a new country, discovering a new place.

The next morning, the teacher from the train showed up at our hotel to take us around the city. We were pleasantly surprised that he came. The more we talked to him, the more we learned about Malaysia: about the political system, the ethnic conflicts, and the recent successes and advancements of the government. He kept reminding us that these were only his opinions, that he was only one person, and that he didn't represent all of Malaysia. As we were to find out later, there was much more to say about local politics; furthermore, it was not unusual to have this type of refreshing, illuminating conversation in Malaysia.

Journal excerpt. Penang, Malaysia. March 30, 1967:

> *We took a bus trip around the island today—46 miles. It's beautiful—high hills covered with trees, rice fields on the flat lands, beautiful beaches. There are lots of coconut palms and rubber trees. (Malaysia supplies 43% of the world's natural rubber.)*

As a free port, Penang was full of shops selling almost everything. We walked around, swam, relaxed. Penang felt different from Thailand, more cosmopolitan. One of the first things we noticed was language. On buses and in stores we often heard people speaking English. Most of the writing on the billboards was multilingual: English, Malay, Arabic, and Chinese. It was nice to see mosques again, after having gotten used to seeing Buddhist temples in Thailand. We had fun guessing the ethnicities of people by looking at their clothes and listening to them speak. People wearing knee-length dresses with ankle-length skirts underneath were probably Malay, those wearing slacks and blouses seemed to be Chinese, and Pakistanis or Indians wore knee-length dresses with pants under. Of course, we were only making playful guesses; many people of all ethnicities wore Western clothes.

We were struck by how much cleaner and more organized Penang was compared with Bangkok. We acknowledged the fact that we had only been in Malaysia for a few days and that we were comparing a small island town with a large capital city, but even so, Penang was impressive. After just a few hours, we could easily get around on local buses. The system was clear; the buses left precisely on the minute. More astonishing were the signs inside the buses: "No spitting," "Wait until the bus stops before leaving," and "Only five standing." Throughout our travel of almost two years, we had not seen such prescribed order. In Thailand, as well as in India, people would run and jump onto buses, often hanging out the doors, barely able to keep from falling. Inside the Thai buses, people were so hemmed in that it was impossible to get a breath of fresh air. In comparison, Malaysian public transportation, from what we could see so far, felt organized and comfortable. Maybe it was the effect of British rule, even though the country had been independent for almost 10 years.

It was in Penang that we decided to try hitchhiking. This was the first time in our travels that we had even considered hitchhiking, but here it seemed possible. For one thing, there were private cars on the road and the roads were paved; for another, many people spoke English. In addition, the country seemed safe, and there was a straight highway to Kuala Lumpur (KL), 250 miles away. My main hesitation was how to begin. I was too embarrassed to stand on the road with my thumb out, so we decided to wait at the Penang customs shed. All cars had to stop there before getting on the ferry, so maybe we could ask people for rides when they were stopped. We walked to the customs shed, where an officer approached us, asking where we were going. We said that we hoped to get a ride to Kuala Lumpur. The officer nodded politely and then proceeded to ask all the cars that came through to help us out. At this, I was even more embarrassed. We stood there by the customs shed looking at the cars, with the drivers looking us over, most of them driving right on. Finally, two Indians said they would take us to Taiping. It was only about 50 miles away, but it was a start. We were glad to be out of the limelight at the customs shed, but also thankful that the officer had helped us.

From the moment we entered the car, the driver and his companion began talking animatedly about the teachers' strike, which turned out to be a fascinating corollary to our conversation with the Malay teacher a few days before. I wondered why the teacher hadn't mentioned it; maybe the teachers in Penang weren't on strike. At any rate, though we didn't comprehend all the details, it was clear that the teachers' union was immersed in a strike against the government. Our driver said that most Indians strongly supported the strike; they felt that Indians weren't getting enough representation from the Malay government. Our 50-mile journey sped by as we learned more about schools and government policies.

The Indians let us out in Taiping, and about 15 minutes later, as I felt a little more comfortable extending my hand out, a truck stopped, picked us up, and took us another 50 miles to the town of Ipoh, the largest tin center in Malaysia. While we rode through gorgeous green countryside on good roads, this truck driver, a Malay who was also clearly involved in local political issues, gave us more information about the teachers' strike, which he supported. When he let us out in Ipoh, a British family picked us up. Again, we had a talkative driver. After driving only a few miles, they said they were stopping at a swimming club, and would we like to join them for a drink? Of course, why not? The man had been in Malaysia for 30 years, and his view of Malaysia differed considerably from those of both the Indians and the Malay truck driver. He was quite happy living there, despite the current economic and political situation. It was clear to us after spending time with the British family that these private clubs and other institutions kept them separated from much of the turmoil that we had been hearing about from the Malays and Indians.

As soon as we got out on the street again, a young couple who said they had seen us at the customs shed in Penang picked us up. They took us all the way to Kuala Lumpur. This ride was the longest and the scariest. The man drove way too fast through the hilly roads. I almost asked him to stop and let us out, especially after we had passed two accidents, but I was too embarrassed to say anything. For one thing, the people seemed kind, and for another thing, we were quite enjoying the conversation. In fact, when we reached KL, they took us to a hotel, the Tai Sun, went in with us, and paid for one night. We kept saying that they didn't need to do that, but they ignored our protests.

After dropping off our few belongings in the room, we walked out to get something to eat and see the neighborhood. I was not impressed with the area, which looked dirty and run-down, but the amusement park looked interesting, so we walked in. Not many people were around outside, but there were noises coming from one building. Not knowing what to expect, we entered and found ourselves at the opening of a Chinese opera.

Journal excerpt. Kuala Lumpur. March 3, 1967:

> *It was quite fascinating—completely alien to our idea of a show. The costumes were magnificent, though. There wasn't much action, but what action there was was very graceful. They spoke in very high shrill voices against a loud background of shrilly instruments. Their faces were painted wonderfully in their opera masks. The stage was so colorful and busy. There wasn't a space left blank. Everything was colored in bright reds, yellows, pinks. There was a funny stagehand who sauntered out every so often to move a chair or table. He had a T-shirt on and a cigarette hanging out of his mouth—very out of place among the brightly dressed actors singing on the stage. All during the show, the audience was quite enthralled, and very noisy. Half the time they were laughing and yelling themselves, along with the shrill voice and tinny instruments. I think it was all very "Chinese-y."*

We weren't anxious to return to the Tai Sun Hotel, since it hadn't looked very clean on first glance. In fact, we wouldn't have stayed there if the room hadn't already been paid for. It was obvious that the sheets on the bed had been slept in. I asked for clean linens, even though we were still carrying our own sheet. After tossing and turning for what seemed like hours, I finally fell asleep but was awakened by more noise than I had ever heard in a hotel. Someone had turned on the lights full blast, and since the paper-thin walls went up only two-thirds of the way to the ceiling, the lights shone in every room. It sounded like someone was throwing water on the floors and scrubbing them while loudly talking and laughing. Furthermore, the people seemed to be wearing wooden shoes that made a loud *clop-clop-clop* sound with every step on the wood floor. Not only was all this noise inside the hotel, but the hotel itself was located on a busy intersection with trucks, buses, and cars honking all night. We left early in the morning.

WE WERE STILL REELING from our first foray into hitchhiking in Malaysia. In three days, we had learned more about local politics, the educational system, and ethnic differences than in three months of living in Thailand. I didn't know if it was because we were hitching or because people were more involved in local politics, or if this was a particularly divisive and engaging time in Malaysia. Maybe those who picked us up were more outgoing and more ready to talk. Maybe the biggest reason, though, was language. We were in a multilingual country with English as a major language, so we could have fluent conversations with most people. Whatever the reasons, our first 250-mile foray into hitchhiking was positive; we were ready to continue after KL despite the one scary driver.

In KL we had people to meet: the Brodies. My mother had sent me their names and suggested we look them up. The Brodies invited us to stay with them, so we stayed two more nights in Kuala Lumpur. They took us to see tin mines, rubber plantations, a new university, and the national mosque. Mr. Brodie had been with the British government in KL and had stayed on after the British left. His wife was Chinese. Their daughter, then about 18 or 19, had a date the first night we were there. When her boyfriend came to pick her up, Mr. Brodie joked to Mick that he didn't know whether to worry more if the boys came or if they didn't come.

From the Brodies we were able to get a clearer understanding of the school strike. The main issue was that the government was establishing Malay as the national language, so now school subjects must be taught in Malay instead of English. Since at least half of the population did not speak Malay, there was much resentment. The switch to Malay was causing additional problems because there were not enough textbooks written in Malay. There was a scramble to write appropriate texts for all levels of education. New words in Malay were being coined or borrowed in order to bring in modern concepts. One of the people we talked to in KL was a Chinese teacher who was working with the teachers' union against the new curriculum. He told us that government investigators said that if he didn't stop his activities, he would be sent to jail. The Malay government had all the power.

The Brodies told us that the Malaysian constitution gave preferential treatment to the Malays, most of whom were Muslim. The Chinese and Indians were angry that government funds were being used to build national mosques. The Brodies also said that there was a clear social hierarchy. The Malays were on top, the numerous and wealthy Chinese were next, the Indians were third, and smaller diverse groups such as Filipinos were at the bottom. The British, he said, many of whom had stayed in Malaysia as plantation superintendents, kept themselves apart from the other ethnic groups through their clubs and associations. The Chinese, though not having the highest social position, were increasingly gaining economic power. The Chinese and the Indians together controlled most of the wealth, but the Chinese also sent a considerable amount of money back to China, thereby angering the Malays. After hearing so much, I felt like the social and political situation in Malaysia was a tinderbox about to ignite.

After two days enjoying the generosity of the Brodies, we were anxious to move on. We had already decided to continue hitchhiking, since it had worked out so well from Penang. We hoped that again we would meet and learn from a variety of people.

WE LEFT KL on April 5 for the 250-mile trip to Singapore. This time I felt comfortable flagging down cars, and fairly quickly a truck driver stopped for us. He was going to Malacca, which was a bit off the main highway, but the driver persuaded us to go with him when he said that Malacca was a beautiful town on the coast with an ancient Dutch history and a canal running through it. It sounded good; we could see another part of Malaysia. We got to Malacca that night, stayed at the International Hotel, and spent the evening walking around town.

Canal in Malacca, Malaysia

The next day, we got a ride with another truck driver, one that took us directly into Johor Bahru, the town right across the causeway from Singapore. We walked across the causeway and got a bus to the White House Hotel, where we stayed for a week.

21.

Singapore and the SS *Vietnam*

Singapore was a large flourishing cosmopolitan city with an impressive harbor full of ships. It had been an independent country for only two years, having seceded from Malaysia in 1965. We heard that the island was about 80 percent Chinese, but many British were still living there, and English was commonly spoken. The shops, many run by Indians and Chinese, were loaded with goods, and there were moneychangers everywhere. The first night, beckoned by the twinkling lights strung around, we walked to the night market, where we were overwhelmed by spicy aromas, sizzling popping sounds, and hot glowing woks. We traipsed from vendor to vendor, tasting a bit here and a bit there, not always sure of what we were eating but loving every moment.

Singapore, view from our hotel

Singapore street

One of the tasks we had planned for Singapore was to get visas for Taiwan. We had already bought tickets for a ship leaving from Hong Kong for Taiwan, but to our dismay we found that there was no Taiwanese embassy in Singapore. We would have to wait until we got to Hong Kong for our visas.

AFTER WE HAD BEEN at the White House Hotel for a couple of nights, who should walk in but Clem and Evelyn Crow. They got the room right next to ours, and we spent the next several days telling travel stories, laughing, walking through neighborhoods, and eating together. Though we had met them for the first time in Bangkok, it was surprising that we hadn't met them before, since our lives seemed to be on the same trajectory. They were married the same summer we were, they left the U.S. on an ocean liner for Europe like we did, and they had been traveling from Europe to Asia during the previous year and a half like we had. People even said that Evie and I looked alike.

Clem, Evelyn, Patti, Mick

One of the people we looked up in Singapore was Mr. Leong, a friend of Peter's, whom we had met in Peshawar six months earlier. The first thing Mr. Leong and his wife did was to take us out to a Chinese lunch that included 13 small courses. It was the most delicious Chinese food I had ever eaten. We also realized how much we had been overpaying for food. Mr. Leong was taken aback when we told him the prices we had been quoted.

Mr. Leong told us that he was a producer's agent, and he explained in detail some of the inside dealings that would take place in Singapore. He said that every day, approximately 60 or 80 boats smuggled goods into the harbor from Indonesia, often copra (from coconuts), rubber, and pepper. This amounted to about $1 million daily. The Singapore authorities not only offered protection to these people but also had special wharves and trucks to accommodate the goods that were brought in. The smugglers would also take Singapore goods back to Indonesia for about 300 percent profit. The U.S. supplied the Indonesian authorities with fast, efficient boats to help stop the trade, but that didn't prevent it. Mr. Leong said that the Indonesians would take a 20 percent cut of the profits and let the smugglers go.

On a related topic, Mr. Leong said he used to trade with mainland China, but now he was getting U.S. contracts, so he was forced to stop all negotiations with China. If he continued business with China, the U.S. wouldn't give him any work. He added that the Chinese in Singapore were quite restricted in their travel. Only those having nonessential jobs could return to China for a visit, and they had to be at least 45 years old. He complained that all the Southeast Asian countries had legalized discrimination against the Chinese, but still the Chinese controlled more than 50 percent of the capital in these countries. He was quite adamant that things would have to change.

AS WE SAID OUR goodbyes to Clem and Evelyn in Singapore, we were sure that we would see each other again somewhere in the world, sometime. And, in fact, we did. Clem and Evelyn live in Honolulu, where they stopped in 1967 and decided to make it their home. We've seen them several times over the years and have children and grandchildren of similar ages. Not only that, but Mick and Clem ended up with similar careers: community college teaching.

SS *Vietnam*

THE SS *VIETNAM*, BOUND for Hong Kong, would take 11 days, with brief stops in Bangkok and Manila. I didn't expect the ship to be very deluxe, and it wasn't. It had three classes: first, tourist, and economy. Our economy class tickets meant that I had to sleep in a women's cabin and Mick in a men's cabin. I didn't like that, but at least our cabins were right next to each other. I walked into mine, not sure of what to expect. The room was quite tiny and dark, since there was no porthole. Two sets of bunk beds were lined up along one wall. The space between the beds and the other wall was barely enough to turn around in, but against that wall was a small sink with a mirror and a tiny toilet room. I put my few belongings up on the empty top bunk.

Later I met my bunkmates: three Chinese women, who spoke continuously among themselves, mostly in Chinese, and rarely to me. One of the women, as I was to find out soon, would clear her throat every morning with a loud gurgle. Mick could even hear it through the wall. I tucked my pillow around my ears to try to block out the sound. In contrast to my bunkmates, Mick had only one—a quiet Malaysian student going to study in Tokyo. I wished I could sneak into his room.

I had hoped that I could pass the time lounging on the deck with a good book, but that wasn't the case. There were very few places we could relax. The only deck we could go to was cluttered with booms, cables, and ropes. There was a dining room, where we could play checkers, but only between meals during the day. At night sometimes dances or movies were held there. The dining room served regular meals, family-style, but the most we could say about them was that they were substantial. On the upside, there was a delightful international mix of passengers on the ship. Most were Asian (Japanese, Chinese, Malay, Filipino, Indian, Pakistani), and there were a few Europeans (Danish, English, French, Italian, German), some Australians and New Zealanders, and a few other Americans. Most were men between about 20 and 35 years old.

I really liked being with this mix of people, many of whom had travel adventures like ours. The person we talked to the most was a Danish engineer who was returning from a difficult year in India. He had been given a grant to assist with engineering projects, but when he got to India, he found that nothing had been prepared for his work, including the required paperwork. It took him a half year just to get the appropriate clearance—in part, he said, because he wouldn't pay the expected bribes. He recounted dismaying stories of poverty, mismanagement, and poor sanitation, but he also brought out the complexities of the issues.

Though Mick's and my life as low-budget itinerant travelers was different from this engineer's life, we had faced similar frustrations with bureaucracy and poverty, especially during the 10 days of travel in India between Kathmandu and Calcutta. Our stress during that period was compounded, since it was the first time we had been without a vehicle and a bed. We had been hungry, tired, and sick. Now, with three months of hindsight and by talking to our Danish friend, we were better able to put our own experiences into a broader context, with more understanding of India as a fascinating multilingual, multiethnic country.

22.

A Day in Manila

After nine days at sea, we docked in Manila. We had one whole day there, from 7 a.m. to 10 p.m. I was especially excited, since it was a return trip for me. Thirteen years earlier, from 1953 to 1954, when I was 12 years old, our family had lived on the campus of the University of the Philippines. As I thought over that year in the Philippines, images came rushing back to me: the juiciness of tree-ripened mangoes, the soft sweetness of fried bananas for breakfast, the delicious feeling of being enveloped in warm humid evening air when stepping out of an air-conditioned theater, the comfort and safety of sleeping under a mosquito net. As we left the ship, I looked forward to sharing more of my memories with Mick.

We used our one day fully. We began the morning by taking the bus about 10 miles outside Manila to the university where I had lived in 1953. Many of the campus buildings that I remembered had been torn down, including the two houses I had lived in and my elementary school. But even with new construction everywhere, I could find my way around. On a whim, I knocked on the door of a house I recognized. I was pretty sure I had been there before, that it was the home of a family that my parents had been friends with. It was, and the family remembered me immediately. We ended up spending three or four hours with them; they served us lunch and drove us around the campus, pointing out all the new buildings. They also warned us to be careful when we returned to the center of the city, since Manila was now quite dangerous; many people they knew had been robbed.

We spent the rest of the day walking around Manila, looking in shops and eating food I had craved. We found sellers of sweet bibingka, crispy lumpia, and spicy *lechon* (pork). The best was when we saw a fruit vendor selling mangoes. We bought 10 and immediately peeled several as we stood on the sidewalk, our hands dripping with sweet juicy nectar. We did see evidence of street gangs, mostly in the form of graffiti, but despite the warnings of danger, I felt safe and happy that day; it more than fulfilled my expectations.

Back on the ship, we learned more about the Philippines from several Filipino fellow passengers. They all corroborated stories we had heard about gangs and robberies in Manila. One man commented that political life was oppressive, that no one could say anything against the government of President Ferdinand Marcos or the U.S. government. Any talk of too much Americanization must be undercover. He added that some duly elected men had not been allowed to be seated in Congress because they had been accused of being communist or anti-government. Another man said that Hukbalahaps (Huks, for short, who came together in 1942 as the military arm of the Communist Party against Japanese occupation) were growing in number and gaining prominence. I was surprised to hear that, since I remembered learning about the Huks when I lived in the Philippines. I thought their rebellion ended in 1954. I wanted to learn more from these men on the ship, but they didn't, or couldn't, elaborate. I didn't have anyone else to ask about Filipino politics.

Journal excerpt. SS *Vietnam*. April 23, 1967:

> *Today is the last day on the ship. We're rather glad. It's not <u>too</u> bad, but eleven days is plenty!*

23.

Hong Kong and the SS *Baikal*

I was eagerly looking forward to a week in Hong Kong. This would be my third time to be in this fascinating city. The first was in summer 1954 when I came with my family after our year in the Philippines. The second was in fall 1961 when I was returning from Taiwan after four months living in Taipei, where my father had another sabbatical teaching year. As we disembarked, I knew exactly where to go—the International Guest House, a perfect place: good location and good price, $2.80/night.

Though we received several newsy letters from home, our first day in Hong Kong was frustrating, to say the least. The main problem was that we couldn't get a visa for Taiwan because our passport indicated that we had been in communist and socialist countries. I wasn't sure what the officials were upset about. Was it that we had been in East Germany and Yugoslavia the previous year? Or was it because of our short visits to Laos and Burma? We were furious; the whole idea seemed ridiculous. The only other way to enter Taiwan, the man in the Tourist Office said, would be to send a cable to someone in Taipei who could cable back a reference for us. There was no way we could do this. Not only did we not know anyone to send a message to, but it might take three or four weeks. We gave up on getting the visa, but we still had our boat tickets on the *Anking* headed for Taipei. We knew we wouldn't be allowed on the ship without visas, so we went to the China Navigation Line office to see if we could get a refund on our tickets. After another frustrating meeting, we finally got the China Navigation Line to refund most of our money; they gave us $51 back, most of the $63 we had spent.

Finally, after still more hours of searching, we found a Russian ship, the SS *Baikal*, that would be leaving for Yokohama the next week, only a day after we had planned to leave anyway. We bought those tickets. At the end of that day, I was exhausted and upset after dealing with government officials. I was also reminded of how much easier it had been to live in our own camper and not have to buy tickets for boats, buses, or trains. How much more relaxing it was when we didn't have to depend on other people's time frames.

WE SPENT THE REST of the week in Hong Kong shopping and sightseeing. On April 29, I wrote in my journal, "Hong Kong seems much the same as when I was here before, but it's ten times more fun with Mick. We have such a wonderful time everywhere."

We had decided to have new clothes made, which entailed finding tailors and arranging for fittings. We also shopped around for the best price for a good camera and ended up buying an Asahi Pentax Spotmatic. We saw a play (Ibsen's *A Doll's House*). We went to the symphony, bought magazines and books, took the tram up Victoria Peak, and visited the village of Aberdeen on Hong Kong Island. We also rode the train through the New Territories, through fields and villages, up to the town of Lo Wu on the Chinese border. At a stop in the market town of Tai Po, we left the train and walked a mile to the next station, passing fishing boats and villages teeming with people. I wanted to keep going. I wanted to walk right into China. We couldn't, of course. American citizens were forbidden by the U.S. government to enter China; the ban was stamped in our passports: THIS PASSPORT IS NOT VALID FOR TRAVEL TO OR IN COMMUNIST CONTROLLED PORTIONS OF CHINA, KOREA, VIET-NAM OR TO OR IN ALBANIA, CUBA.

Hong Kong Island

Sampans in the New Territories

While in Hong Kong, we were aware that China's Cultural Revolution, which had been launched the year before, had made an impact on the city, but I didn't realize the depth of the issues.[4] It was unfortunate for us that Hong Kong was one of the few places we had stayed where we didn't meet any residents who could tell us about their own lives. Mick in his journal, though, did comment on Chairman Mao and the Cultural Revolution.

---

4   A few weeks after we left, in mid-May 1967, there was a large-scale pro-communist labor dispute, referred to as "1967 Uprising" or "1967 Riots" or "1967 Protests." The actions continued for several months by people in sympathy with the Cultural Revolution and against British rule.

Mick's journal excerpt. May 3, 1967:

> *With the last few months, since the "cultural revolution" in China . . .*
> *there have sprung up in Hong Kong a number of Chinese propaganda*
> *stores. These stores have books, papers, articles, and all types of pro-*
> *paganda including Mao buttons, of which I acquired three. . . . People*
> *were always crowded in [the stores] and there were particularly long*
> *lines waiting for more Mao buttons. This Mao fascination appears*
> *to be a personality cult of the first order. What a charismatic symbol*
> *he must be in China, and what a point of solidarity and unity for the*
> *people. I suspect in a worldwide election he would be number two,*
> *trailing only Bobby Kennedy with Nasser a distant third. Interesting*
> *government! In any case, "Mao Speak" appears to be increasing rather*
> *than subsiding as many Americans would hope.*

BEFORE LEAVING HONG KONG, we gave our parents our next address for picking up mail: American Express, Tokyo. I also bought another small satchel to replace the one with holes. I wasn't surprised that it had barely lasted a few months, since I had paid only 80 cents for it. I still preferred a flimsy satchel to a regular suitcase, but I hoped this new one, at $3, would last for at least three months.

WE BOARDED THE RUSSIAN ship SS *Baikal* on May 2, 1967, for the four-day trip to Yokohama. The ship had a huge hammer and sickle on its red smokestack, so we assumed they didn't care that we had been in both socialist and communist countries. The ship could take 250 passengers, but only 50 were on board. We had purchased economy-class tickets but were in for a surprise. The Russian captain, who spoke some English, seemed delighted to meet us. He asked us all sorts of questions about where we had been traveling and living and working. He asked us how long we had been married, and when we said two years, he offered us the honeymoon suite. I didn't feel like we were still having a honeymoon, but I was happy to oblige.

We were given a first-class double room that had a couch and a desk. It was on the top deck, and it had a large picture window overlooking a small, covered promenade deck. We also had the run of the ship, from bow to stern and even the bridge. I loved being on the ocean, especially in this very clean ship with its spacious stateroom. What I liked most was leaning over the very tip of the bow and watching the knife-edge front of the ship slice through the water.

I was surprised, and pleased, at the number of women working on the *Baikal*. On the ships we had previously been aboard, I rarely saw a female crew member. I was also surprised that the women working on the *Baikal* seemed so large, especially after being in Southeast Asia for four months. Though most of the crew members were men who smiled but didn't speak to us, we met one friendly member of the crew who greeted us in English. She said that we were the first Americans she had ever talked to. I was surprised at that until I realized that she was the first Russian woman I had chatted with. The Cold War was in full swing, so it was nice to be able to comfortably talk with "the enemy."

In all the rooms of the ship there was Soviet propaganda: signs, pictures, posters, and literature in several languages showing such topics as the growth of Soviet industry and number of women working. There were free booklets on communism, Marxism, socialism, and freedom. There were movies with subtitles twice a day. One was about the period leading up to the 1917 revolution that was blatantly skewed. I realized, though, that Americans were doing the same thing. At USIS offices all over the world there were brochures, literature, and films about how good America was.

To call the passengers to meals, a snappy little tune blared out of the microphones in every room of the ship. No matter what we were doing, the tune reached us loud and clear, seemingly demanding, "Get up and go to the dining room right now." The tune itself was not bad, but hearing it three times a day for meals and other times for announcements began to be annoying. In fact, both of us continued to hear this tune in our heads for months after we left the ship.

Though I was relaxed and happy to be on this ship, I never got used to the food, especially breakfast. One day we were served seaweed noodle soup and vegetable stew for breakfast. Another morning we had a meat and onion mixture, bean curd soup, assorted seaweeds, and rice dotted with seaweed. And on another day, we had cucumber, tomato, and lettuce salad with slices of salami. I didn't know if this was Russian food or if they were aiming to please the Asian passengers, but it was not what I felt like eating first thing in the morning. Besides breakfast, the other meals were passable, nothing to rave about. As it turned out, we both got a bit sick on the *Baikal,* as did many of the other passengers. It wasn't seasickness. Maybe the food?

SS *Baikal*

24.

Comfort in Japan

Journal excerpt. Tokyo, Japan. May 7, 1967:

We arrived in Yokohama yesterday afternoon and had quite a frantic and frustrating time getting a place to sleep. We finally settled on the YMCA for Mick and the YWCA for me. Together it cost us $7.00. We haven't ever before spent so much in all the time we've traveled. The only other time that comes close to that much was in Calcutta, where we splurged one night and took a fancy tourist hotel for $5.00. Tonight is a bit better—50 cents for each of us. That is what we are used to! We are in the Ichigaya Youth Hostel (which was full last night). Our stay here is restricted to three days, so we'll probably leave Tokyo after three more days.

Today is Sunday . . . and we found several wonderful department stores and had a fascinating time browsing through them. They are better than U.S. department stores. There are several nice Japanese touches, such as a lady standing by each entrance bowing at all incoming people, a lady standing at the foot of the escalators wiping the handrail [with her white glove], bowing and saying something (it sounded good!), and such extras as playgrounds for children; wonderful restaurants, snack bars, and tea corners; art exhibitions; and of course wonderful things to buy. We found one basement floor containing "Round-the-World" snack bars. Germany, Italy, China, United

*States, and Japan were represented with pictures from one major city
and light lunch food from each country. It was all so clever and appe-
tizing! We couldn't help but sample different foods. I'm pretty excited
about our two forthcoming months in Japan and Korea.*

ON OUR SECOND DAY at the Ichigaya Youth Hostel we struck up a conversation with Fumiaki, a young man about our age. As I was thinking about
how much I liked talking to him, I was surprised, and pleased, to hear him
invite us to join him in Yokohama the next day for the Port Festival. We
had been planning to leave Tokyo anyway, so this sounded perfect. We took
the train, meeting Fumiaki at the Yokohama station; he took us downtown
to watch the parade. Much of it was like American parades, but I was especially intrigued with the float that showcased old costumes from the time
of the opening of the port to foreign trade in 1859. I was also impressed
that the parade began right on time, unlike so many U.S. parades. It began
to feel like *everything* in Japan was well organized and orderly.

After the parade, we had a frantic time trying to find a hotel. Fumiaki
called every hotel he knew, but they were all full. Just when we had given
up and decided to take the train back to Tokyo, Fumiaki called his mother
and told her that he was bringing two foreign guests home. We found out
later that she was anxious and worried, since she had never had foreign
guests before, but for us it was a stroke of luck. We were getting a chance
to stay in a Japanese home. We did not know then how much we would
enjoy that evening, nor did we realize how much we needed to learn about
Japanese culture.

The Satos' apartment was small and traditional, with tatami mats,
shoji screens, sliding doors and windows, and low tables and cushions. It
was exactly how I imagined it would look. When we arrived, Mrs. Sato
presented us with kimonos to wear that evening; she said she wanted us
to be comfortable. I was certainly comfortable wearing a kimono, but that
evening as we sat in the living room, I wasn't sure what to expect or how to

be polite. We talked to Fumiaki, but I felt awkward, knowing that he had just sprung our visit on his mother. At about 10 p.m., just when I thought it was time to go to bed, Mrs. Sato brought out basins, soap, and towels, telling us that we would go with them to have a bath.

Under the evening moon, we followed Mr. and Mrs. Sato and Fumiaki down the quiet, narrow, dimly lit street to the public bath. Fumiaki told us that his parents had decided that we should go quite late to the bath since they were worried that people would stare at us. Was the late timing for our benefit or theirs? I didn't know, but certainly they were being polite. As we entered, we saw a single screen about eight feet high separating the women's and men's parts of the bath. A female cashier sat at the end of the screen within view of both sides of the bath, though in such a way that we could not see into the other side. The cashier was joking and talking to the men on their side, and then turning to talk with women on the other side. It all seemed so strange to me. I guess the cashier did not "count" in terms of looking at naked men. Or maybe the men had towels on at that point. For whatever reason, there was certainly a lot of laughter and a jolly atmosphere.

I entered the wash area with Fumiaki's mother. She didn't speak English, so I followed what she did. The bath wash area was wonderfully hot and steamy. There were several small waterspouts on the floor for washing and three hot pools at one end. A constant flow of water cascaded into the pools over perfectly positioned rocks. I felt at ease. Everything was clean and pleasant. We sat and soaked in the almost-too-hot water and then stepped onto an outdoor balcony where we could dry off in the night air while gazing at trees, bushes, and a little brook. I could go to baths like this every day. When we returned to the apartment, our beds, made of thick futons and soft quilts, had been rolled out on the floor. It was luxurious. That day had been way more enjoyable, way more special, than I had imagined. We thanked Mrs. Sato as best we could; I hope that she knew how much it meant to us that she would open her home and let us take a peek into her life.

Journal excerpt. Japan. May 14, 1967:

> *We are on the New Hokkaido Express now, zooming between Tokyo and Nagoya. It's quite a fancy train—smooth and almost noiseless as we race along at speeds between 80 and 120 miles per hour.*

FOR THE NEXT SEVEN days we traveled south on trains, staying in *ryokans* in Nagoya, Matsusaka, Nara, Kyoto, and Kobe. The *ryokans* were always immaculately clean, with tatami mats on the floor, sliding doors, and small gardens. Since we now had been introduced to public baths by the Sato family, our evenings usually found us in these public baths and then back at our *ryokan*, wrapped up in kimonos, lying on our futons, feeling that all life should be this enjoyable.

Usually when we visited castles, museums, or parks, we wandered around by ourselves, but at one temple, we joined a Japanese tour, since there was an English translator. It was less than optimal. The translator repeated the guide's information in a soft voice and with such an accent that we had no idea what she was saying. We didn't continue to search for translators but sometimes were able to find English-language brochures. The more I visited Japanese gardens, the more impressed I became. In one Zen garden I was enthralled by the perfect placement of three elements: water, trees, and stone. Tall trees symbolized mountains, and ponds symbolized the ocean. I was hungry to learn more.

A major problem for us was that it was hard to communicate. We managed with hand gestures and the few phrases we had picked up, but I wished I could really speak Japanese. In Nara, I walked into a beauty salon to get my hair washed and cut. I didn't know the routine, and I couldn't talk to the hairdresser. I tried to demonstrate ("just a little shorter, please"), but when I came out, Mick said I looked like I had gotten the standard "Japanese schoolgirl's cut." My hair was chopped off, with straight edges and bangs. I looked terrible. I felt like a little girl.

From Nara we took a bus to Toba and to the Mikimoto Pearl Island. Evidently, as we were told, the pigtoe shells that were used as a nucleus for the pearls came from the Mississippi River. Pigtoe shells? I had never heard of them, and I certainly didn't know there was any connection to the U.S. or to the Mississippi River. I hadn't thought much about Mikimoto pearls before that day, but I decided that I really must have a necklace. After all, Mr. Mikimoto's motto (aptly written on his statue) was "To decorate the necks of all ladies in the world with the strings of Mikimoto pearls." How could I fight such an honorable aim in life? I justified buying a pearl choker by convincing myself that it was an early birthday present.

FROM KOBE TO HIROSHIMA, we decided to try hitchhiking, since it had worked well in Malaysia. There was one main highway between the two cities, so we thought it would be easy to get a ride. In fact, it did work out quite well. A truck driver stopped right away, and we easily got three more rides before arriving in Hiroshima. All the people who picked us up were friendly and kind; one couple gave us some sake and raw fish as they let us out. Our lack of a common language, however, contributed to a very different hitchhiking experience compared with Malaysia. Whereas in Malaysia we had learned a tremendous amount through conversations about the politics and social issues in that country, in Japan we gained an understanding of the kindness and generosity of those who picked us up.

One of the immediate issues for us hitchhiking in Japan was that our drivers wouldn't let us get out on the highway. They insisted on taking us to the center of the city, where we could take a train or bus. We tried to explain that we didn't want a train—the edge of the city was better for hitchhiking—but we couldn't make ourselves clear. And probably it seemed too rude to our drivers to leave us standing on the road. Several times we ended up having to walk a long way back to the highway so we could get another ride. That was frustrating and exasperating, but we kept at it, realizing that our drivers were just being polite.

On my 25th birthday, after a cozy night at the Hiroshima Youth Hostel, we ventured into the Peace Memorial Museum, with its sobering but well-presented display of the disaster following the atomic bomb that

Americans had dropped in 1945. Only 22 years had passed since then, but even though I had been born during World War II, the war had meant little more to me than a chapter in a history book. But now, after seeing the museum display, I realized that the wounds must still be extremely raw. It was especially disturbing to know that it had been my country that had dropped that bomb. Was there an ethical or legal justification for the bombing? Did it bring a quicker end to the war? All I saw was destruction.

Outside the Peace Memorial Museum area, Hiroshima was a thriving city. A sweet aroma wafted out to us from a small bakery, where a fresh strawberry-and-cream cake was just waiting for us to buy it. I couldn't pass that up. We carried it carefully out to a small ferry that took us to the island town of Miyajima. The famous shrine, *torii* gate, and pagoda on this tiny island were built by the Heike clan in the 1500s, when they still reigned supreme in Japan. The huge red *torii* gate still stands offshore, where, we were told, it looks to be floating when the tide is in. Unfortunately, when we were there, the tide was at an all-time low, so we didn't get the famous floating view. Instead the gate was completely visible in the sand. Barnacles covered the lower section. Groups of schoolchildren gleefully ran around gathering shells. We found a secluded spot to gaze at the site while we devoured my whole birthday cake in one sitting. On the ferry back to Hiroshima, loudspeakers blared out "Auld Lang Syne." We had been hearing this song off and on for the past week and were getting quite tired of it. Why in the world was this song so popular?

Journal excerpt. Hiroshima, Japan. May 22, 1967:

> *Even when our short ferry trip (ten minutes) was docking at Miyajima people were throwing streamers and Auld Lang Syne was blaring out! The boat was so small that the two people on the dock were higher than the boat. But still the streamers were thrown. A few days ago we walked to the port at Kobe and saw a whole ship full of school-girls leaving for a group trip. This time there were hundreds of colored streamers [with] all the mommies waving goodbye. What an institu-tion! (At this youth hostel, Auld Lang Syne was just played over the intercom as a "good-night, lights out" piece.)*

We tried hitchhiking again, this time from Hiroshima to Shimonoseki, the city at the southernmost part of Honshu Island. It's only a distance of about 120 miles, so we thought it would be an easy trip. In retrospect, it was somewhat comical. We got our first ride right away, but the driver took us back to Miyajima, where we had just left a few hours earlier. That driver let us out, and a businessman picked us up. We tried to communicate with him, but it was too difficult, so we all rode in silence to the next town. We could tell that he was on his way to the train station in the center of town, so we tried to ask him to let us out, but he wouldn't stop. At the train station, as we were getting out, he changed his mind. He said to get in again, so we did. We had no idea what was happening. The man then drove around town until he found someone who spoke English, and he asked that person to drive us to Shimonoseki. Now we were quite embarrassed, especially when the English-speaking driver said he couldn't take us all the way to Shimonoseki, but he could take us to a site about 50 kilometers from there.

We got into his car, feeling like we were a terrible burden. The man didn't say much, and he didn't smile, but he ended up being overly accommodating. He stopped at tourist sites along the way. He also made some business stops and even bought us lunch. And then, when he got to where he had arranged to take us, he decided to go out of his way and continue taking us all the way to Shimonoseki. We couldn't tell if he was pleased or not at having us in his car, and we didn't know how to respond. We felt like we were taking advantage of him, but we hadn't arranged anything with him and didn't know what the other man had told him about us. When we arrived in Shimonoseki, we simply smiled and said *"Arigato"* in the best manner we could. Maybe he was as perplexed as we were.

OUR GOAL IN SHIMONOSEKI was to find a boat going to Korea. At the Japan Tourist Bureau, we asked if we could buy tickets across the Korean Strait to Pusan (now Busan). Luckily, there was a boat leaving in 45 minutes. We ran to the dock, getting there just in time to buy tickets. As we were getting in the boat, Mick bumped into one of the short doorways, cutting his head. It wasn't bleeding much, but it was swelling a little. I cleaned up the wound a bit and dabbed it with an antibiotic. This wasn't the first time he had trouble getting his head through a door. Then we learned that there would be no food for this overnight trip, so Mick dashed back onshore to buy us something to eat. I waited on deck, anxiously scanning the dock, worried that he wouldn't get back in time. I was afraid the ship would start pulling out to sea. How would I tell the captain to stop? Would he do it? I breathed a sigh of relief when I saw Mick running back toward the boat.

In Shimonoseki Harbor leaving Japan on the *Kansui Maru*   Taken from our "room" below deck on the *Kansui Maru* headed to Pusan, Korea

The MS *Kansui Maru* sailed at 5 p.m. for the overnight trip to Korea. Our economy tickets put us on the bottom deck in a large room that was bare except for wall-to-wall tatami mats and some blankets. Knee-high wooden walls divided the tatami mats into sections, and since there were only a few other people, we were able to claim a somewhat private space in the corner. We spread our food out on the blanket and settled in for the night. The sea was calm; the room was quiet. We were able to sleep quite well. Even with all the rush to buy the boat tickets, find some last-minute food, and suffer a bloody head bump, Mick had not wavered in his joy of traveling.

Mick's journal excerpt. Aboard the *Kansui Maru*. May 24, 1967:

> *Now we are about to disembark on Korean soil, the land of the morning calm. As always, I have that good excited feeling that comes with entering a new country. I'll be sorry to have this trip end.*

25.

Trains and Buses in Korea

Korea was not a new country to me. My father, a child of Methodist missionaries, was born in Pyongyang in 1909 and lived there and in Seoul until he went to California for college at age 18. I had uncles, aunts, cousins, and grandparents who had lived and worked in Korea. When we had family reunions, we'd hear Korean phrases, Korean songs, and stories about Korea. For all my father's life, Korea was, in a basic sense, home. I had visited Seoul with my parents in 1961 and now looked forward to going again with Mick. I wanted to revisit my father's boyhood home and meet some of the people he knew. I had already sent a letter to my folks giving them the address of the American Express office in Seoul and asking them to send me names and addresses of people we might be able to visit there.

The *Kansui Maru* arrived in the southern port city of Pusan at 8 a.m. We were immediately aware of being in a new country. Japan and Korea may have been close in distance, but they were miles apart in ways of living.

Journal excerpt. Pusan, Korea. May 24, 1967:

We've spent a day here in Pusan and we know we're out of Japan and back into more "earthy" people. I must admit that I'm a little tired of it. We're back in a land of spitting, pushing, and staring. All of a sudden again I have to be conscious of moving for everyone on the sidewalk

or else get knocked by everyone. Again, we sit in a restaurant and see
people (and hear them) spitting on the floor. Again, all eyes turn as
we walk down the street.

Though I didn't like being stared at, I still wanted to explore Korea. It was a new country to travel in, and I was ready to enjoy whatever came our way. Besides, while we were being stared at in Pusan, we were also staring at everyone and everything around us. We noticed things we hadn't seen since West Asia and South Asia, such as men carrying or pulling heavy loads by hand. There were fix-it men everywhere, molding items such as old tin cans into spray cans or selling things that looked like rubbish to me: rusty knives, old scissors, can openers, and discarded U.S. mess kit utensils. Everything seemed to be getting a second life.

An express train would get us to Seoul in seven hours, but we decided to travel by various local trains and buses so we could see the country. It took us four days. My previous experience in Korea had been only in Seoul, hosted by friends in their homes or at universities. I didn't realize there would be such a difference for us as itinerants traveling by ourselves.

On our way north to Seoul, we stopped overnight three times: in Kyongju (now Gyeongju), Taegu (now Daegu), and Taejon (now Daejeon). As we walked around Kyongju, people stared at us, poked each other, and giggled. The atmosphere felt friendly, but clearly we were an oddity. I wondered if my skirt was too short for this culture. Or maybe it was just that people were curious. We sat down on a park bench, and an old man in a horsehair hat and traditional white starched robe smiled as he came over and sat beside us. He put his hat on Mick's head and laughed. Then a woman came over, sat beside Mick, and pulled at the hair on his arm. She unbuttoned his shirt and stuck her head right by his chest, obviously quite fascinated with all his chest hair. Mick's blue eyes, reddish skin, and hairy body made for a good laugh for everyone. We thought it was as funny as they did. Near the temple was a group of people dancing and playing drums of all sizes. Many were wearing traditional outfits.

The old man lets Mick wear his hat.

Examining the hair on Mick's arm

Dancing in the park

We had no problem finding hotels as we traveled up the country, but some looked like they might have been built in the early part of the century when Japan ruled Korea. Tattered tatami mats were partly replaced by faded linoleum. In Taegu, we didn't have any running water, the toilet stank, and the bath was scummy. It was so bad that we didn't even brush our teeth. Even with our own sheet, we hesitated to lie on the bed. In Taejon, the hotel was much better, but still there were no clean sheets on the bed and no regular running water. Sometimes the toilet flushed and sometimes not.

Regardless of the state of the hotels, I was excited to be in Korea. Here I was in a country that I knew from family stories and pictures, a place that was both familiar and yet far away. The countryside was green and well cultivated; the mountains were rocky, just like the ones in my father's old family pictures. From the train we saw houses of mud and rock with thatched roofs. We continued to see men in their white robes and horsehair hats; we even saw one man smoking an old-fashioned long bamboo pipe. Many women looked clean, fresh, and springy in their traditional dresses made of pink, blue, and yellow fabrics. To that extent, Korea felt familiar to me. My emotions fluctuated between the excitement of being in Korea and the reality of dealing with the daily life issues of a low-budget do-it-yourself traveler in this country.

Journal excerpt. Taejon, Korea. May 27, 1967:

We had our second trip on a third-class local train today and are almost fed up. It was quite a hassle getting on. We got to the station at about 9:45 a.m. for the 10:20 train. Already there were lots of people on the platform. We found a front place and waited. When the train came, it was already loaded, or rather overloaded, but most of the people were getting off. As the train came to a stop, everybody on the platform rushed for the door, pushing anybody in their way. The rush and pressure took me by surprise, and I was pushed backward about two yards. Then I took hold of things, planted my feet, and started shoving to stand still. I made it. Mick had made his way to the front right by the train door. Now the people were trying to get out of the train, but they couldn't because of the crowd trying to push on. Finally, the crowd outside fell back (with some pushing) and left a bit of a place for those on the train to get off. This worked fine until the last few people were getting off. The crowd outside couldn't wait any longer. The last lady had a bag of apples and she almost couldn't get out of the train. People were shoving her, and she didn't have a chance. She really had to fight the crowd, but I guess she finally got out. It really took strength to hold one's own against that crowd, but finally I was on. An old man behind me fell as he was coming up the train steps. He almost got trampled. The rest of the train trip was uneventful except for the crowds, the stuffy heat, and the little boy who urinated by Mick's feet in the center of the aisle. Tomorrow we're taking the express train with reserved seats.

After four days, we arrived in Seoul. We went right to the Banda Hotel. I wasn't sure what to expect, but I knew the name of the hotel from my father's stories. Before asking about rooms, we stopped at the Korean Travel Bureau office in the lobby. Here we met Mr. Hahn, who seemed delighted to talk with us. His English was excellent. I told him briefly about my family history with Korea. He told us that he had lived in Monterey, California, for three years, from 1953 to 1956. As we talked, Mr. Hahn was on the phone trying to find a place for us to stay that was inexpensive but clean. Suddenly he stopped, looked up, and said, "Why don't you come sleep at my house?" Once again, here was a kind and welcoming person, like so many others we had met throughout our travels.

We stayed with the Hahns for the next three nights. They lived in a middle-class suburb of Seoul with their two children, ages five and two. Mr. Hahn told us the economy was booming; prices for land jumped up every month. There were several tract-type homes going up all around his home, and bulldozers were leveling out plots for more new homes. South Korea—or at least Seoul—seemed to be in the throes of modernization. From his house there was a clear view of the mountains, but I wondered if his beautiful view would disappear in time with all the new building.

On May 29, we went to the home of Maud Jensen, an old friend of my father's who was five years older than he. She went to Seoul as a missionary in 1926, met her husband there, and spent the rest of her missionary career in Korea. When we met her in 1967, she was a widow at age 63, living in the house where my father had grown up. She recalled meeting my father and his twin brother when they were high school boys; they were playing unrehearsed duets on the piano.

I enjoyed every minute with Maud Jensen, listening to her stories and imagining my father as a boy. She walked us through each room of this large, comfortable house. In the dining room, she pointed up to the corners of the windows and doorways where I could barely make out the small royal blossoms that had been painted or carved there when the house was built. She told us that my grandparents had been given royal permission to use that particular design in the house construction.

Mrs. Jensen pointed out the stone blocks in the yard that had been left from the old city wall that had passed right by the house. She also imitated my grandfather grinding coffee beans at the dining room table so that everyone was sure to have the freshest coffee possible. He would say, "Now Mattie [to my grandmother], I think this mixture needs more mocha." And he would add chocolatey beans right at the table. I had heard many stories about my grandfather's joviality and kindness, but I had never known that he liked fresh-ground mocha coffee.

After a delicious lunch, Mrs. Jensen drove us around the beautiful large campuses of Ewha University and Yonsei University. My relatives had been associated with the early days of both. After saying goodbye to Maud Jensen and thanking her profusely, we did more sightseeing on our own in Seoul, visiting palaces and gardens. The parks were lovely and peaceful, and the public buses were easy to use. There was still the issue of pushing and elbowing to get on or off. That part of being in Korea never ceased to be a real fiasco.

Man on Namsan Hill, Seoul   Women in the park, Seoul

While in Seoul, we decided to try again to get visas for Taiwan, and this time we got them with no trouble. I don't know why the office in Hong Kong hadn't given them to us. Sometimes things seem to depend on who's in charge or who's behind a desk or what day it is. Anyway, now we knew we'd get to Taiwan for sure, but first we needed to get back to the port of Pusan.

I was not looking forward to two more days of train travel, but that was what lay ahead. On the way to Pusan, we stopped in Chonju (now Jeonju) and then Chinju (now Jinju). We were back to inns with no running water. But also, in both towns, we met kind people who took care of us. In Chonju, a smiling young man stopped us on the street. He attached himself to us as we walked around town, talking and talking and asking all sorts of questions. He even bought me a beautiful hand-painted silk fan. I was embarrassed at that, and also exasperated with all his questions, but I didn't know how to politely get rid of him. Finally, when he accompanied us back to our inn, I was ready to thank him and say goodbye. But no. He insisted on going with us into the inn, where he made the staff reduce the price of our room from 500 won to 400 won ($1.47). I'm not sure why he did this. Maybe he was embarrassed at the condition of the hotel or maybe at the price we were paying. I suppose we were always charged more than local people, but we really hadn't minded paying that 500 won. In the end, I hoped that talkative young man enjoyed being with us, was pleased to be able to practice his English, and hadn't realized that I wanted to get rid of him.

In Chinju, we walked into a Japan Air Lines (JAL) tourist agency to see what kind of information they might have. The staff looked up in amazement. No one, at least no Western tourists, just ambled into their office. They hadn't seen any tourists for a long time and were clearly happy to talk to us, to speak in English. A few of the staff members took us out to two teahouses and bought us some fruit. Then they said they would arrange for us to stay at one of the JAL men's apartments. No one was living in his room, they said; it was one of the rooms in a small building that housed 10 families. We told them that we had already paid for an inn, but they insisted that we stay in this room that night. We couldn't turn them down, so we walked back to the inn to explain that we didn't need to stay there after all. The receptionist gave us our money back, and we gave her a tip for partial payment of the room we hadn't used. Then we went back to the apartment of the JAL man. It was bare, but fine. We slept well until 5 o'clock the next morning, when someone in the building turned on a radio. Through the thin walls in the building, it blared out. We couldn't go back to sleep, and it was too early for breakfast. Annoyed, we tried not to think that this was rude as we huddled under the covers.

ON JUNE 2, WE were back in Pusan ready for our return boat trip on the MS *Kansui Maru* to Shimonoseki, Japan. I had looked forward to getting on the boat, but that night ended up being miserable. We had both picked up a bug in Korea that gave us sharp stomach pains and terrible diarrhea. We took turns at the tiny squat toilet above our sleeping deck. I would run into the smelly room, not knowing whether to squat or lean over, ready for both. I threw up three times. Both of us had had diarrhea often over the past year, but this was the worst case either of us had ever had. Luckily it was all over in about 24 hours.

26.

Okinawa to Taiwan

Exhausted after being sick all night, we were delighted to find a small, very clean private youth hostel in a quiet location overlooking the hills of Nagasaki, Japan. Not only did we have a room to ourselves, but I was allowed to use the washing machine. I threw everything in, even our sheet. The quietude of the afternoon belied my realization that we were again in a city that had been destroyed by an American bomber 22 years earlier. It was hard to imagine that horrendous moment, in which 70,000 people were suddenly killed. As we viewed the placid bay and shipping yards of this modern port city, we felt too worn out to visit the Atom Bomb Museum. Instead we spent that evening soaking in the marvelously hot, steamy water of our Japanese bath. My tenseness and exhaustion of the previous days slowly subsided.

Hitchhiking was easy as we made our way to Kagoshima, the port city at the southern tip of Kyushu Island. It took seven or eight rides to get there. We chatted with the drivers, feeling quite relaxed on our rides through the countryside. Our last ride, in fact, dropped us off right in front of the main ferry company, RKK Lines. *What luck*, I thought. I didn't know yet that our luck had run out.

The ticket agent looked at us kindly as we showed our Taiwan visas and asked about the next ship. "I'm sorry," he said. "That ship has already left. There will be one next week." What? We could not wait a week. Though dismayed and disappointed, I was determined to get to Taiwan. The ticket agent, evidently realizing our anguish, tried to be helpful. "There is an overnight ferry going to Naha, Okinawa, tomorrow," he added. It was not where we wanted to go, but after some discussion we decided to take it. At least in Naha we'd be halfway to Taiwan, and from there somehow we would find a boat going to Keelung, Taiwan. We bought two round-trip tickets on the *Otohimaru*, bound for Naha.

The ship was clean and beautiful, but the ocean swells were enormous. I was seasick and still queasy the next morning when we disembarked in Naha. I suppose it had been the best decision to take the ferry but it seemed that shipping agents in Naha were not used to itinerant travelers dropping in to find a ship going to Taiwan. What began as another long, anxious-filled day ended with a surprise decision.

Journal excerpt. Taiwan. June 7, 1967:

> *This morning we arrived in Naha, Okinawa, after a <u>very</u> rough sea. (I threw up about eight times.) We began looking around for ships going to Keelung and, as usual, had a terrible time dragging information out of people. . . . At three p.m. when everything seemed hopeless for several days ahead, we suddenly decided to fly on the local airline CAT (Civil Air Transport). At 5:30 we were in Taipei. It all happened so quickly that we're still reeling. In fact, I can still feel the ship moving [from this morning], and since then we've been in two countries and had an hour's jet ride. Taiwan looked beautiful from the air. It's so easy and painless to fly compared with taking little boats.*

I HAD LIVED IN Taiwan six years earlier, in 1961. That year, my father had received a Fulbright grant to teach biology at National Taiwan University. I took a semester off from college so that I could go with them to Taiwan, where I stayed for four months. Now, almost six years later, I was tickled that I could show Mick the people and places I remembered. We spent three days exploring Taipei. I found the house I had lived in during the fall of 1961 without much trouble, though it was an exhausting walk, longer than I had remembered.

What I was anticipating the most was seeing my Mandarin-language teacher: Dung TaiTai ("TaiTai" means "Madam" and is used for a married woman). For four months in 1961, I had daily, intensive, one-on-one Mandarin classes. Dung TaiTai had been an excellent teacher. I had thoroughly enjoyed the language study, and at the end of four months I felt generally competent in my use of Mandarin. Now, however, as we were on our way to have dinner at her house, I was embarrassed at how much language I had forgotten. Though I was recalling more each day, I felt terrible when I would recognize a word but couldn't remember what it meant. Despite my feelings of inadequacy, I did manage to carry on a conversation that evening. As we were led to the dinner table, Dung TaiTai said that we were having "Peiping food." On the table was a large stack of flat round breads and several other dishes. We watched our hosts to see how to handle this meal, and then proceeded to pick up a round bread and pile it with onions, brown sauce, pork, duck, beansprouts, vermicelli, egg, and other ingredients, and then roll it all up. Delicious! Since then, I've often had Peking duck, but it has never been quite as good as what we ate at Dung TaiTai's house in Taipei that evening.

Dinner with Dung TaiTai and her husband

The next four days went by quickly, as we explored places south of Taipei by bus. At Sun Moon Lake, though it had rained all night, the morning was bright and clear, so we rented a little rowboat for an hour. That afternoon in the Teachers' Hostel, as we were trying to figure out where to go next and what bus might take us there, a man came over and began chatting in English with us. He was the leader of a group of educators from South Vietnam who were ending their three-month tour of the U.S. that had included visits to 11 schools in 10 states. I was surprised, and pleased, to hear that there were such tours for Vietnamese educators since, of course, this was at a time when the U.S. military was fighting in their country. I hoped to talk more with the people in the group, so I was happy to hear the man say that they had room in their tour bus. "Please come with us," he said. "We're going south to the town of Chiayi." Having no other plans, we joined them; the teachers were full of energy and fun to talk to. They asked us all about where we were going and how we were traveling. They seemed surprised that we were traveling on our own on local buses. I wanted to find out more about the war from their perspective. I wondered if they had come across any antiwar attitude in their U.S. travels, but I never did get a chance to broach the topic. The time just didn't seem right. And the whole mess seemed so far away from our day-to-day travel life in Taiwan. After a day in Chiayi, we spent a couple of more nights in Taichung and Hsinchu before going back to Taipei.

Journal excerpt. Chiayi, Taiwan. June 11, 1967:

> *A sad thing has happened to us. I believe that our trip has ended (in the John Steinbeck sense in his book Travels With Charley). We have just felt it all of a sudden. Suddenly, going places and doing things seem secondary or "extra." We seem to be thinking more of what we'll do in the U.S. than where we are going next. We still have about three weeks more of traveling, but somehow it seems gone. Everything from now on is returning—returning to Taipei, returning to Okinawa, returning to Kyushu, returning to Tokyo, and then returning to the U.S. We aren't*

"doing and exploring" much anymore—or anyway the feeling of it seems to be gone. It's quite sad.

We had five more days in Taipei before going north to Keelung to get the boat back to Naha, Okinawa. We could have traveled around Taiwan more, but we decided to stay in the Hotel Golden City in Taipei, to enjoy the pleasure of staying in one place for a while. We relaxed, read books, ate good food, and went shopping for gifts to take back to our families. No rushing around to get tickets or wait in a line or plan where to go next. For Mick, the best thing in Taiwan was the food. One of the most memorable meals was a delectable Szechuan duck dinner at the January restaurant near the Taipei train station. Mick still contends to this day that this was the best meal he has ever eaten.

Mick's journal. On the boat to Naha, thinking about Taiwan. June 19, 1967:

The food was excellent! I only regret that I had but one stomach to fill at every meal. Peiping Duck is a gourmet delight, and of course Szechuan duck is a heaven of spices. Best food in the world.

ON JUNE 18, WE embarked on the SS *Miyako Maru* on our return trip to Naha, Okinawa. Surprisingly, there was only one other passenger, but even so, "Auld Lang Syne" rang out as we pulled away. The three of us slept below on bench cushions that night. Before reaching Naha, we stopped on the island of Ishigaki, another of the Ryukyu Islands.[5] While the ship had been calm and quiet on the way to Ishigaki, suddenly it was now overflowing with passengers. More than 50 people crowded into one small room and the same number in other rooms. The officers moved us upstairs to a nicer room with fresh air, but it was still packed with about 30 people. As

---

5   Ishigaki is both the main city and the name of the island. It is part of Okinawa Prefecture of Japan and includes the disputed territory of the uninhabited (but reputedly located over oil reserves) Senkaku Islands, claimed by China and Taiwan as well as Japan. The Chinese name is Diaoyu Islands ("Tiaoyu" in Taiwan).

we got ready to pull away from the dock, we had not only the repeat joy of hearing "Auld Lang Syne" but also the crash of cymbals clanging, the sobs of people saying goodbye, and the flapping sound of multicolored serpentine streamers blowing in the wind. A ship's steward was passing out rolls of serpentine, so I took one, held the end tightly, and threw the rest of the roll down to the dock. Someone picked up the other end, but I had no idea who it was. All I could see was a tangled mass of colorful streamers between the ship and the dock. As the ship slowly pulled out, my serpentine tightened and then broke, and, like everyone else's, it ended up floating in the water. I loved the ritual.

Leaving for Okinawa with streamers and "Auld Lang Syne"

27.

Japan Again

After two more nights on the *Miyako Maru* and another night on the *Otohimaru*, we disembarked in Kagoshima, Japan, where we headed toward the town of Beppu and its famous hot springs. We had decided to hitchhike again, but traveling on this rainy day was worse than ever.

Journal excerpt. At a railroad station in Kyushu. June 22, 1967:

> *We've been trying to hitchhike to Nobeoka, and it's difficult in the rain. We're over halfway there now, and we're stuck in a railroad station in a little town off the highway. This last man turned off the highway and deposited us at the station before we could object. Now we are sitting here. The train costs too much, and it is too far to walk to the main highway in this rain. We are off the main route down Kyushu, and there are very few trucks here. One man stopped and wouldn't pick us up because he wasn't going exactly where we were. He was very polite and kept suggesting trains, buses, and taxis. We would have liked a ride as far as he was going, but this was too much to understand. It's only 3 p.m. I guess we can afford to wait here a while longer before braving the rain.*

I was ready to quit that afternoon, to give up trying to get a ride. I was cold and tired. All I could think of was relaxing in a hot bath and climbing into a warm bed. I really didn't want to leave the railroad station for a long walk in the rain. But finally we did. It was better than standing around doing nothing. We managed to reach the highway, where, after a half hour of getting soaked, we got a ride to a place close to Nobeoka. The *ryokan* was a welcome haven, and the next day it was easy to get to Beppu. My spirits were rising, but I was disappointed in the Beppu hot springs; I thought they would be larger, more like Yellowstone. Maybe I was still feeling jaded after that rainy day of hitchhiking. In fact, we didn't spend much time exploring the area and didn't even try soaking in one of the famed *onsen* baths.

Hitchhiking to Tokyo with *all* our luggage

The next 10 days passed leisurely, as we hitchhiked our way up the northern coast of Honshu. We had plenty of time and didn't want to deal with buying tickets or changing trains and buses. We knew we wanted to end up in Tokyo, but our route was dependent on whoever picked us up. Each night, we stayed in a youth hostel or *ryokan*, but in the city of Kanazawa, as we knew our days in Japan were coming to an end, we chose an especially fine one.

Journal excerpt. Kanazawa, Japan. June 27, 1967:

We're splurging tonight. Our first night in a fancy ryokan. It's really living! When we walked in, we were immediately led to a side room for tea and cakes while the ladies took our bags and made our room ready. In the tearoom, a woman performed a special ceremony (like the tea ceremony or maybe it was the tea ceremony). It was wonderful to watch and of course to take part in the drinking of the green powder liquid. She was so graceful in every action. By this time all was ready; we were refreshed, and a lady came to lead us to our room. There all our bags were arranged, and our kimonos laid out. After a few minutes' interval, she came again (each time with all the appropriate bowing and polite phrases) to lead us to the bath. What a wonderful bath—large pool, rock garden by the pool, etc. There's nothing better than a hot Japanese bath after a long day of traveling. After the bath we went back to our room, where dinner was properly prepared and waiting for us. We had raw fish, soy sauce, rice, relishes, soup, cooked fish, salad, and watermelon. Most of it was delicious, some . . . hard to get used to. (The raw fish is delicious though.) After a nice leisurely dinner, our lady came again to prepare the bed at about 8 p.m. It always looks so good and comfy. In the morning she will come in as soon as we are up, to put away the bed and bring our tea. What a pampered life.

Three days before the SS *President Wilson* would be leaving, we arrived back in Tokyo. What we were most looking forward to was checking for mail at the American Express office. It had been a long month since we had been able to receive any, and we weren't disappointed. There was a pile for us, and it included Mick's acceptance letter from the University of Pittsburgh grad school. Both of us were relieved to know for sure where we'd be living for the next few years.

Our days in Japan ended with an invitation to lunch at a Chinese restaurant in Yokohama owned by Dung TaiTai's brother's wife's family. It was delightful, not only because of the nine delicious courses, but because of the camaraderie that developed among all of us. That afternoon brought together our love of Chinese food with a now-extended-family feeling with my former Chinese teacher.

Part Six

The Journey Home

July 1967

28.

Reflections

The SS *President Wilson* sailed on July 5, 1967, for the 12-day voyage to San Francisco. Since we had bought the cheapest tickets, Mick was assigned the men's dormitory with 42 other men. "Quiet, though stuffy," he wrote in his journal. There were no dormitories for women, so I was put in a room with three Chinese women. We saw many U.S. military personnel, but they were in first class. The best and biggest surprise was that we saw a familiar face as we boarded the ship. It was Hein, a German we had first met in Baghdad a year earlier. We had crossed paths with him in Kabul, in India, and in Nepal. What a perfect coincidence: meeting like-minded travelers had been one of the consistent joys of our travels.

Mick's journal excerpt. SS *President Wilson*. July 6, 1967:
> *Yesterday we left Yokohama, the beginning of the end for the trip. After two years, now it's over—a bit sad. These have been two years we can never, nor will ever, attempt to duplicate. . . . My only consolation is that I know this is just the first of a great many and possibly more exciting ventures to come.*

I shared Mick's sadness over ending this vagabond way of life. Though I looked forward to seeing family and friends, and even setting up a household someplace, I knew I would miss the spontaneity of travel and the excitement of being in new countries. For almost two years, from day to day we had never really known exactly what would happen next. Now, on shipboard, each day was pretty much the same. I spent my days reading books I found in the ship's library; Mick was writing an article on our travels for a University of Maryland newsletter. We talked, played, and hung around with Hein. Being on the ship was somewhat akin to living in no-man's-land. We were stuck in one place; we couldn't leave, yet we were moving forward, returning home, completing a circle.

The slowness of life on the sea allowed me time to reflect. Two years previous, I had been a bride of two months; now I felt "seasoned" at age 25. Was this as a wife or as a traveler? It was impossible to separate these two facets of my life. Mick and I had rarely been separated—either day or night—for two years. We had learned to work together as a team while navigating the globe. We had trusted and relied on each other; we had been "buddies." With so much changing every day in the world around us, we found solace in being able to count on each other. We rarely needed anything more.

This bond in our relationship was one that developed over time. When we began our trip in Europe, we focused mainly on the day-to-day issues of living in our camper; we enjoyed having a vagabond life, visiting sites, meeting people. The turning point occurred while we were in Spain meeting other travelers; we began to view ourselves as part of a subculture. We were not just living in our camper moving from here to there; we were WTs, world travelers, part of an amorphous group of people for whom traveling was a lifestyle, not a trip. We were spending as little as we could, not only so we could keep traveling but also because we wanted to live this way. We chose it, not because we had no money, but because we knew we could—and would—return to another life.

As we became increasingly comfortable with a nomadic life, we needed fewer items. We did make a practice of buying small gifts for others as well as ourselves, but we mailed them back along the way. We had jettisoned our steamer trunk a year into our journey. We had sent back our suitcases, duffel bag, and briefcase. All of this represented a move to being less encumbered, less tied to things. Most of the time in East Asia, we carried only one tote bag and one or two small shoulder bags. That was plenty, with even more clothes than I needed; I didn't feel the need to vary what I wore. Washing everything out at night, stringing it up around the room, and sometimes putting on damp clothes the next morning was a usual routine. It would have been impossible to travel as we did if we hadn't been able to easily carry everything we owned.

In thinking over the two years, I realize that I had rarely felt fear, but there were a few scary times. One was the hot night in Baghdad when a tire in Bernd's Mercedes went flat and a crowd gathered, pressing closer and closer in. It seemed like any spark could turn the crowd into an uncontrollable mob. Another was riding on the Thai bus north from Bangkok with a driver speeding around bends. But more common than fear were my feelings of anger or frustration at being stared at or being pushed and shoved in crowds. I worried at times, but usually these worries were short-lived and associated with daily events such as getting gas, buying food, or finding a comfortable place to sleep. And then there was always money to think about, whether it was waiting to receive it, as in Spain, or planning how best to carry it. We divided our cash between us; Mick would wrap most of his in a handkerchief and pin it to his inside front pants pocket. But in general, over these two years, our days were relatively worry-free.

Before we began our travel, I had not realized how much I felt drawn to people, how much I enjoyed learning from them. In almost every country, regardless of their languages and cultures, people welcomed us into their homes, gave us food, shared their stories. Sometimes we initiated the visits, such as when we walked across the desert in southern Turkey to say hello to Kurdish women in their tents. Or hiked for a day to the Karen hill tribe in northern Thailand. But more often, other people would spontaneously initiate the visits, such as Mr. Hahn in the Seoul travel bureau, who invited us to stay with his family for three days. Or the man in Jordan who invited us to swim in his pool. Or the family in Yugoslavia who gave us fresh mushrooms. Or Ravi's family in Delhi, who took us in for a week. People may have felt drawn to us in part because we were a young couple who didn't look threatening. Furthermore, as a woman, I could relate to other women and their families in ways that may not have been possible for a single man. In general, our meetings with people were accompanied by smiles and welcoming gestures, even if we didn't speak the same language. Underlying this openness and graciousness was a sense of trust and an eagerness for all of us to learn from each other.

AS WE HEADED TOWARD California, I looked forward to seeing friends and relatives, and to entering a new phase of life, though not without some trepidation. I knew we would be moving to Pittsburgh, where Mick would start grad school; I knew I'd be looking for a teaching job. I also knew we were going back to a country that had changed. When we left in 1965, the civil rights movement was mostly centered on the U.S. South. Sit-ins and bus boycotts had helped lead to the passage of the Civil Rights Act of 1964 and the Voting Rights Act of 1965. But now there were new political movements. The civil rights movement was encompassing a larger area with a broader focus. Protests against the war in Vietnam were increasing. What we didn't yet know was that in San Francisco that summer, tens of thousands of people—musicians, artists, hippies—were descending upon Golden Gate Park and the Haight-Ashbury neighborhood to participate in the countercultural phenomenon known as the "Summer of Love." We were not the only ones whose lifestyles would be changing.

AS OUR SHIP NEARED the coast, I scanned the horizon. And suddenly there was the Golden Gate Bridge. I looked up into its delicate arches as we sailed under, and I shivered with joy. What more perfect ending could there possibly be than to sail into San Francisco Bay? As we slowly pulled into the dock at Pier 50, I saw a small crowd waving to us: parents, siblings, various other relatives, and a horde of friends. It was a gorgeous blue-sky sunny day. I was wearing my new blue tailored dress from Tokyo and my Mikimoto pearls; Mick was wearing the new suit that had been tailored for him in Hong Kong. We walked off carrying one small hand tote bag each plus my shoulder bag. After one year, 11 months, and two weeks, we were back in California.

Approaching the Golden Gate Bridge

July 17, 1967: San Francisco, ready to disembark

Afterward

Our arrival in San Francisco in July 1967 did not bring an end to our travels. In fact, it initiated a lifetime of working and traveling throughout the world.

After two years in Pittsburgh, where Mick was taking graduate classes and I was teaching school, Mick received a grant that would allow him to do field research almost anywhere in the world. It didn't take either of us long to decide where we would most like to live for a year. The answer came immediately: Afghanistan. Of all the countries we had lived in or traveled through, this was the one most fascinating to both of us. And so it was that in the summer of 1969, we packed our bags and, along with our new baby daughter, spent the next year living in Kabul. Mick conducted his dissertation research at Kabul University, I taught English in classes offered by the United States Information Service (USIS), we studied Dari (a dialect of Farsi), and we traveled throughout most of the country. We never regretted that decision.

In the many years after 1967, regrettably we lost contact with most of the people we had met. It is surprising to me now that we did not exchange contact information, but of course there was no email then, nor were there mobile phones. In addition, most of the travelers we met were young people with no permanent homes, so, like us, they got mail through their parents' addresses. We do keep in regular contact with Clem and Evelyn, our Hawaii friends that we had met in Bangkok. For several years, we also kept in contact with Ravi's family in Delhi; and with Per, our Norwegian fellow traveler in India. We later reconnected with Peter, whom we had traveled with in Pakistan; with Clarke, whom we had met in Bangkok; and with the family of Jim, who had been such a help to us when he was the

U.S. consular officer in Basra, Iraq. I would love to sit down now with the many other travelers we met so we could rehash old memories and share more recent life stories.

In the years after the 1970s, Mick and I continued to travel both for fun and for work. While I was finishing a master's degree at the University of Hawai'i in 1979, I heard that China was hiring foreign-language teachers. I was especially excited about the idea of living in China; I had wanted to go there ever since being in Taiwan in 1961 and 1967. And so, after an unsuccessful search for an application form or a hiring office, I wrote a letter directly to the Chinese government in Beijing, outlining my experience and my desire to work. That unsolicited letter led to a welcome invitation to teach at the Shanghai Foreign Language Institute (now the Shanghai International Studies University) from 1981 to 1982. My students were dedicated, hard-working college students sponsored by the Chinese government and selected to study English; many were hoping to go to the U.S. for future study or work abroad. Mick and our children, ages nine and 12, accompanied me for most of that year. The children attended Chinese schools, but they also studied at home using correspondence school materials. During vacations we traveled on trains throughout China, from the northern city of Urumchi in the Xinjiang Uyghur Autonomous Region to southern subtropical areas of Xishuangbanna near Kunming.

In 1980, the year before going to China, I had begun teaching in the Department of Education at the University of California, Santa Cruz, a position that continued until 2001. During that time, I was able to combine teaching in Santa Cruz with work abroad in Vietnam, Turkey, and Ukraine.

The opportunity to go to Vietnam dropped into my lap when I was in working on a PhD degree at the University of California, Berkeley in 1993. I was asked to supervise several Stanford University undergraduates who had been selected through the VIA program to teach English in Hanoi. I jumped at the opportunity and began studying Vietnamese. During that summer in Hanoi in 1993, I made the decision to return there for my doctoral research. The next spring and summer, 1994, I lived on the campus of Vietnam National University, where I conducted interviews and observed classes, documenting ways that Vietnamese culture and history were an inseparable part of the Vietnamese teachers' methods of teaching English.

A few years after completing my doctorate, I received a Fulbright grant to be the director of a master of arts degree program for Turkish teachers of English in Ankara, Turkey. My two years there, from 1997 to 1999, not only gave me administrative experience but also allowed me to become immersed in Turkish life. Though I traveled extensively during vacations, from the far east region around Lake Van to the southern coast on the Mediterranean Sea, I did not see nomadic camps like those that had so impressed Mick and me in 1966.

When I heard about a career as a Regional English Language Officer (RELO) in the U.S. State Department, I applied and was accepted, after which I retired from UC Santa Cruz. Between 2002 and 2005, my office was in the U.S. Embassy in Kyiv, Ukraine, but my job entailed working not only with university English-language teachers in Ukraine but also in the nearby countries of Moldova, Belarus, Georgia, Armenia, and Azerbaijan. It was a fascinating period for me, both professionally and personally. My work as a RELO included conducting seminars, establishing libraries, planning conferences, and consulting on textbook development. During the years after my full-time retirement from the State Department, between 2007 and 2010, I continued to lead short-term teacher-training workshops through the State Department in Mongolia, Guatemala, and Bosnia & Herzegovina. In 2011, 2012, and 2013, I was able to return to Vietnam each fall to teach MS-TEFL graduate degree courses through a joint partnership program with Southern New Hampshire University.

People often ask me how Mick and I managed to keep our relationship healthy through the years that I was teaching abroad. It wasn't always easy, but it worked out. Mick was able to take leaves from his community college teaching and administration work in California, so he could join me, often up to six months at a time. It also helped that he was as flexible, adaptable, and drawn to the excitement of living in a new country as I was. Maybe the times of being apart helped us enjoy the times we had together.

Like most people, when I read about an event in a place I've lived, my mind is filled with images from that time. When I think about the horrendous 2001 destruction of the colossal Buddha statues by the Taliban in Bamiyan, Afghanistan, for instance, I not only shudder at the loss of such a treasure, I also remember the coolness in the caves as I climbed up into the statues to gaze out at the expansive view of Bamiyan Valley. In 2014, when I first read about war in the Donbas region of Ukraine, I remembered meeting with teachers at Donetsk National University and at Luhansk Pedagogical University, where I presented books as we sat around a table with cookies and juice in a corner of the school library. Now, in spring 2022, as Ukraine is engulfed in a wider war, I feel the anguish of my Ukrainian friends and former colleagues. I can only hope that I might again be able to share cookies and juice with teachers in a peaceful Ukraine.

My life has been enriched by working with people of ethnicities, languages, regions, and cultures that differ from my own, but these differences pale in comparison to our similarities. As Maya Angelou states so well in her poem "Human Family": "we are more alike, my friends, than we are unalike."

Kabul, Afghanistan, 1970

China, 1981

Lhasa, Tibet, 2011

New Zealand, 2014

Acknowledgments

In my first attempt, years ago, at turning my travel notes into a story, many of my family and friends graciously offered to read early renditions. Special thanks go to my sister Sylvia Tesh, my sister and brother-in-law Katrine and Gary Watkins, my cousins John Huyler and Steve Huyler, and my friend and colleague Nick Royal. All of you not only gave me the encouragement I needed to proceed but also made comments and suggestions that continued to strengthen my writing as I delved deeper into this travel memoir.

Thanks to the many teachers in classes I took from the Writing Salon, especially to Allison Landa and Marisa Zeppieri, who gave me a start on the road to publishing. I gained a needed perspective from editor Melissa Cistaro, who read an early version of the manuscript. My developmental editor, Elizabeth Rosner, helped enormously by encouraging me to expand and deepen my writing. My copy editor, Elissa Rabellino, added precision with her detailed and careful reading, observations, and corrections. Thanks to John Byrne Barry, who drew the maps for the book, and to the many members of the Bay Area Independent Publishers Association (BAIPA) who helped me through the steps of publishing. Many of those in BAIPA, as well as family members including Rebecca, Adam, and Angela, were crucial in the brainstorming process of coming up with a title. And most of all, to Mick, for reading uncountable versions of the book, making insightful suggestions, checking out facts on the Internet, and adding his own memories to mine. He has not only been part of the journey from the beginning but also a partner in turning 55-year-old memories into a book.